The Last WORKS MINIS

The end of a legend

www.veloce.co.uk

First published in September 2007 by Veloce Publishing Limited, 33 Trinity Street, Dorchester DT1 1TT, England. Fax 01305 268864/e-mail info@veloce.co.uk/web www.veloce.co.uk or www.velocebooks.com
ISBN 978-1-845840-87-7. UPC: 6-36847-04087-1

Bryan Purves & Tim Brenchley

The **Last**
WORKS
MINIS
The end of a legend

VELOCE PUBLISHING
THE PUBLISHER OF FINE AUTOMOTIVE BOOKS

Dedicated to our wives – Elizabeth and Nicki respectively – who have supported us throughout our research and the rebuild of the two cars.

Publisher's note –
Photograph quality. When the majority of the photographs for this book were taken, it was not known that they would one day form part of a book. Unfortunately, because these original digital images are of relatively low resolution they will appear a little fuzzy and grainy in print. Despite the problem of reproduction, these photographs form an essential part of the Works Minis story, therefore they have been included for the sake of completeness.

CONTENTS

ACKNOWLEDGEMENTS

We would like to express our warmest thanks to the following people and organisations – listed alphabetically – who assisted us with information, photographs and support in our quest to write this book, and without whose help it would not have been possible.

AP Racing, *Autosport*, Conrad Avey, Aymami Foto Racing, Ken Ayris, Simon Ayris, Keith Bird, Gerard Brown, Geoff Bullen, Wayne Butterworth (West Pennine Motorsport), Lucien Campello, Corgi Classics, Robert Clayson, Stuart Craddock (Weston Park), John Colley, Gary Dixon, Scott Dukes, Robert Dyson, John Edge (John Edge Graphics), Echappement, F'Autodelta, Dominic Farley, Peter Farley (Rover Cooper Registrar), Glen Fisher, Peter J Fox, Richard Franklin, Trevor Godwin (Coventry Automotive), Bob Green (B G Developments), Philippe Gutierrey, Mike Hally, Daniel Harper (Mini Sport), Amy Hodge (*Mini World* magazine), Martin Holmes, David Jane (British Motor Heritage Ltd), Reinhard Klein, Les Kolczak (*Mini* magazine), Lynxsigns Ltd, Martin Kernahan (Kernahan of Witney), Maurice Louche, David Lucas, Lee McNair (Bill Richards Racing), Kevin Malloy (ATL Ltd), Ian Moore, Max Mosam (Bremax Electronics Ltd), RAC Motor Sports Association Ltd, David Paveley, Piranha Models, Miguel Plano, Pro-rally Photography, Elizabeth Purves, *Rally Sport* magazine, Bill Richards (Bill Richards Racing), Dave Richards, Tom Seal (D R Developments), Seat, Shenstone and District Car Club, Penny Smith, Steve Smith, Stack Instruments, Stena Line, Marc Stretton (*Mini* magazine), Nick Swift (Swiftune), David Savage (British Motor Heritage Ltd), Dave Tippett, Roger Tristram (Owen Motoring Club), Monty Watkins (*Mini World* magazine), Ronnie White, Frank Williams (Speedsport), John Yea (British Motor Heritage Ltd), Philip Young (Endurance Rally Association), Robert Young Photographic.

Special thanks go specifically to Mike Southall (Enterprise Garage and Racing), without whose initial help we would never had got started with this project, and Peter Barker, Simon Cottingham, Donald Farr, David Paveley, Basil Wales and Robert Young (ex-works registrar, Mini Cooper Register) for their time and effort with proofreading. Our thanks also go to Basil for penning the Foreword and David for the Afterword.

Every effort has been made to trace the origin of photographs used within this work not taken by ourselves; should appropriate credit not have been made, please accept our sincere apologies.

We appreciate that we have not been able to include all of the details of the cars. Should readers have additional information in terms of specifications, photographs and history which they feel may benefit the content of a later edition of this book, we would be pleased to hear from them.

FOREWORD By Basil Wales

The Mini concept, as developed by the late Sir Alec Issigonis, established itself as an icon of the age like no other car. Many books have already been written, and many more of a general nature will doubtless follow; some, perhaps, documenting particular cars or aspects of the Mini's illustrious heritage. Bryan Purves and Tim Brenchley have researched and written about activities concerning several cars toward the end of the model's long production period in a way that helps the

Lars Persson and Lars Ytterbring prior to the 1966 Scottish Rally in conversation with Basil Wales. (Bryan Purves Collection)

reader to understand the problems and pitfalls of competition activity.

I first met Bryan at Silverstone in 2000 when he was parting with his few MGA Twin Cam components, which evoked happy memories of my long-gone BMC company apprenticeship. Bryan's infectious enthusiasm drew me to him as we spoke about the heritage of the engine. Later, we met on a Minis-to-Monte run, after which we have maintained regular contact. With so many books having been written about the Mini I guess that I was one of the few people who had not already been invited to pen words of encouragement to potential bookworms, who might not get further than the start of this, the latest Mini book on the shelves.

Those of us involved in the most popular competition activities of the Mini and Cooper variants believe we lived through the most interesting and exciting period, and now enjoy the nostalgia of the past. As we that are left grow older, let us leave a reminder of what was done in our time. This sort of competition activity was important in establishing the heritage of the Mini which ably demonstrated what once was acclaimed as the Best of British, and not without good reason! In my

Basil Wales with his MkII Cooper 'S'. (Bryan Purves Collection)

humble opinion it is vital that the facts are documented whilst we are still around and can produce the documents to support a distant memory. It was with this in mind that I arranged to have video recorded what I entitled "Classic Experience" evenings, bringing out rally drivers, co-drivers, racers and mechanics to tell their stories and relate their experiences to a receptive audience and a video camera whilst still in their prime.

The current owners of all these ex-works cars mostly recognise that they are only custodians and the full heritage needs to be accurately maintained for future generations to enjoy. Bryan and Tim have researched in great depth the work undertaken by a wide range of people connected with just a few specific Rover Coopers, and written in much detail in what is an almost unique approach to the task.

It must be acknowledged that BMW played a major part in maintaining production of the classic Mini beyond its economic life, to ensure that the new Mini developed by Rover engineers at Gaydon was ready and in production at Cowley as soon as Longbridge stopped making the classics. The value of this classic heritage is still under review at Mini headquarters but the recent acquisition of one of the best genuine ex-works Mini Coopers for display to plant visitors can be taken as an indicator, coinciding as it did with the release of the latest second generation Mini.

Much additional information is included in this book, such as the considerations necessary to decide tyre choices; the meaning of tyre markings on Michelin covers; the main suppliers to BMH; the wide range of scale models of Minis available from European and Japanese sources; steel specifications for different tasks, and a valuable record of all the cars linked to BMH and Rover that were modified for competition of one form or another from 1994 to 2001. I am sure there are still people around who could help with a few unanswered questions that come to mind when reading this absorbing book, and the authors do invite their input. A supplement ready for the inevitable reprint would be a fitting tribute to the work already undertaken by these two diligent owners.

Basil Wales

Basil Wales

INTRODUCTION

Having bought my first Mini – a 1963 Morris Super deluxe in Surf Blue, registered 940 RFC – in 1965, I was impressed by the vast amount of modifications that were possible on what was to become 'The Car of the 20th Century'. I spent many hours developing this little car with the aim of achieving the maximum power from the 850cc engine. The late Clive Trickey was at the time writing Mini articles in *Car and Car Conversions* magazine, and also wrote a wonderful book, *Tuning the Mini*.

My 850cc Mini then gained a 1098cc engine taken from an Austin 1100, and eventually this was changed for a 1275cc Cooper 'S' power unit. I had so many switches on the dashboard that when my father-in-law decided to drive the car back from our wedding reception I had to give him a lesson on how to start the engine!

Now deep into Minis, from 850s to full-blown 1330cc Cooper 'S' models, along with my brother Norman I decided in 1970 to enter our own home-built car in the Mini Seven Championship, undertaking all the work ourselves. We modified a 1959 shell, which, as you might not realise these days, was 40 pounds lighter than its 1960 counterpart. The only exception was that we had Chris Tyrell of Leatherhead prepare the cylinder head for us. The car we affectionately named 'Omemade'.

Over a period of several years numerous Cooper 'S' models came and went, and then in autumn 2004 the opportunity to own a 'works' car came my way when Tim Brenchley spotted a for sale advert for not just one but two examples. (Tim had never owned a Mini but, having regularly navigated with me in my 1964 Mk1 Cooper 'S', had begun to realise what wonderful cars they are.)

What was this all about, I wondered; two cars at the same venue, a Group 'N' and a Group 'A', both entered in the 1997 Monte Carlo Rally? Curiosity compelled me to make contact with the owner of the two cars to learn the details, and this is where the story really begins ...

In April 2005, after five months of contemplation, I eventually decided to purchase a car – but which one? A decision had to be made, which was not easy as the Group 'N' had actually

''omemade' at Thruxton in 1970. (Bryan Purves Collection)

finished the Monte Carlo Rally and the Group 'A' had retired with mechanical failure, although it had gone on to take part in numerous other rallies. The Group 'A' was complete and virtually turn-key, whereas the 'N' had the sub-frames and engine removed. But was it complete?

A decision was made; I would purchase the Group 'N' car, regardless of the work involved. The car was transported to my home, which immediately prompted Tim to seriously consider buying the sister car. By June 2005 we were transporting the second car down the M25 to be reunited with her sister.

During my period of indecision from December through until April, research had begun, and it was surprising what Tim and I discovered. The cars had featured in numerous national magazines, had raced in Germany, competed in the WRC Catalunya, Jim Clark Memorial, and Manx and Ulster rallies. They also formed the basis of the 1997 ST Special Tuning catalogue. What we had purchased were the last two genuine 'works' Minis ever to be produced and undoubtedly the most technically advanced in both body and mechanical design.

Our original intention with this book was to catalogue the story of these two cars, the likes of which will never be produced

again with Mini production ending on 4th October 2000 and the collapse of the Rover Car Company. But questions and suggestions such as: "Why do you not consider compiling a book relating to all of the 'works' 1990s Rover Coopers, and include their racing and rallying history?", and "Encompass all this information all within one tome" threw down a challenge that Tim and I could not refuse, and so we have tried to bring you as near as we are able to establish the complete history of what can only be described as the last of the 'works' Minis.

Bryan Purves

Above and right: Bryan and Tim rallying Bryan's 1964 MkI Cooper 'S'. (Courtesy Pro-Rally Photography)

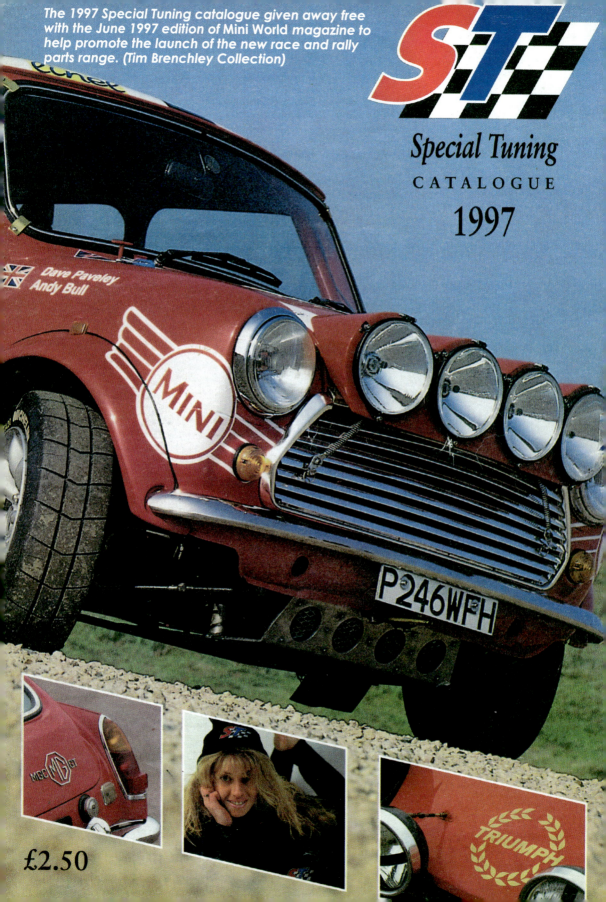

The 1997 Special Tuning catalogue given away free with the June 1997 edition of Mini World magazine to help promote the launch of the new race and rally parts range. (Tim Brenchley Collection)

S·T

Special Tuning

CATALOGUE

1997

Dave Paveley
Andy Bull

MINI

P246WFH

£2.50

A LEGEND BEGINS

Much has been written about the Abingdon Competitions and Special Tuning Departments, but still there is a place within this work for a brief résumé of how it all began and ended.

In 1952 the merger of the Austin Motor Company and the Nuffield Organization amalgamated a great number of motor manufacturers with numerous different models under one management structure. Essentially, there were two large retail names – Morris and Austin – neither of which had any form of in-house motorsport policy.

John Thornley, at that time General Manager of the MG Car Company based at Abingdon in Oxfordshire, proposed that some sort of professionally managed department be established in order to promote motorsport, which would then boost sales of the numerous marques. Thornley – Abingdon-based, with direct experience of the halcyon days prior to the Second World War, and the numerous competitions and events that the MG models had been involved

Right and overleaf: The BMC rosette was used as the basis for the Competitions Department logo. (Bryan Purves Collection)

15

in – proposed that a true competitions department be set up at the Abingdon site. Eventually, having gained the approval of Leonard Lord, Chairman of the Nuffield Organization, the BMC Competitions Department was formed on 1st December 1954.

Abingdon then began to produce a continuous stream of race and rally cars, all of which have become household names, to this day held in high esteem. The organization of drivers, cars, mechanics and office staff needed management, and Marcus Chambers was appointed as the first Competitions Manager. He came to Abingdon with a wealth of experience of pre-war racing with the likes of Bentleys and HRG, and his initial brief was to prepare a car for the Le Mans 24 Hour Race in six months' time. The car was EX182, which was to become the prototype for the new generation of MG sports car, the MGA.

At the same time, and having just taken on his new role with the company, Marcus was informed that he had to oversee the 1955 Monte Carlo entry which consisted of three Austin Westminsters and three MG Magnettes. The former were prepared at Longbridge and the MGs at Abingdon. The cars, crewed largely by amateurs with little international experience, were all overweight, and the fact that they achieved only very poor results emphasized the weakness of BMC's entry. There were but two exceptions to the amateur nature of the crews, namely John Gott and Willy Cave. It was Gott who quickly introduced recceing to the team and Cave the fine ability of co-driving.

Three cars were entered in the 1955 Le Mans 24 Hour Race with two cars finishing 12th and 17th, a result which put the Competitions Department on the motorsport map, and the genesis of what was to arguably become the most successful factory team ever! The 1955 RAC Tourist Trophy Race at Dundrod in Northern Ireland with the 'works' car EX182 was unfortunately the scene of fatalities, as a result of which Leonard Lord quite openly stated that any future competition activities would be in the areas of rallying and record-breaking.

Bolstered by the enthusiasm of the staff in the department, and external support of the general public, Marcus Chambers lost no time in looking for experienced personnel to make up his teams in the driving and navigator seats. John Gott and Willy Cave were already onboard, soon to be joined by Nancy Mitchell, Bill Shepherd and Pat Moss. Nancy Mitchell soon made an impact, becoming the 1956 FIA European Ladies Champion. Ann Wisdom, Val Domleo, Donald and Erle Morley also became part of the rally scene. Support team members were now an important part of the works rally teams, with Doug Hamblin, Doug Watts, Den Green and Tommy Wellman making up the initial team. Next came Bill Price who eventually became Assistant Competitions Manager.

Although there was a ban on the works entering any form of racing, it continued to support numerous privateers, and in 1959 an MGA Roadster was entered in the Le Mans 24 Hour Race. In 1960 the same car – now a coupé built by the Abingdon team – took part again, ostensibly entered by the North West Centre of the MG Car Club, and finished 12th overall.

Success after success began to fill the record books. September 1959 saw the competition debut of the car that was going to change the face of rallying for the next decade: the Mini. An Austin Se7en 850cc Mini driven by Marcus Chambers took 51st place on the Viking Rally. Then, just one month later, with Pat Moss behind the wheel of TJB 199, an 850cc Morris Mini Minor, and the experienced Stuart Turner as co-driver, an outright win by some ten minutes was achieved at the Mini Miglia National Rally organised by the Knowldale Car Club, Lancashire, the first national rally in which a Mini appeared. Stuart Turner is quoted as saying: "I can remember sitting in the Mini with my feet in water and Pat complaining how slow it was".

In 1960, in an Austin-Healey 3000, Pat Moss and Ann Wisdom snatched outright victory on the Liège-Rome-Liège Rally, BMC's first victory in Europe.

Having overseen establishment of the new Competitions Department, Marcus Chambers resigned after seven very challenging years to take up an appointment as Service Manager with the BMC garage Appleyard in Yorkshire. It was here that he spotted the talents of a young Tony Fall, later to enjoy great success with the 'works' Minis.

Upon Marcus Chambers' recommendation Stuart Turner was persuaded to move from his current position as Sports Editor of *Motoring News* to Manager of the BMC Competitions Department. The department was now well established on the rally scene, with the Big Healeys demonstrating their potential, the MGA enjoying racing success, and the little Mini showing a vast amount of as yet untapped potential.

Turner studied the form of those drivers showing promise on the world motorsport stage, recognising that many of the Scandinavians had driving skills which could benefit the Abingdon-based team. Rauno Aaltonen of Finland was invited to drive a Mini in the 1962 Monte Carlo Rally. Paddy Hopkirk – who really wanted to drive a Healey – joined the team. Timo Makinen was loaned a Mini Cooper for the 1962 RAC Rally in which he finished seventh. Co-drivers included Paul Easter, Tony Ambrose and Henry Liddon.

In 1962 the MGB was launched and, being built at Abingdon, had immediate access to parts bins. A car was prepared under the management of Peter Browning for the 1963 Le Mans 24 Hour, with Paddy Hopkirk and Alan Hutcheson taking a class win. In 1964, nobody was prepared for Paddy Hopkirk's outright win of the Monte Carlo Rally in the Mini Cooper 'S' with Henry

BMC

SPECIAL TUNING

FOR THE

MINI

848 c.c.

Issued by:

THE B.M.C. SPECIAL TUNING DEPARTMENT

THE M.G. CAR CO. Ltd., ABINGDON-ON-THAMES, ENGLAND

Left: The first BMC Special Tuning booklet offering tuning parts for the 850cc Mini. (Bryan Purves Collection)

Liddon navigating. With this resounding success, the Competitions Department was constantly in demand by sporting car owners for those special parts used on the rally cars, which gave an ideal opportunity to employ staff from the ex-Service Department that had just closed down. John Thornley then set up the Special Tuning Department as a subsidiary of the Competitions Department. In the first instance the venture was a loss-maker, and Basil Wales was asked to take over the management. With Basil's careful planning, and managed to a very high standard, the department began to flourish, but when British Leyland's new Managing Director, George Turnbull, took over he had the department accounts checked out by company chief accountant, John Bacchus, to establish that Basil was not cooking the books to his advantage. With a clean sheet Basil was given full autonomy to run the department until he left

The early days of the Special Tuning Department. Left to right: Michael Cox, Bill Richardson, Basil Wales and Henry Chapman. On the wall is a gallery of photographs capturing some of the Abingdon competition history. (Bryan Purves Collection)

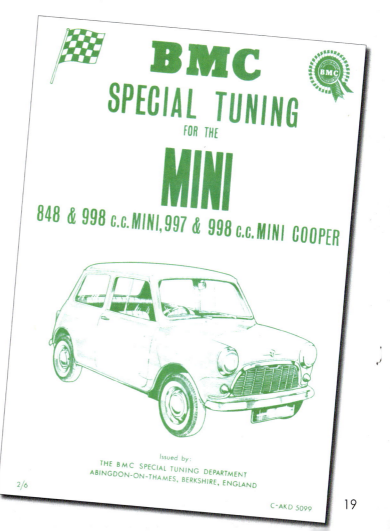

The later BMC Special Tuning booklet offered parts for the 850cc to 998cc Mini Cooper also. (Bryan Purves Collection)

JOIN THE BMC TEAM OF WORLD-WIDE ENTHUSIASTS

Fit BMC SPECIAL TUNING Parts as used by Works Team Cars Full Factory Approval

Then in 1966 the first five cars to finish – including the BMC Minis which finished in 1st, 2nd and 3rd places – were disqualified for the infamous infringement of the lighting regulation that the French had imposed. Not to be deterred, 1967 saw Rauno Aaltonen and Henry Liddon claim a third outright victory. The Mini Cooper 'S', in all its glory, continued to achieve outright victories on the Circuit of Ireland, Acropolis, 1000 Lakes and Alpine rallies.

In 1967 Stuart Turner moved to Castrol. Peter Browning took over his role and further development of the range continued. Along came the MGC-GTS and long-distance racing came to the fore with entries at Sebring and Marathon de la Route. Later that year there was another merger with the BMC name dropped in favour of British Motor Holdings. In 1968 the concern was taken over by British Leyland which encompassed the arch rival company to the MG name, Standard Triumph.

The Competitions Department now concentrated attention on endurance rally events such as the 1968 London to Sydney Rally and the World Cup Rally. Finally, a Rover 3500 was prepared for the 1970 Marathon de la Route but never took

ten years later in 1975 to help develop the interchange ability of the Unipart range at Garsington Road, Cowley.

Back to the rallying scene and again in the 1965 Monte Carlo Rally we saw another Cooper 'S', driven by Timo Makinen and Paul Easter, perform what has been described as "the greatest rally drive ever".

We'll bring out the beast in your car.

Under British Leyland, Special Tuning marketing took on a higher profile with "We'll bring out the beast in your car" as a slogan. (Bryan Purves Collection)

part due to closure of the Competitions Department. This important announcement in the history of the department was made by Sir Donald Stokes on 19th July 1970, and on August 24th Peter Browning passed the news to staff that the Competitions Department would close in October that year. Lord Stokes has a tremendous amount to answer for: the loss of an important part of Britain's motoring heritage!

The Special Tuning Department carried on, now flying the British Leyland flag in international motorsport with the budget provided by the marketing departments of both BL UK and international divisions, although the income generated by the

The Leyland logo that featured for several years. (Bryan Purves Collection)

The new British Leyland Special Tuning Abingdon logo. (Bryan Purves Collection)

The Leyland badge, in the form of a crash helmet, could be seen on many a racing/ rally overall. (Bryan Purves Collection)

sales of tuning parts became very low-key. The department achieved many successes with the Triumph Dolomite Sprint and the much-maligned Morris Marina.

In 1974 Bill Price rejoined the team as Workshop Supervisor. In 1975, after Basil Wales had left the company after immense success in the world of rallying, Bill Price continued the workshop activities with the TR7, along with Richard Seth-Smith who was brought in as Department Manager, and supported by John Kerswell as Public Relations Manager. Seth-Smith's term as manager lasted just one year with Bill Price then promoted to that position. But this was not the end of the legend, as will be revealed ...

One of the last British Leyland Special Tuning brochures. Note the basic styling of the ST logo, which featured in the 1990s resurrection. (Bryan Purves Collection)

The last ST Special Tuning booklet relating to competition parts for the Mini was issued in 1980. (Bryan Purves Collection)

BRITISH MOTOR HERITAGE

(Courtesy British Motor Heritage Ltd)

British Motor Industry Heritage Trust was initially established in 1983 as part of Austin Rover Group, with the primary objective of keeping alive many of the great marques intrinsic to the history of the British motor industry. At its Syon Park location was a range of cars for public viewing, the most notable of which were the MG and Triumph marques.

Over time it became obvious that there was a need to source previously unobtainable parts, and this requirement was met by a division of the industry, with British Motor Heritage beginning small batch production.

Approved and selected dealer outlets were established and granted permission to trade under the banner of the Association of Heritage Approved Specialists, and it was from these retail outlets that the general public was able to purchase Heritage manufactured bodyshells and panels.

On 18th September 1996 BMH issued a document *The Mini – Proving It Just Can't Be Beaten*, which emphasized the fact that, since the Mini's return to international rallying on the 1994 Monte Carlo rally with Paddy Hopkirk, there had been a steady resurgence of individuals competing with the new Rover Cooper Mini. To quote: "Of all the things that the Mini is known for, its achievements in motorsport stand out above all else – in particular its giant-killing feats have given it almost legendary status."

To that point in time BMH had an interest in the model but very little exposure within the Mini market place. Initial thoughts were that it would become involved in the manufacture of key obsolete parts, such as Mk1 and Mk2, Countryman and Pick-up

bodyshells, whilst raising awareness of the company as a supplier of high quality Mini products.

The Mini market was now saturated with sub-standard copy parts and bolt-on goodies, the majority generally of inferior quality, a fact made obvious by the lack of engineering integrity of the 1996 Monte Carlo car, which was essentially constructed from the parts that were generally available in the marketplace. BMH then went on to determine how it could re-establish the Mini as a winner. One particular model was considered to be the Mini's direct competitor: the Fiat Cinquecento.

In January 1996 a document detailing the company's concern about the lack of Mini sales worldwide was produced by Patrick Flemming of Rover Group Marketing and circulated to all dealers. The document set out suggestions for a marketing strategy and objectives to try and develop the Mini brand toward the year 2000 and launch of the new Rover-produced Mini. Comparisons were made with six contemporary vehicles, with the Mini achieving the greatest power (kW) and 0-100kph (0.60mph) time. It was claimed that the Mini had unparalleled handling, city car practicality, and strong emotional appeal. Two European and three Japanese derivatives were considered, bringing the models inline in terms of internal fittings and seating with similar models from other manufacturers. Highlighted were the new

Sports-Pack options that had been used very effectively on the 'Silverstone' Special Editions sold in Germany. Sales volume was also a key factor, as can be seen in the accompanying chart 1.21.

Launch plans were made as Rover admitted it had not really marketed the Mini during the past few years; the 1997 model Mini was set to be launched in October 1996 at the European Motor Show in Paris (1-13th October); Birmingham (15-27th October), and Berlin (19-27th October). Prior to these dates the 1997 model was on sale in Europe from late September 1996. Initial exposure of this model was expected to be via press activity and advertising commencing January 1997.

It was considered that the homologation specification (refer to Appendix 1) for Groups 'A' and 'N' was inadequate for re-establishing the Mini in motorsport. A comparison was made by looking at Fiat Cinquecento homologation papers which highlighted areas that could be exploited and where Rover/BMH should be working. There was an obvious window of opportunity for homologation to the 'Kit Car' VK (Variant Kit) rules which would serve two purposes: first, it would make the Mini a car to be contested within the 1300cc Class and, second, it would give BMH the opportunity to produce unique engineered components and kit parts.

The 1997 homologation papers permitted the addition of twin point injection and changes to the external body profile.

	1994 Actual	1995 Budget	1996 Budget	1997	1998	1999	Lifetime
UK	5713	6745	6520	3000	3000	3000	9000
France	2710	2500	2000	1450	1350	1250	4050
Italy	2425	1800	1300	700	700	700	2100
Germany*	2600	2600	3500	3000	3000	3000	9000
Japan	8097	8362	7500	7500	7500	5500	20,500
Total	21,545	22,007	20,820	15,650	15,550	13,450	44,650

Table 1.21: Sales volume (Courtesy Rover Group Marketing. Mini 97 MY)

The evolution papers for homologation allowed competitors to select the best of the old, plus development modifications. At the time the cost for the preparation of the homologation papers was estimated to be around £12,500 (Table 1.22).

BMH considered that media exposure would play a large part in the promotion of the Mini and the only means of attracting this would be for the cars to be competing in prestigious events, not just in Europe but throughout the world. Financial implications had to now be seriously considered and table 1.23 gives an insight to the considerations for the forthcoming three years.

Reference to Appendix 1 (BMH forward strategy 1996-2002) and Appendix 2 (Mini development) record how BMH/Rover Sport envisaged budget expenditure, development of the cars, and the retail aspect during the forthcoming three years.

During 1996 numerous changes were

Variant Options	ER	Variant kit
Twin point injection	Inlet/exhaust port sizes	Bodywork
Front radiator	Front view of car	Rear wing
Repositioned oil filter	Crankshaft material	Suspension
Distributorless ignition	Flywheel material	Engine bore and stroke
Side impact bars		
New dashboard layout		
New wheelarches		
Gear ratios/final drive		
6-speed gearbox		
Sequential change		
RAC skid set		
John Cooper head		
Type of disc/caliper		

Table 1.22: The suggested part grouping for the 1997 homologation.
(Courtesy Rover Group Marketing)

	1997	1998	1999
Costs			
Development	141,000 (inc. 1996)	0	0
Homologation	12,500 (1996)	0	0
Car	92,000	46,000	92,000
Maintenance	42,000	42,000	42,000
Events	211,000	153,000	213,000
Marketing	TBA	TBA	TBA
Revenues			
Parts contribution	437,000	393,000	353,000
Sponsorship	TBA	TBA	TBA

Table 1.23: The estimated costs and revenues between 1997 and 1999 for two Minis.
(Courtesy British Motor Heritage)

Brian Cameron was appointed MD of BMH in 1995. (Courtesy Richard Franklin)

of the Rover organization, and eventual demise of Mini production could now be clearly seen. Under the leadership of Brian Cameron, who was appointed MD in late 1995, along with John Brigden of Brigden Associate (a consultant specialising in PR, marketing and advertising, and former journalist with *Car and Car Conversions* and *Mini World* magazines), BMH was determined to look at the marketing aspect of the company. The Mini means many things to many people – especially because of its famous exploits on the world rally stage during the 1960s. Used and developed by the enthusiast for over three decades in all areas of motorsport, the Mini's real magic has been in the

occurring in the world of the Mini. The Rover name was dropped from badges, and British Motor Heritage (BMH), based in Faringdon near Witney, Oxfordshire, arrived on the scene and was putting a considerable amount of effort into the manufacture and supply of Mini parts. It also offered the facility to build complete cars suitable for competition use whether on the track or in rallying, and all alongside the supply of new bodyshells for the MGB, TR6, and MG Midget, and panels for the Morris Minor. BMH was also sponsoring the British Motor Industry Heritage Trust Museum at Gaydon, Warwickshire.

BMW had now taken overall control

rally scene, and it was a great shame that the Competitions Department was shut down by Lord Stokes.

Up until 1996 the Mini had been running on nostalgia, with Paddy Hopkirk in 1994 driving a Brigden-Coulter Motorsport-entered Mini in the Monte Carlo Rally, and Russell Brookes taking a car on the RAC Rally. In reality, what chance did they have against the modern technology used in rally cars of this period? At least Class divisions meant that they had things to themselves in their class. Since the 1996 Monte, the Mini had to face stiff opposition from the sporting Fiat Cinquecento, considered the Mini Cooper's replacement.

With BMH a wholly-owned subsidiary of the Rover Group, it cannot be claimed that the later generation vehicles are 'works' cars in the 1960s sense, though they are still 'works' cars in essence. If a car and its associated development is totally paid for by the manufacturer – be it built at Abingdon or elsewhere – then it must be considered a 'works' car. Should a car be only part-funded by the manufacturer then, in our opinion, it cannot be classified as 'works'. During our research we discovered that the 1994 BCM cars cannot be fully classified as 'works' vehicles due to their outsourced sponsorship. However, we decided to include these very important cars anyway as we feel that they illustrate how the rallying Mini reached its ultimate specification in the 1990s when it was entered in the 1997 Monte Carlo Rally. The last two Rover cars – P245 WFH and P246 WFH – were to become something special due to the technology that was more readily available, and were what can only be described as the ultimate development of the last 'works' Minis.

Without a competitions department the obvious course of action was to go to the experts in the field. Tom Walkinshaw Racing developed a programme for the Rover SD1, and who better than Enterprise Racing to develop the Rover Mini? Enterprise Racing had been involved with the production of Leyland and Rover race and rally cars since 1980, from the Metro to the 6R4, achieving extremely commendable results over the years. What now became apparent is the re-establishment of sub-contracted competitions departments, usual practice for world rally championship teams.

In their infancy the 1996 BMH Rover Minis were fitted with twin point injection engines, six-speed gearboxes, 13 inch wheels, larger brake discs, four-pot callipers, adjustable suspension, rose-jointed linkages, and state-of-the-art dashboard instrumentation, with the immediate objective of entering two

BMH Mini Motorsport - Actuals 1996					
Event	Publication	Space	Ad cost	Value	Notes
1996 Monte Carlo Ral	Autosport	Half page	750	3000	Value of
	Mini World	2 pages	2400	9600	editorial
	CCC	6 pages	11250	45000	is 4 times
	Complete Car	5 pages	12500	50000	ad rates
	Motoring News	Qtr page	450	1800	
	UK papers	10 pages	1200	4800	
	AMS	4 pages	20000	80000	
	Satellite - Vox	7 minutes	21000	84000	
	Satellite - WDR	6 minutes	18000	72000	
			87550	350200	
Nurburgring 24-Hours	Autosport	Qtr page	450	1800	
	Motoring News	Eighth page	300	1200	
	Mini World	Half page	700	2800	
	CCC	8 pages	13,125	52500	
	Complete Car	2 pages	5,000	20000	
				0	
	AMS	2 pages	10,000	40000	
	WDR TV	6 minutes	18,000	72000	
	Vox TV	2 minutes	6,000	24000	
	German papers	6 pages	6,000	24000	Estimate
	Auto Zeitung	3 pages	6,000	24000	
			65575	262300	
Nurburgring 6-Hours	Mini World	2 pages	2,400	9600	
	Mini Magazine	1 page	600	2400	
	CCC	3 pages	5,625	22500	
	Auto Express	Eighth page	300	1200	
				0	
	Vox TV	4 minutes	12,000	48000	
	Auto Aktuel	2 pages	5,000	20000	
	Auto Zeitung	Half page	500	2000	
			26,425	105700	

BMH outgoing costs of actuals for the 1996 entered events. Attention is drawn to the first section of this document, which relates to the 1996 Monte Carlo campaign driven by Dron and Douglas. This then leads on directly to the two new cars that were being prepared for the Nürburgring races. Major companies often invite the media to events to experience the product first-hand and also to write an article promoting their products. Consider the amounts paid to the media as shown, and also that the projected financial value of each promotion was envisaged to be four times the outlay. (Courtesy British Motor Heritage – Rover)

Dave Paveley driving the new Rover Cooper, Andy Bull navigating, on the 1996 Mull Rally with the aim of testing the full potential of the car. (Courtesy Speedsport)

Nürburgring races during the 1996 summer racing season.

Given the enthusiasm of Brian Cameron and John Brigden it was felt there was every reason to promote what was later declared 'The Car of the 20th Century', but in this case a fully competitive car. Brian Cameron recognised that the nostalgia trip was over for the Mini: it had to prove itself against modern competition and win again if it was ever going to move on. BMH was also considering retailing or renting what it described as a 'kit' suitable for serious rally enthusiasts, and it was now that a car was entered in the 27th Philips Tour of British Mull Rally for testing purposes. The idea was that Special Tuning (ST) would be reformed to offer prospective rally enthusiasts the opportunity to purchase appropriate parts to build a Group 'A' car

into what was anticipated to be a 135bhp 'screamer'. The thinking went that, maybe with this arrangement, a suitably built car could possibly take over from the Group 'A' cars, and participate in the World Rally Championship where the rules on build are surprising relaxed. Other ideas were maybe a mid-mounted engine, 4x4, or even turbocharged – who knows?

In 1997, and with the Mini becoming further removed from the mainstream BMW/Rover new car range, BMH decided to make inroads into the Mini market, starting with remanufacture of numerous hard-to-obtain parts for the earlier models, though not, unfortunately, MkI bodyshells. Production began with the MkIV version and then later the MkV as either Standard or Sports-Pack variants. In order to promote the Heritage name in the marketplace,

The front sections of the bodyshells waiting to be welded to the floorpan and rear sections. (Courtesy British Motor Heritage Ltd)

The British Motor Heritage logo and its construction. (Courtesy British Motor Heritage – Rover)

Roll welding the roof panel to the lower body section. (Courtesy British Motor Heritage Ltd)

what better way forward than by having a 'works' sponsored Mini both on the track and in rallying? BMH backed the Mini project whilst Rover Sport took over the business side of things.

A completed bodyshell reaches the end of the assembly line in the BMH factory. (Courtesy British Motor Heritage Ltd)

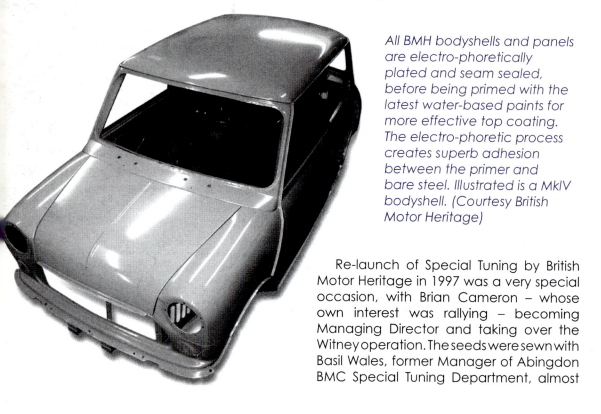

All BMH bodyshells and panels are electro-phoretically plated and seam sealed, before being primed with the latest water-based paints for more effective top coating. The electro-phoretic process creates superb adhesion between the primer and bare steel. Illustrated is a MkIV bodyshell. (Courtesy British Motor Heritage)

Re-launch of Special Tuning by British Motor Heritage in 1997 was a very special occasion, with Brian Cameron – whose own interest was rallying – becoming Managing Director and taking over the Witney operation. The seeds were sewn with Basil Wales, former Manager of Abingdon BMC Special Tuning Department, almost

Although rejected by some Mini purists, Clubman production sales amounted to 626,312 units across the range. (Courtesy British Motor Heritage – Rover)

A range of Special Tuning marketing products. (Tim Brenchley Collection)

coming out of retirement to give the project his support and encouragement.

In November 2001 the company that was once a subsidiary of the former Rover Group was sold off by BMW as an independent business. The legacy consortium consisted of a group of three ex-Rover Group/Unipart employees headed by David Bishop. Since taking over the company these individuals have worked extremely hard to provide good quality replacement parts by building upon the work of the former company, and still using much of the original tooling and production procedures. A dedicated team of staff caters admirably for the enthusiast, and must be commended for its work. There is nowhere else in the world that manufactures classic car parts so comprehensively.

 British Motor Heritage Special Tuning

Personal Accessories

In addition to the range of exciting product already listed here, we are able to obtain to order the full range of Special Tuning products as featured in the British Motor Heritage 1997 brochure. Please telephone your preferred branch for more details.

Lapel Pin Badge	HMP190147
Special Tuning Space Pen	HMP190148
Special Tuning Rollerball Pen	HMP190185
Brass Special Tuning Key Ring	HMP190149
Special Tuning Mouse Mat	HMP190151
Vinyl Decal	HMP190152
Enamel Car Badge	HMP190153
Special Tuning Accessories Brochure	HMP990012

THE ROVER GROUP

It is important that mention is made of what the Longbridge produced Rover Mini was all about and how it came to be. It was the Rover Group's intention to make the Mini once again more prominent in the world's small car market with production commencing in June 1990. Numerous different models were produced, incorporating a great many product differences, including Limited Editions, although not all models were Cooper-based. (Appendix 3 has a list of models.)

Initially, the John Cooper conversions (MCC542) were based on the 1000cc engine, and coincided with the Racing Green, Flame Red, Checkmate LE model and Mini 30. All these variants made a good basis for future models. Now that the model was established, Rover's MD, Graham Day, worked closely with John Cooper on full reintroduction of a Mini Cooper which was to be based primarily on modified Mayfair and City models.

The Mini Cooper, the first Rover Cooper since 1972, was to be classified as the RSP (Rover Special Product). A total of 1650 were built with 1050 units intended for the UK market. They were fitted with the MG Metro 1275cc power unit producing 61bhp.at 5550rpm, and a top speed of 92mph. The engine also had an oil cooler and a modified exhaust system.

The RSP models were available in three colours: Racing Green, Flame Red and Black, all with a white roof. It seems apparent that they were, in the majority, built from whatever parts were left in the parts store at Longbridge at the time. They featured standard trim, Webasto glass sun roof, wheelarch extensions, and door mirrors painted to match body colour, plus a Cooper bonnet badge, white Cooper laurels on the boot lid and on the rear side quarter panels,and two white coach lines down the sides. Twin white stripes incorporating John Cooper's signature attached to the sides of the bonnet, leaving a small gap before the bonnet lip. The front of the car was fitted twin driving/ spot lights directly in front of the grill. A further feature was different road wheels identical to those on the Mini 30 and later Racing Green cars. These wheels were easily identified as the wheel stud holes were in line with the spokes.

Rover's new Mini Cooper with a 1967 model. (Courtesy Rover)

The Rover RSP model was available in three duotone colours: Flame Red, British Racing Green, and Black, all with a white roof. The price was £6995 without any extras. (Bryan Purves Collection)

The RSP engine bay. (Bryan Purves Collection)

The chassis number on an RSP car always started with SAXXNNAMBAD, and introduction of this model eventually led to reappearance of the legendary Cooper 'S' logo. The first three letters of the VIN details were always SAX, which was the world make identifier; the fourth and fifth letters – XN – denote that the car is a Mini; the sixth letter, N, that the car is a Cooper; the seventh letter, A, that the car is fitted with two doors. The eighth letter was either a Y or M: the Y denoted a fuel injection Cooper whilst the M indicated that the car was a carburettor model. The tenth letter could be either B, C, M or N. B denoted right-hand drive with carburettor, or right-hand drive with injection if it was a C. If the car was left-hand drive with carburettor/injection, then an M or N would be used accordingly. The final letter D stated that the car was built at Longbridge, Birmingham.

During March 1994 the German manufacturer BMW purchased the Rover Group; an acquisition, it was felt, that could have major repercussions for production of the Mini. BMW did quite categorically state that part of the reason for the takeover was its wish to increase volume production of the small car range. Second only to Japan, Germany was the biggest importer of the beloved Mini, although volume sales worldwide were declining.

Another aspect had also to be considered: the 1996 introduction of the new emission and safety regulations which could quite possibly sound the Mini's death knell ...

THE 1994 RALLYE MONTE CARLO

Date: 22-27th January 1994
Distance: 3058km including 588.42km
 over 22 different stages
Special Stage surface: asphalt
Participants: 186 at start; 94 finishers

The Rallye Monte Carlo is possibly the most famous motor rally in the world, and also the most prestigious. It is every motor rally enthusiasts dream to take part or just spectate at this event.

The rally is always run on asphalt roads, but due to the time of the year these become an ever-changing surface when it's dry and clear, rainy and wet, or icy and snowy, and in many instances a combination of all three! The driver is constantly changing his or her driving style and rhythm in an effort to drive as fast and as safely as possible on whatever road surface encountered.

The competition cars have team members who drive the route in advance of the event and report back to the team prior to the start of a Leg or Stage. This gives the driver the opportunity to select his/her tyre preference according to road conditions they are likely to experience.

By tradition the Rallye Monte Carlo posters always depict the winner of the previous year's rally. (Tim Brenchley Collection)

The manner in which the car is set up is also extremely important as it must handle well in every conceivable condition, even when environmental conditions necessitate a performance compromise, compelling the driver to change driving style to deal with those stressful moments as they arise.

The car's engine must be set up to give good torque output as the driving on this event is generally erratic with many stop/go scenarios; slowing for ice on the road and then accelerating away without losing traction.

The Rallye Monte Carlo is an event where risks must not be taken; one of the biggest mistakes made by inexperienced drivers is to drive too fast when conditions become tricky. One rule that should always be obeyed is only drive fast when it's known to be safe, even on the last night Leg where there is a possibility of a higher placing.

Project Mini Monte Carlo

CLASSEMENT

COMMUNE

FINALE

THE 1994 MONTE CARLO RALLY JANUARY 22-28, 1994

Project Mini Monte Carlo, 38 West Street, Marlow, Bucks, SL7 2NB.
Tel: 0628 473311/0732 740216. Fax: 0628 483029/0732 462359

In 1994 a higher proportion of the route ran over new stages than it had in previous years, with more night stages.

The Mini has always been synonymous with the Rallye Monte Carlo, and in 1994 famous racers were to be entered by two new teams: Brigden Coulter Motorsport with Hopkirk at the wheel, and D R Engineering with Makinen/Needel in another two cars. The BCM entry was initially conceived as a way to commemorate Hopkirk's and Liddon's 1964 Rallye Monte Carlo victory in a Mini Cooper with the registration 33 EJB. The initial idea was that John Brigden would compete in one car, Jeremy Coulter in a second, and Paddy Hopkirk in a third. However, rallying had changed quite considerably since the Mini Cooper's 1960s heyday, and the logistics of entering World Rally Championship events had become immense.

Issue · Number 143

1994 · 1 · 1994
RALLYE MONTE-CARLO

RALLY INFORMATION

62nd Rallye Automobile Monte-Carlo
22-27 January 1994

World Championship - Round 1

TIMETABLE

Total Distance: On average 3058km
Stages: 23 (none tackled twice)
Stage Distance: 621.95km
Stage Surfaces: Closed asphalt public roads
Reconnaissance: FIA rules, from 9-19 January
Rally Headquarters: Hall de la Permanance.
Sporting d'Hiver, Place du Casino, Monte Carlo.
Parcs Fermes: Valence - Parc des Expositions
Gap - CMCL, Blvd Pierre et Marie Curie
Monaco - Quai Albert 1er
Rest Halt Headquarters:
Valence - Parc des Expositions
Fuel: FIA control fuel
Servicing Restrictions: None
Sun Rise: 0746 Sun Set: 1603
11 Stages in Darkness

Time of Day
(Monte Carlo follows Central European Time)

New Zealand	CET + 12 hours
Australia (East)	CET + 10 hours
Japan	CET + 8 hours
Middle East (UAE)	CET + 3 hours
South Africa	CET + 1 hour
Finland	CET + 1 hour
UK	CET - 1 hour
Argentina	CET - 4 hours
USA (East)	CET - 6 hours
USA (Pacific)	CET - 9 hours

Scrutineering
Before the start in each of the starting towns on Sat 22 Jan

Concentration (no stages)
Cars leave six starting towns on Sat 22 Jan as follows:

City	Provisional start time	Length
Bad Hombourg (D)	1747	1205km
Reims(F)	1902	1162km
Lausanne (CH)	2112	1084km
Monte Carlo (MC)	2130	1081km
Barcelona (E)	2205	1088km
Turin (I)	2235	1152km

Cars arrive in Valence from 1800 on Sun 23 Jan.

Etape de Classement (stages 1 - 6)
Start: Parc des Expositions, Valence
Mon 24 Jan 0900
Regroup: St Agreve Mon 24 Jan 1411-1426
Arrive: Parc des Expositions, Valence
Mon 24 Jan 1820
Distance: 409.55km
6 special stages, 179.97km

Etape Commune - first part (stages 7 - 12)
Restart: Parc des Expositions, Valence
Tue 25 Jan 0800
Regroup: Allevard les Bains
Tue 25 Jan 1340-1355
Arrive: CMCL, Blvd Pierre et Marie Curie, Gap
Tue 25 Jan 1918
Distance: 511.26km
6 special stages, 180.44km

Etape Commune - second part (stages 13 - 16)
Restart: CMCL, Blvd Pierre et Marie Curie, Gap
Wed 26 Jan 0500
Arrive: Quai Albert 1er, Monaco
Wed 26 Jan 1257
Distance: 434.86km
4 special stages, 106.47km

Etape Finale (stages 17 - 23)
Restart: Quai Albert 1er, Monaco
Wed 26 Jan 2200
Regroup: Digne les Bains Thur 27 Jan 0414-0429
Finish: Quai Albert 1er, Monaco Thur 27 Jan 1033
Distance: 573.82km
7 special stages, 155.07km

Times given for the first car.

Monte Carlo · **Distance chart (km)**
Note: + via autoroute

177	Digne				
263	86	Gap			
+400	203	161	Valence		
+460	263	221	60	St Agreve	
402	220	143	138	198	Allevard

Chambery

Allevard les Bains

9   10

Grenoble

St Jean-en-Royans

8

St Agreve   6   4   5

VALENCE   7   11   12

3   Crest

1   GAP

2   Vals-les-Bains
Aubenas

13   Serres

Bad Hombourg
Paris · Reims
Lausanne
MONTE CARLO · Turin
Barcelona

14   Sisteron   15   Digne-les-Bains   18
20 21 22   Puget-Theniers   17
16   19   23
Castellane   St Auban   Nice · MONTE CARLO

37

Initially, cars had to be available, so it was essential to gain the support of Rover and convince the management that it needed to see the Mini once again competing on the world rally Stage. Some claimed that the Mini was out-of-date and nearing the end of its production life; why should Rover need any further publicity for a car that was out-of-date and uncompetitive compared with its foreign counterparts?

Jeremy Coulter and John Brigden were two individuals with experience of rallying Minis: Jeremy won the 1991 FIA European Historic Rally Championship and John contested some of the FIA European rounds. John and Jeremy also ran their own company which, at the time, was responsible for the public relations of a subsidiary of the Rover Group, namely British Motor Heritage. With in-house knowledge of relevant personnel within the Marketing and PR Departments, Kevin Jones agreed to act as their spokesman to persuade Rover of the merits of the project. Rod Ramsay, Rover Cars' Marketing Director, then became involved and ultimately had the final say about whether the project could proceed. Rover Brand Manager, Nicki Darzinskas, had also to be convinced, along with Rover Sport, which controlled all of Rover's motorsport activities.

During January 1993 a letter was sent to Rover setting out the project, and meetings were arranged with Nicki Darzinskas and Kevin Jones of the PR department. The objective now was to get Paddy Hopkirk onboard and willing to drive one of the cars. Louise Aitken-Walker and Tina Thorner were also considered to drive a second car. A team for a third car had yet to be chosen by Rover Japan, which was considering making an entry.

As this was, in part, a celebratory event, plans for the financing, car build and entry had to be made well in advance of January 1994 as it was essential that the Mini had a high profile. The decision to proceed with the project was finally made

Rover External Affairs official release letter of support for the Mini's return to Monte Carlo. (Courtesy Stephen Smith)

in September 1993, leaving just four months in which to build, test, raise sponsorship and turn the idea into reality. In order to ensure that the project was successfully overseen, the task of managing the whole ensemble was assigned in October 1993 to both John Brigden (*Heritage* Editor) and Jeremy Coulter (*Mini World* Sports Editor). These two men formed a consortium called Brigden-Coulter Motorsports Ltd – generally known as BCM – with 1000 one pound shares distributed between John Brigden (600), Shirley Brigden (150), and Jeremy Coulter (250). The company continued to trade until 1995.

Rover, having agreed to become associated with the venture, donated one of the factory cars that had been used for company testing purposes and then written off, and sold a further two units at cost price to the consortium. It also donated £15,000 in cash. In the meantime, Rod Ramsay spoke to David

New bodies came directly off the production line devoid of sealant or paint, and were delivered directly to Safety Devices of Soham where the integrated roll cages were tailored to each bodyshell. (Courtesy John Colley)

One of the bodyshells in the process of having a roll cage fabricated to fit. (Courtesy John Colley)

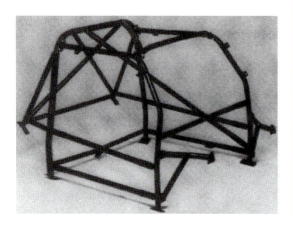

The roll cage that was fitted to the BCM Monte cars. (Bryan Purves Collection)

Nick Chalkley building one of the 1994 Monte Cars at the Canterbury workshop. (Courtesy Mini World)

Bloom of Rover Japan which, in turn, offered a further £75,000 in sponsorship money. This Rover Japan sponsorship was subsequently withdrawn and given to Tom Seal to develop an entry for Timo Makinen. At the same time British Aerospace, which had expressed an interest in assisting with sponsorship, withdrew its offer of support. It was now that John Brigden made contact with Sanwa Trading and Co in Japan which agreed to support the venture.

In the first instance one development car was built under the watchful eye of Simon Skelton at his Auto Auctions workshop at Thannington Without, Canterbury, Kent. This car then appeared at the London Motor Show at Earls Court on the Haymarket Publishing stand. Whilst it had been hurriedly completed and not built to full Group 'A' specification, it was to then provide the basis for a test car which was taken to Valence in France in December and used by Paddy Hopkirk and co-driver Ron Crellin as a test car. The car received its first experimental engine, built and fitted by Bill Richards Racing.

It was initially thought that the power output of the engine would be constrained by the injection throttle body, but on testing it was discovered that the limiting factor was the size of the exhaust valves. Due to the restrictions that applied to Group 'A', the size of the valves could not be changed, although they could be manufactured from a different material. Time was then spent working on the gas flowing of the head and matching of the engine parts. Piper Cams designed a special camshaft with characteristics to suit the small valves. The dynometer figures were impressive: 96bhp at the flywheel and torque peaking at 80lb/ft at 4500rpm.

One clever feature of the Weber Alpha system fitted to the car was that the ECU was fully programmable by using a lap top computer with appropriate software. The engine had then to be run through to the point of detonation up to 60 points on the power curve. With the ECU permitting 16 throttle positions and 16 engine speeds, this equated to 156 points of calibration. In real terms only around 60 visits to the map were generally required with each point being logged, recording the injection pulse and the ignition advance. The readings built up a map which was appropriately tweaked to permit snap throttle opening along with cold starting. With the full range of datum established, the information was then blown onto a chip.

Apart from the Weber Alpha ECU the car also used the Weber distributorless

The test car being unveiled by Paddy Hopkirk at the Earls Court Motor Show. (Courtesy Mini World)

Paddy Hopkirk, having just unveiled the Rover Cooper entry in the 1994 Rallye Monte Carlo, with John Cooper in the background. This car was destined to be driven by Phillippe Camandona and not Paddy Hopkirk. (Courtesy Mini World)

ignition system which replaced the standard distributor with twin static ignition coils. This, in turn, increased and made a more consistent spark voltage. The crank sensor was removed and a modified reluctor ring fitted on the flywheel, which passed through a magnetic sensor that told the ECU when the engine was at top

As a mark of respect Paddy had the honour of having his 1964 rally number on his 1994 entry. (Courtesy Mini World)

The car was very well presented and received a great deal of enthusiastic support from the general public at the Motor Show. (Courtesy Mini World)

Working on the test car which eventually went to the Earls Court Motor Show. For homologation purposes the car had to weigh at least 750kg. Phillippe Camandona drove this car, although it then carried the registration L33 EJB which was later to become K33 EJB and K764 VKM. (Courtesy Mini World)

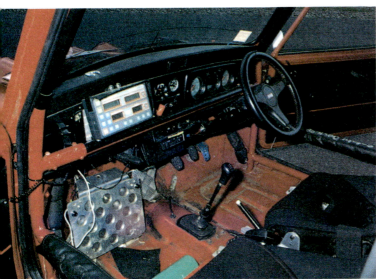

The cockpit of car number 37. (Courtesy Mini World)

British Motor Heritage dealership trading as Sanwa Trading, Castrol Oils, BCM, Autocar, Dunlop, Southern Carburettors, Autosport, Classic Cars, Your Classic, NGK, Ripspeed Racing, Spax, Safety Devices, PIAA, Jack Knight, Kent Auto Auctions, Stena Sealink, Corbeau, Paddy Hopkirk Automotive, Ferodo, Classic and Sportscar, Newton Commercial, Jack Knight,

dead centre in order to index the whole system. By now, Bill Richards had built two engines.

When the car returned to the workshop it was dismantled in order to evaluate where parts and components could be modified and developed. In the meantime, communication had been established with Rene Isoart, Commissaire General of the Automobile Club de Monaco, who agreed to allow Paddy Hopkirk to run as car number 37 – the start number he had in 1964. At the same time the registration L33 EJB was purchased from the DVLA at Swansea.

Sponsorship deals for the British entry were arranged with a large Japanese Spax. Barretts of Canterbury assisted with the main service vehicles and also the Mini Cooper Register. The service vehicles consisted of a Range Rover and trailer, two V8 Sherpa vans, two Range Rover Discoverys, a Granada, Subaru and a Ford Maverick.

Five right-hand drive cars were built. One car was for Hopkirk with the second originally intended as the team recce car but actually driven by Swiss driver, Philippe Camandona. The third car was for the Rover France entry driven by Philippe Chevalier (son of Maurice Chevalier, the singer), and owner of the Rover dealership, Carbury Automobiles in Valence. The fourth

The internal layout of the boot with a specially manufactured ATL fuel cell and the spare wheel strapped down over the battery box. (Courtesy Mini World)

car was built for promotional purposes and was later a competition prize. The fifth car, registered L54 CVP, was purchased from Rover and was to be the Russell Brookes car entered in the 1994 Network Q RAC Rally, and later driven by Tony Dron in the 1996 Rallye Monte Carlo.

Three BCM competition cars were built to full Group 'A' specification, the engines built by Bill Richards Racing working in conjunction with Laurence Mahon and Peter Cook of Southern Carburettors, Wimbledon, the company responsible for the unique Weber Alpha engine management system. Between Bill Richards' engine build and setting up on the rolling road an engine output of 104bhp was achieved with a torque of 85lb/ft at 4500bhp. Helping to achieve extra horsepower, the regulations also permitted the catalyst exhaust to be discarded and leaded fuel to be used.

Inside the cars were Corbeau Sprint design race seats, Safety Devices roll cages, an intercom, four-point harnesses,

The Group 'A' engine built by Bill Richards fitted with distributorless ignition. The standard coil and distributor were replaced by two double-ended static ignition coils that fired alternately, ensuring the coils delivered consistently high voltage. The air filter fitted to the BCM cars had the potential to increase power output by as much as 6bhp. (Courtesy Mini World)

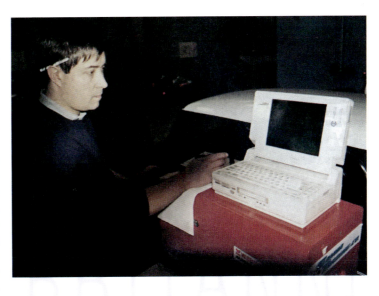

and an electronic fire extinguisher system. The cars were devoid of all usual interior trim with a standard dashboard and instrument layout but with the panel constructed from Kevlar. Additional instruments were fitted in the dash centre to monitor oil pressure, fuel pressure and oil temperature. Attention to detail also included a green change-up light situated above the rev counter. A brake balance bar was fitted and also regulation fire extinguishers. Gear change was via a quick shift lever.

The car – along with Paddy Hopkirk and Ron Crellin – was taken for testing on the special stages at the Northampton Silverstone Rally School, which gave Paddy and Ron the opportunity to test the car and discover all its idiosyncracies. An aspect that Paddy didn't like was the seat wings adjacent to the occupant's head, and this was easily and quickly remedied with a hacksaw! The car was then fitted with a five-speed Jack Knight gearbox but Paddy felt that a four-speed, involute dog-type, non-synchromesh unit would be stronger, a modification carried out prior to further testing at Millbrook. Paddy then used the vehicle as the Course Car on the RAC Rally Britannia on November 21st 1993.

In order to establish what would become the final specification of the car for homologation, comprehensive testing was carried out in the mountains around Valence, the Rover dealership in Valence generously allowing full use of its workshop facilities. The aim was to determine the appropriate gear and differential ratios in the Jack Knight dog box and the state of engine tune required in the mountains. Bill Richards tells the tale of the car coming in at the end of a day's testing when he and his team of mechanics had to remove the power unit, and then rebuild it to a revised specification in preparation for the next day's testing before it came back the next night for more modification. The

RALLY BRITANNIA

HISTORIC

RALLY CAR REGISTER

NOTTINGHAM 1993

(Tim Brenchley Collection)

Phillippe Camandona, who began his Concentration Run from Lausanne, Switzerland. (Bryan Purves Collection)

ultimate straight cut final gear ratio fitted to Paddy's car was 4.66: 1, which gave a top speed of 92mph with a 0 to 60 time of 5.5 seconds.

Upon returning from France the car had to be stripped and re-prepared for the start from Bad Hombourg in nine days' time, which required a concentrated effort on the part of all team members. With Bill making further modifications to the power unit, an increase in power to 97bhp at the wheels was recorded, equating to 115bhp at the flywheel; torque increased to 87.5lb/ft. It was also decided to run the car on 13 inch wheels which gave a wider choice of tyres: tarmac tyres were readily available; snow tyres could be supplied direct from Japan; and studded snow tyres were especially manufactured for the team.

Although Hopkirk's car was built to Group 'A' specification, he achieved better braking by using the standard brakes as opposed to the Group 'A' units. The castor and camber angles were constantly changed according to the different Dunlop tyres fitted. Eventually,

the car was set up with what some might regard as a rather considerable amount of castor angle.

The ultimate idea and thought behind the BCM project was to enter a team of three identical cars painted red with white roofs, and to finish with a big splash in Monte Carlo. This, unfortunately, did not happen.

Jerry Brown, formerly of Brown and Gammons, along with Richard Barnet and Simon Warner, an experienced rally logistics man, took responsibility for all service arrangements. Bill Price and Den Green were to be responsible for en route servicing, along with mechanics who had worked on the cars when they were being built. Bill Richards, who built the engine, was on hand to ensure the cars arrived at the finish.

The team of three BCM Rover Coopers were, in the event, all in Group 'A' Class 5. Car 37 was driven by Paddy Hopkirk and Ron Crellin, car 44 by Philippe Chevalier alongside Moins Bernard, and the Swiss entry number 40 by Philippe and Francine Camandona.

Getting ready for the start at Bad Hombourg with the Hopkirk car leading the Rover France entry of Philippe Chevalier. Paddy's and Ron's food requirements whilst on the rally consisted of ham and/or cheese baguettes, apples, pears and bananas, coffee/tea (Paddy, black and sweet/Ron, white and sweet) Badoit sparkling water, Twix and chocolate caramel bars. (Bryan Purves Collection)

To date, all Monte Carlo Rallies started with a Concentration Run, competitors this year had a choice of six European cities and then a drive to Valence, a distance of 1129km from where the full event started.

Paddy Hopkirk and Ron Crellin elected to start from Bad Hombourg in Germany, so part of the service crew went to the

*Enthusiastic support for the Mini at the start of the Concentration Run.
(Courtesy Mini World)*

Leaving the starting ramp at Bad Hombourg.
(Courtesy Mini World)

start venue whilst the remainder departed for Valence, where the Concentration Run finished. The Classification Event then started from Valence the following morning.

On the Concentration Run to Valence, which encompassed eight en route service points, both Hopkirk's and Chevalier's cars were found to be overheating. Hopkirk's problems were easily resolved by the service crews fitting a mechanical fan to support the electrical one already installed. It was later discovered that Chevalier's car, having completed just 80 kilometres of the Classification Run, had a cracked cylinder head so the team had no alternative but to retire from the event.

When the cars arrived at Valence they were met by the truck of sponsor Dunlop, driven by Tony Leek, carrying approximately 150 different tyres for use on the event, compared to 1966 when there was a four-car Mini entry with 730 tyres offering 13 different options. The cars were also backed up by eight service cars, forty personnel, plus additional support from both Castrol and Dunlop. At strategic points around the route there was the equivalent of 890 gallons of petrol contained in 4-gallon rubber bags.

The French entry driven by Phillipe Chevalier with Moins Bernard navigating. (Courtesy Lucien Campello)

Once the build of the car had been completed, and Timo was satisfied with the general layout and set-up, it was taken to the British Aerospace complex at Dunsfold for testing purposes and a general shake down. Minor points were highlighted and rectified on-the-spot. Testing also took place using the facilities at Gaydon.

The car was now fully prepared and ready to be transported to Monaco, where it was intended to start the Concentration Run which finished in Valence with all the other teams. On the day before the team was due to depart, the car was loaded onto

Another story relates to a Rover Cooper, number 101, which had been built for Rover Japan with Tom Seal of D R Engineering having overall responsiblity for the project. Tom had been involved with Timo Makinen for many years, building rally cars for him. Timo, in the meantime, had managed to secure sponsorship from Rover Japan and contracted Tom to build a car for him. Paul Easter had agreed to accompany him as navigator. The majority of the build was to be undertaken in B & P Classic Development's workshops over a six-week period, with both cars being constructed to Group 'A' specification.

Meanwhile, the rally organising body had also offered Makinen the chance to run at number 52, the number he was originally issued when he rallied the Mini in 1965, an offer he declined.

Three engines were built by Tom Seal, two of them fitted with five-speed dog gearboxes of which there were only two. It was planned that two cars would be constructed for this event, leaving one engine free if required.

a trailer attached to a new Range Rover Discovery. Paul Taylor, one of the mechanics, took it home to Hinckley, Leicestershire, anticipating a 4.00am departure the following morning. Just prior to midnight Paul checked the car and the tie-down straps before getting four hours' sleep. He awoke to discover that whilst asleep the car had been removed from the trailer ... It was later reported that the car had been seen at 3.30am heading towards Nuneaton on the A5 around Smockington Hollow, with a green Mini-Cooper following closely behind.

At the same time as the Makinen/Easter car was being built, another vehicle, owned by Keith Dodd of Mini Spares, was also being rally prepared for Tiff Needell. Unfortunately, due to internal politics, work was halted and the car remained partially built in the workshop.

By 6.30 that morning it had been decided that a Rover Japan-entered Mini would be on the starting ramp with Makinen behind the wheel. Fortunately, the spare unfinished car scheduled for Tiff

... continued p55

Construction of the dashboard in the original Makinen car ... (Courtesy Tom Seal)

... and fuse board and switch panel layout. (Courtesy Tom Seal)

Timo could not read the dash display so this was changed to the conventional three-instrument arrangement. (Courtesy Tom Seal)

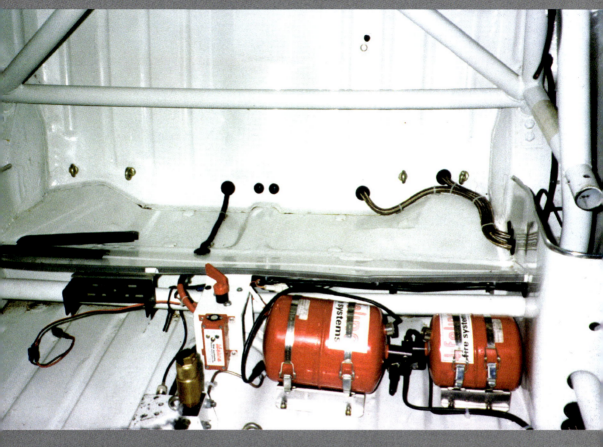

The inside of the car was painted white. (Courtesy Tom Seal)

Group 'A' grooved discs and large calipers. AP supplied blank mounting, 4-pot calipers and Tom Seal re-designed the mountings to fit modified Metro flanges; machining was carried out by Precision Engineering of Coventry. (Courtesy Tom Seal)

The partially built Makinen/Easter car. An ATL fuel cell was fitted with an external filler cap on the left-hand side. The registration of this car was L66LBL. (Courtesy Tom Seal)

The Group 'A' engine virtually built, which was fitted to a five-speed dog gearbox and a modified Metro clutch cover. (Courtesy Tom Seal)

A dynamometer printout for the Makinen engine. (Courtesy Tom Seal)

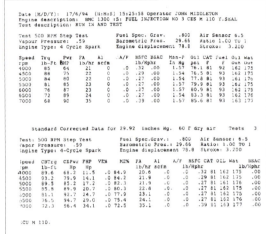

```
Date (M/D/Y): 17/6/94  (H:M:S) 15:25:58 Operator JOHN MIDDLETON
Engine description: BMC 1300 1S: FUEL INJECTION NO 3 CES M 110 T.SEAL
Test description: RUN IN AND TEST

Test 500 RPM Step Test        Fuel Spec. Grav.   .800   Air Sensor 6.5
Vapour Pressure: .59          Barometric Pres.  29.66   Ratio 1.00 TO 1
Engine Type: 4 Cycle Spark    Engine displacement 78.8  Stroke: 3.200

Speed  Trq  Pwr  FA   A1       A/F  BSFC BSAC  Man-P   Oil CAT Fuel Oil Wat
rpm    lb-Ft BHP  lb/hr scfm         lb/Hphr   In Hg   psi  F    F  Out Out
4000   85   64   21   0    .0  .32  .00        1.57 76.1 81  92  162 175
4500   88   75   22   0    .0  .29  .00        1.54 76.5 81  93  162 175
5000   84   80   22   0    .0  .27  .00        1.54 77.8 81  93  161 176
5500   81   85   23   0    .0  .27  .00        1.57 79.9 81  93  162 175
6000   76   87   23   0    .0  .27  .00        1.57 80.9 81  93  162 175
6500   72   89   24   0    .0  .27  .00        1.54 83.3 81  93  162 176
7000   68   90   35   0    .0  .39  .00        1.57 85.6 81  93  163 177


    Standard Corrected Data for 29.92 inches Hg.  60 F dry air     Tests  3

Test: 500 RPM Step Test        Fuel Spec.Grav.:   .800   Air Sensor: 6.5
Vapor Pressure: .59            Barometric Pres.: 29.66   Ratio: 1.00 TO 1
Engine Type: 4-Cycle Spark     Engine displacement 78.8  Stroke: 3.200

Speed  CBTrq  CBPwr FHP  VE%   ME%  FA    A1  A/F  BSFC CAT OIL Wat   BSAC
rpm    lb-ft  Hp    Hp              lb/hr scfm      lb/Hphr              lb/Hphr
4000   89.6   68.2  11.5  .0 84.9   20.6  .0   .0  .32 81 162 175   .00
4500   93.2   79.9  14.1  .0 84.2   21.9  .0   .0  .29 81 162 175   .00
5000   89.5   85.2  17.2  .0 82.3   21.9  .0   .0  .27 81 161 176   .00
5500   85.8   89.9  20.7  .0 80.3   22.8  .0   .0  .27 81 162 175   .00
6000   81.1   92.7  24.7  .0 77.9   23.1  .0   .0  .27 81 162 175   .00
6500   76.5   94.7  29.0  .0 75.4   24.1  .0   .0  .27 81 162 176   .00
7000   72.3   96.4  34.1  .0 72.5   35.1  .0   .0  .39 81 163 177   .00

:CU M 110.
```

Dynamometer testing prior to fitting the engine to the car achieved 96.4bhp. (Courtesy Tom Seal)

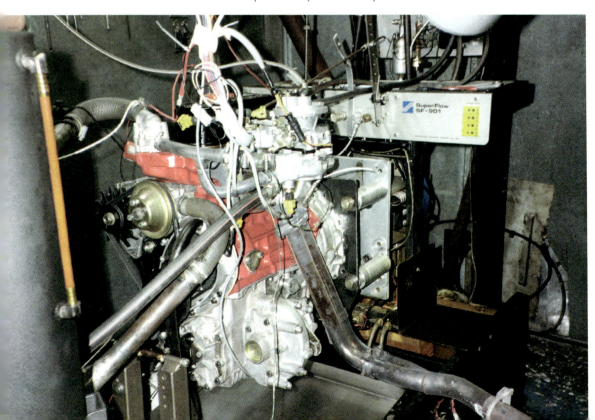

The engine now installed in the car. (Courtesy Tom Seal)

Timo and Paul testing road-holding capability. (Courtesy Tom Seal)

The engine kill switch was set in a bucket recessed in the top of the scuttle. A central bonnet catch pin was fitted to the leading edge with the location plate attached to the closure panel. (Courtesy Tom Seal)

Timo Makinen's car was finally tested at the British Aerospace complex at Dunsfold in Surrey. (Courtesy Tom Seal)

The Makinen/Easter car now ready for transportation to the start of the Concentration Run at Monaco. (Courtesy Tom Seal)

Needell was in a corner of the workshop, complete with suspension, roll cage in place and fully painted. A fully-built, bench run-in engine was also available. The team of mechanics intended to support the original car on the event had already left, en route to Dover. It was here that they were intercepted just prior to boarding the ferry, whereby they quickly returned to Coventry.

In the meantime, given the added interest in a Japanese entry, Japanese enthusiasts had chartered a Jumbo jet to fly 450 Japanese Mini enthusiasts to France from Tokyo to watch the rally!

John Smith, Lucas wiring guru from the Abingdon

Looking through what was initially intended to be Tiff Needell's car, at the Timo Makinen and Paul Easter car in the background. (Courtesy Tom Seal)

The partially constructed second car. (Courtesy Tom Seal)

A bolt-in roll cage was fitted to both bodyshells. (Courtesy Tom Seal)

Additional spot welds were added to strengthen the area around door apertures. (Courtesy Tom Seal)

days, was called back for the second time to wire up this new car. Brian Wood and Paul Taylor of B & P Developments made all of their facilities available, and, with the immediate support of all the Mini spare suppliers and the dedication of the staff, the car began to come together very quickly.

A driving factor was that the car had to be fully built by midday Friday, and on the trailer ready for transportation to the scheduled start venue for the Concentration Run. In the meantime, The Automobile Club de Monaco had been contacted and agreed that the car could be the last scrutineered at 3.00pm on the Saturday afternoon. A BBC television team heard about the race against time and arrived to record Tom Seal drive the car onto the trailer for the journey to Monte Carlo.

On the start day of the Rallye Monte Carlo, Saturday January 22nd, Tom Seal received an anonymous telephone call telling him the whereabouts of the first car. It was found in a remote lane outside the gate of Mancetter Quarry in Nuneaton with just the engine, gearbox and front sub-frame removed. It can only be assumed that it was taken to a facility with the equipment necessary to remove the engine

The completed Needell rolling body waiting to have the inside sprayed white. (Courtesy Tom Seal)

Tom Seal looking at the engine waiting to be installed in the new Makinen/Easter car. John Smith (hands in pockets) stands back whilst undertaking the wiring. (Courtesy Tom Seal)

assembly and entire front sub-frame, leaving the remainder of the car complete. The police were completely baffled about why the car had not been stripped. The car was rebuilt subsequently and given to Keith Dodd of Mini Spares. The car that did take part in the rally was sold to Neko Publishing in Japan.

John Smith, the wiring guru from Abingdon days. (Courtesy Tom Seal)

The engine bay of the second Makinen/Easter car. (Courtesy Tom Seal)

Finally complete and ready to go after 48 hours of work by a team of truly dedicated people! Standard Mini instruments were fitted as requested. (Courtesy Mini World)

It was fortunate that the full rally included the Concentration Run as on this event it was discovered that the charge time on the standard coil was not correctly mapped to engine output. Tom Seal, fortunately, had all the data saved on his lap top computer, so was immediately able to rectify this problem.

The Classification Run from Monaco on the morning of Monday January 24th consisted of 409.55km, comprising six stages over 179.97km, passing through St Pierreville on Stage 1, through St Agreve and returning to Valence, driving on snow-covered roads throughout. Makinen was running 26 seconds slower than Hopkirk. Hopkirk and Camandona

A large capacity steel fuel tank and twin fuel pumps fitted on the rear bulkhead. (Courtesy Mini World)

successfully completed the La Souche Stage 2, where, unfortunately, Timo had to retire due to running out of fuel. (For

The second car was built and ready for scrutineering in 48 hours. Ron Elkins, wearing glasses and standing at the back of the car, was responsible for all publicity whilst the car was on the event. (Courtesy Tom Seal)

Finally, the Makinen/Easter car was on the Concentration Run. (Courtesy Mini World)

Timo Makinen completed the first stage only, after running out of fuel in the second – thereby ending the biggest 'human interest' story since the disqualification of the 1966 Works Rallye Monte Carlo Minis. (Courtesy Robert Young Photographic)

B & P Classic Developments' advertisement prior to the start of the Monte Carlo Rally. (Bryan Purves Collection)

participating in this event Timo Makinen was handsomely rewarded.)

Stage 3 was possibly the most difficult of the day, passing through Burzet and Lachamp Raphael to St Martial. It was on this Stage that spectators threw snow on the road, causing Armin Schwarz in a Mitsubishi Ralliart to go off the road. Whilst trying to avoid his car, Colin McRae hit a tree. Colin finished the day placed 121st.

After Stage 3 the Hopkirk car fractured the exhaust downpipe. The problem was radioed through to the service crew, which

The driver's view, with enthusiastic crowds in the village of Lachamp Raphael making for difficult driving. Crowd control was the responsibility of the police. (Courtesy Robert Young Photographic)

With the cars having departed, the service crew had a period in which to relax before heading off to the next venue. L to R: top row: Messrs Chalkley, Skelton, Higgs, Williams. Bottom row: Peter Cook, and Bill Richards with hammer. (Bill Richards Collection)

was ready and waiting prior to the start of Stage 4. Complete removal and reassembly – including refitting of the injection system – was achieved in just 18 minutes.

In the meantime the ice note crew of John Flynn and Terry Dear reported back that Stage 5, St Bonnet le Froid, was basically ice, snow and slush, and advised fitting snow tyres for this section.

At the end of day 1 only two of the Rover Cooper cars remained in the event, with Phillippe and Francine Camandona lying 58th and Paddy Hopkirk and

Philippe Camandona on Stage 8, Ponte-en-Royans to St Pierre de Cherennes. (Courtesy Robert Young Photographic)

Ron Crellin in 59th place. They were 3rd and 4th in class with the World Champion Skoda in front.

The second day began with a Common Run from Valence to Gap where teams were

Roadside servicing had designated venues set out in the team itinerary, that included car parks, lay-bys and garage forecourts.
(Bill Richards Collection)

Camandona departing from a passage control.
(Courtesy Martin Holmes)

Section 13, Special Stage 9e showing the start and finish on the left-hand page and, on the right, the start of the route information set out in the Carnet D'Itineraire. (This example belongs to Bill Richards, service crew for car number 37.)

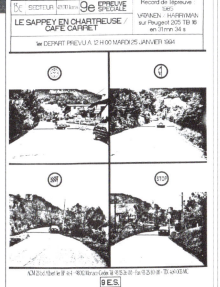

confronted by six stages covering 180.44km of a 511.26km route. Car 37 now experienced windscreen wiper failure and the horn decided not to work, which is always a problem when driving through enthusiastic crowds. During the day's activities the downpipe on the Hopkirk car had to be changed on another two occasions.

The factory rally teams were constantly in danger of being swamped by the hype which surrounded the Mini's return to the Rallye Monte Carlo. (Courtesy Autosport)

Bill Price, who serviced in the 1960s, working on the Hopkirk car in 1994. (Courtesy Rover Group)

Unfortunately, Paddy had been 'off' during the latter Stage and at the night service halt at Col Bayard the sump guard had to be removed, the front panel straightened, and a replacement number plate fitted. When the time came for the car to restart, it was discovered that the pick-up sensor for the timing, situated by the flywheel, had been removed and not replaced. Once reinstated the car instantly fired up and was on its way.

Wednesday 26th saw a 5.00am pre-dawn start for the run from Gap to Monaco. This Leg consisted of four stages totalling 106.47km within the 434.86km route to Monte. Tyre choice was now extremely important with some stages as much as 40km in length, so varying driving conditions were assured with anything from dry tarmac to rutted, snow-covered roads. The intermediate tyre was selected, which proved an ideal choice.

The ice note crew sent the message that the 2km Sisteron Stage was sheet ice, so John Flynn was despatched to arrange a pushing crew in the event of need. Paddy, unfortunately, took the car off the road at one point, sustaining what seemed to be slight damage to the exhaust once again. A quick push, however, and they were on their way again.

The service crew working on Paddy's and Ron's car, rectifying the damage sustained on the last stage. (Courtesy Robert Young Photographic)

A 5.00am start with Paddy closely followed by a local French Mini enthusiast. (Bill Richards Collection)

The Camandona car pressing on hard on closed roads. (Courtesy Rover Group)

Ron Crellin clocking in at a control. (Courtesy Mini World)

At the end of the day's final Stage service crew 'B', consisting of Richards, Skelton and Watts, set about once again replacing the exhaust system on Paddy's car, at the same time carrying out a full service and tyre change. Service Crew 'A' – Higgs, Williams and Chalkley – were established in Monaco awaiting arrival of the two cars to give them a quick service before they went into Parc Ferme.

To qualify as a finisher on the Monte the car has to reach Monte Carlo within the time limit, which both Rover Coopers achieved. With the Minis placed at 47th and 52nd at the Monaco break, they qualified for the final night Leg which the regulations permit only the top 100 cars to undertake.

Wednesday night January 26th. The event now took in the Mountain Circuit – Monaco to Monaco, departing the wrong way up the Formula 1 circuit and heading into the night with the drive encompassing six stages totalling 121.55km within a 573.82km route. All this was undertaken in the mountains behind Monaco, in the dark on snow-covered

The Sisteron Stage. (Courtesy Robert Young Photographic)

Concentration. Listen to co-driver's instructions and drive with caution! (Courtesy Rover Group)

Control is essential on the narrow, twisty, snow-covered Sisteron stage. A patch of black ice unfortunately saw the car leave the road. (Courtesy Rover Group)

Keeping tight to the corners, but now with a damaged front end. A replacement front number plate was attached using tie-wraps, the original discarded by the roadside after going off on the Sisteron Stage. (Bryan Purves Collection)

Throughout the rally car 37 experienced problems with the exhaust system. (Bill Richards Collection)

Pressing on after the Sisteron Stage and now on dry tarmac heading towards Monaco. (Bryan Purves Collection)

roads. It was on the Col de Turini, undoubtedly the most famous venue on the rally calendar, that Hopkirk drove the studded-tyred Mini into a controlled skid on the hard-packed ice to a huge reception by the waiting crowd. After the Turini Stage the tyres were changed for intermediates and the route headed off from La Bollene in the direction of St Saveur.

The Camandona car originally wore the registration number K33 EJB. (Bryan Purves Collection)

Support for the Minis throughout the event was stupendous. (Bill Richards Collection)

The historic Col de Turini, where thousands of enthusiastic spectators gather to enjoy the sight and sound of the rally cars passing through the night Stage. (Bryan Purves Collection)

Arriving at a control during the night leg. (Bill Richards Collection)

Paddy slid the car on the Col de Turini Stage to the roar of the crowd. Ferodo carbon metallic brake pads were fitted for this Stage. (Courtesy Robert Young Photographic)

A Rover Switzerland publicity poster prior to the rally in which Philippe and Francine Camandona finished 47th overall. English registered, K764VKM is not listed with the DVLA or Experion. (Bill Richards Collection)

Later, during the night section, the fan belt came off the pulley on the uprated 100amp/hour alternator on Hopkirk's car. Without giving it any thought he proceeded to cut it off, only to find that the replacement belt in the boot did not fit as it was a production part. Consideration had not been given to the fact that the alternator was running with a non-standard pulley, hence a longer belt should have been in the boot kit. A replacement belt was eventually

The night rally route as issued to the service crews, illustrating the route after the initial climb to the Col de Turini before the return to Monaco. (Bill Richards Collection)

The very early hours of the morning – 00.35 – and the start of another Special Stage. The scrutineer's pass is stuck on the roof. (Bill Richards Collection)

fitted but to no avail as they were out of time. Also during the night and on the next section Philippe Camandona experienced electrical problems which were found to be related to the in-line fuse to the fuel pump that had actually broken rather than blown. Camandona's mechanic was quickly on the scene but, in the dark, it is often difficult to detect minor problems and again the team ran out of time.

The very last scheduled Stage (SS 23) was cancelled due to a landslide. Cars that retired during the final Leg – Etape Finale – were still officially classified; a total of 113. Both Minis arrived at the finish ramp to huge media attention and qualified as finishers. Phillipe Camandona was placed 47th overall and 3rd in class, with Paddy Hopkirk 52nd overall and 4th in class.

At the end of every Monte the cars line up in the finishing order and drive around the town, ending at the castle where Prince Rainer resides and the prize giving ceremony is held. On this occasion the tradition was broken with Paddy and Ron placed 4th in the parade as acknowledgement of their achievement in 1964. They drove the Mini to the plinth where they were presented with Honore of Paris watches in commemoration of their participation.

The final Secteur information set out in the Etape Finale. (Bill Richards Collection)

34	SECTEUR	Km 3.290	T.I. 00:10	moy./h 19.740		
ROQUEBRUNE (Beach) MONACO (Parc Fermé)					Carte Michelin N° 115	
DISTANCE totale	partielle		DIRECTION		INFORMATIONS	DISTANCE TOTALE DEGRESSIVE
0.00	0.00	1	PARKING (car park)			3.29
0.46	0.46	2	MONTE-CARLO			2.83
1.56	1.10	3			FILE DE GAUCHE (Keep Left)	1.73
1.66	0.10	4				1.63
2.53	0.87	5				0.76

ACM 23, Bd. Albert 1er BP 464 - 98012 Monaco Cedex - Tél. 93.15.26.00 - Fax 93.25.80.08 - Tlx 469 003 MC

69

Philippe and Francine Camandona,
having arrived in Monte Carlo.
(Bill Richards Collection)

*Front end damage during the Sisteron
Stage did not prevent Hopkirk and Crellin
finishing the rally! (Courtesy Chris Harvey)*

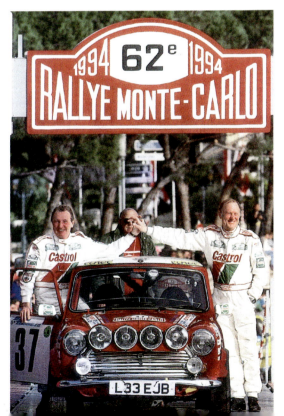

*Relaxing on the harbourside at
Monte Carlo. L to R: Philippe and
Francine Camandona, Paddy Hopkirk,
Ron Crellin, and Timo Makinen.
(Bill Richards Collection)*

This year was the first Rallye Monte Carlo win for Ford since 1953 when Maus Gatsonides and Peter Worledge were victorious with a Ford Zephyr.

Brigden-Coulter Motorsports published a leaflet – Project Mini Monte Carlo – which gave information about how the company could build replicas of Hopkirk's Monte Carlo car for between £25,000 and £30,000, subject to the customer's personal specification (see Appendix 4). One car was built for Stephen Smith, a replica of the Paddy Hopkirk/Ron Crellin car. Stephen, wanting to be part of the project, sourced a six month old Rover Cooper, registration L283 APL, along with many of the component parts. The staff involved in the original project then built the car, which was then displayed on the BMH exhibition stand at the National Exhibition Centre, Birmingham. The car made an impression on John Brigden who offered Stephen the registration number L333 EJB to replace the one originally issued to the car.

After the rally Dave Johnson – a member of the rally ice notes crew – obtained from

Stephen Smith at Castle Combe. (Stephen Smith Collection)

BCM a dismantled Mini that was claimed to be one of the original Rover test cars. Dave, along with John Flynn, built it up to Group 'N' specification and competed in the Mobil 1/*Top Gear* British Rally Championship in 1995.

Prior to the rally a 'show' car was displayed at the Earls Court Motor Show, the occurrence heralded

Simon Cottingham being presented with the keys to his Monte Carlo replica car by Paddy Hopkirk. (Courtesy Simon Cottingham)

as the official launch of the Monte Carlo campaign. *Autocar* and *Motor* magazines, in conjunction with support of the Monte Carlo entry, ran a phone-in competition with four questions. Those who answered

The so-called Paddy Hopkirk rally replica on the day that Simon collected it from John Brigden's home. (Courtesy Simon Cottingham)

correctly were entered in a draw to win a replica of the Earls Court Motor Show Mini; Simon Cottingham was the lucky winner. When Simon collected his prize from John Brigden's home the car featured 5 inch x 13 inch Minitor alloy wheels fitted with Dunlop 505/13 rally tyres, Silverstone wheelarch extensions, and a Kevlar dash panel. In 1995, Simon purchased a lamp pod from Mini Machine and a wiring loom from BCM in an attempt to replicate the Hopkirk Mini. In 1999 he acquired an appropriate number plate – C3 EJB – and replica mud flaps were fitted.

The car was essentially a standard Rover Cooper with the addition of a rear roll over cage and semi fitted out rally dashboard. A selection of appropriate decals were mounted on the external body. Mechanical specification was as per

Simon purchased a lamp pod in order to recreate the Hopkirk replica car. (Courtesy Simon Cottingham)

The 1994 car which was the prize in a phone-in competition, now fitted with new registration and mud flaps. (Courtesy Simon Cottingham)

BILL RICHARDS
Racing

THEY ALL SAID THAT A MODERN INJECTED COOPER ENGINE RUNNING ON STANDARD VALVES COULDN'T PRODUCE ANY REAL POWER. WE PROVED THEM WRONG ON THE 1994 MONTE CARLO RALLY...

Using a Weber Alpha engine management system developed by Southern Carburettors, Bill Richards Racing found the power to make the Brigden Coulter Motorsport 1994 GpA Mini Coopers not only quick but reliable as well. Paddy Hopkirk's engine didn't miss a beat over more than 500 stage miles which saw our lead car at one point up to an amazing 39th overall, up among Cosworth Escorts and Lancias.

We have also supplied Mini engines and competition gearboxes for many of the most successful Historic Rally Minis, including 850s, 997 Coopers and Cooper S models. We can also offer Minicross and full race Mini and Metro engines in a variety of specifications using our own special camshafts and components developed through more than 30 years' experience building and tuning A-series engines.

Bill Richards Racing, Unit 86, Ellingham Ind. Estate, Ashford, Kent TN23 2JZ. Tel: 0233 624336

"We proved them wrong on the 1994 Monte Carlo Rally". (Bill Richards Collection)

a 1.3 SPi Cooper. The door and rear side trim panels had the 'Lightning' trim correct for 1993/94 production, with front and rear seats from a carburettor model. The VIN plate was correct for a 1990 RSP Cooper, the bodyshell and rear screen details were identical to those of L33 EJB.

The front windscreen carried the number SAXXNNAYCBD060898, which was identical to that of a car sold in Germany. Another interesting fact is that the engine number was virtually identical to that of the engine fitted to the Paddy Hopkirk car, with just one difference: the fourth digit had been changed to a 'Z' (12AZEF...) where it should always read as a '2' (12A2EF...) This featured on the V5 registration document.

John Brigden on one occasion said: "We were perhaps guilty of underestimating the size of the problem of building a modern rally car and, with hindsight, if we had known the problems we probably wouldn't have started the project".

Which begs the question: why didn't Rover – the main beneficiary – not become fully involved and co-ordinate this very fragmented project?

Network Q
RAC Rally 1994

Date: November 20-23rd 1994
Total mileage: 1468 miles starting and
  finishing in Chester
Stages: 29 timed over 323.37
  competitive miles
Surface: tarmac on first day and then
  mainly gravel
Participants: 178 starters, 97 finishers

This event was a qualifying round of the FIA World Rally Championship for Drivers, the FIA World Rally Championship for Manufacturers, the FIA Ladies Cup, the FIA Cup for Drivers of Production Cars (Group N), and the FIA World Cup for Manufacturers of 2-litre Cars. It also incorporated the Millers Oils Historic Rally of Great Britain, the National Rally Britannia, and the Classic Rally Britannia.

After a much celebrated return to international rallying on the Rallye Monte Carlo, BCM decided to enter two Minis in one of the toughest three-day rallies in the world – the RAC – through the forests of Great Britain. This was always a tough rally where, in order simply to reach the final flag, it was felt that a car had to be built using the latest available technology.

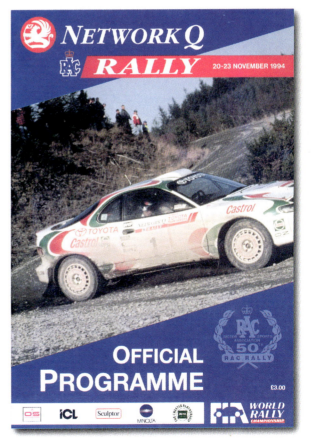

(Bryan Purves Collection)

1468 miles, 29 timed Special Stages covering 323.37 competitive miles during a four-day period. (Network Q RAC Official programme, courtesy 1994 RAC Motorsports Association Ltd)

NETWORK Q
RAC RALLY
20-23 November 1994
OFFICIAL RALLY ROUTE MAP PROVIDED BY ORDNANCE SURVEY

REGROUP Low Cranecleugh

MONDAY 21st NOVEMBER

Stage No.	Location	Time	Rating
Start	Harrogate	05.00	★
SS8	Hamsterley	07.04	★★★
SS9	Shepherdshield	09.10	★★★
SS10	Pundershaw	09.34	★★★
SS11	Chirdonhead	11.13	★★★
SS12	Wauchope	12.20	★★
SS13	Kershope	13.02	★★★
SS14	Grizedale West	16.04	★★★
SS15	Grizedale East	16.43	★★★
Halt	Chester	20.00	★★★

Ordnance Survey®
MiniScale mapping
© Crown copyright 1994   0703 792802

0 10 20 30 40 50 km
0   10   20   30 miles

WEDNESDAY 23rd NOVEMBER

Stage No.	Location	Time	Rating
Start	Chester	05.15	★
SS23	Pantperthog	07.41	★★★
SS24	Dyfi	08.10	★★★
SS25	Gartheiniog	08.53	★★★
SS26	Penmachno South	10.52	★★★
SS27	Penmachno North	11.13	★★★
SS28	Clocaenog West	12.20	★★★
SS29	Clocaenog East	12.32	★★★
Finish	Chester	14.55	★★★★

RALLY HQ—Chester
START / FINISH
HALT Monday 21st
HALT Tuesday 22nd

HALT Harrogate
Sunday 20th

Days 3 and 4. (Network Q RAC Official programme, courtesy 1994 RAC Motorsports Association Ltd)

REGROUP Llandovery

Star rating for public viewing, Day 2. (Network Q RAC Official programme, courtesy 1994 RAC Motorsports Association Ltd)

SUNDAY 20th NOVEMBER

Stage No.	Location	Time	Rating
Start	Chester	08.00	★★★★
SS1	Ferodo Carden Pk	08.31	★★★★
SS2	Tatton Park	09.51	★★★★
SS3	Chatsworth	11.43	★★★★
SS4	Mobil 1 Clumber Pk	13.18	★★★★
SS5	Jamo Donington	15.02	★★★★
SS6	Jamo Donington	15.14	★★★★
SS7	Leeds Harewood	17.44	★★★★
Halt	Harrogate	18.58	★★★★

TUESDAY 22nd NOVEMBER

Stage No.	Location	Time	Rating
Start	Chester	05.00	★
SS16	Dyfnant	06.49	★★★
SS17	Sweetlamb Hafren	08.22	★★★
SS18	Brechfa	10.48	★★★
SS19	Trawscoed	11.43	★★★
SS20	Crychan	13.33	★★
SS21	Hafren 2	15.11	★★★
SS22	Dyfnant 2	16.55	★
Halt	Chester	19.30	★★★

SPECIAL STAGE STAR RATING

★   Poor viewing facilities. Limited car parking and access difficult by foot. Not advisable unless really keen.

★★   Limited car parking with minimal viewing facilities. May involve long walks – you may not be troubled by massive crowds.

★★★   Good viewing with car park and reasonable access. Traffic may delay access.

★★★★   Full viewing facilities with commentary and ample car parking. Good for family viewing and recommended for newcomers.

The other Mini entries posing for a team photo. The crews are: L to R back row: Dave Lucas, Trevor Godwin, David Wyer and David Johnson. L to R front row: Kevin Moore, Robert & Michael Plant and John Flynn. (Courtesy Dave Lucas)

(Bryan Purves Collection)

This event marked the climax of the World Rally Championship season and was the deciding event for that Championship.

Didier Auriol came to the final round with an 11 point lead over Carlos Sainz. Didier knew that everything could be lost here, and the RAC was not one of his favourite events. Sainz described the RAC as "... the most difficult event on the World Championship calendar ..."

Ford Motorsport had decided to enter a six-car team for the final round of the Championship to mark its last appearance in the series. Colin McRae, driving for Ford, was pleased to see that the spectator vantage points had been improved this year, especially on the first day and in particular at the Donnington Stage. This year also happened to be the 50th anniversary of the running of the RAC Rally which first occurred in 1932.

It was the original intention of BCM to enter both a Group 'A' and a Group 'N' specification car, but the latter did

not materialise and this challenge was then taken on by John Flynn outside of what can be called the remit of a 'works' car. The Group 'A' car – registration number L54 CVP – was to be driven by multiple British champion, Russell Brookes, with Neil Wilson alongside, and the Group 'N' car – registration number Q441 NUR – by David Johnson and John Flynn.

Russell Brookes had a vast amount of experience of this particular event, having already competed in 24 RAC events, finishing second overall in 1979. Between 1969 and 1971, he competed in no fewer than five RAC Rallies in Minis. In 1971 Russell achieved the fastest stages on five occasions using a 'works' engine. The 1994 event commemorated 25 years of RAC participation for Russell; his first rally in 1969 happened to be in a Mini Cooper.

This year there were five Mini entries: Russell Brookes and Neil Wilson; David Johnson and John Flynn; Trevor Godwin and David Wyer, and Kevin Moore and David Lucas, together with twin brothers Robert and Michael Plant.

The Russell Brookes car started life as an L registered 1994 Rover Cooper 1.3i, originally a Longbridge 'pool' car supplied to Barretts of Canterbury, where it was dismantled to become the donor car for

The design of the ATL fuel cell allowed the spare wheel to just fit into the remaining space. (Bryan Purves Collection)

the Brookes/Wilson entry. The required parts were then built into a new, fully-prepared, seam welded and appropriately modified shell put together by Safety Devices at the end of 1993. The original bodyshell – used for approximately 5000 miles only – was then sold to David Harper of Mini Sport.

Mini Sport was directly involved in supplying many parts such as the suspension, brakes and numerous other small components. It had already considered fielding its own entry, prior to this opportunity arising, so in turn became involved in the preparation alongside Brigden Coulter Motorsport Ltd (BCM). Bill Richards Racing was commissioned to build the Group 'A' 1293cc engine which produced 93bhp at the front wheels and 91lb/ft of torque. The 0 to 60 time was calculated to be 5.7 seconds using a 4.66: 1 final drive and Jack Knight four-speed, straight cut dog gearbox coupled to uprated driveshafts from ST Transmissions, and a four-

Left and centre: A compact and easily manageable cockpit. (Bryan Purves Collection)

The fully prepared engine bay prior to the rally. (Bryan Purves Collection)

pin differential. This put the top speed at just over 90mph. Due to homologation regulations many of the components, such as manifolds, injection body, valve sizes, crankshaft and conrods, had to remain standard. Omega pistons were fitted, along with an uprated camshaft. Modifications were permitted to the injection system which incorporated a Weber Alpha set-up.

On the suspension side of the build Mini Sport supplied its Adjusta-Ride suspension system along with rose-jointed, adjustable tie rods and negative camber bottom arms. The rear sub-frame was fitted with adjustable negative camber brackets.

Dunlop supplied new tyres, recently developed

Mini Sport supplied many of the parts that were fitted to the car. (Courtesy Mini Sport)

especially for the event. The design of the tyres was based upon a casing that was intended primarily for racing using a mixture of composite materials and steel.

With just two weeks to go before the rally, Mini Sport offered to field a service crew with two service vans, plus three chase cars. In total there were fifteen members of staff from Mini Sport and

Barretts of Canterbury who had never worked together, so strict guidelines had to be established with personnel responsible for specific elements of the en route servicing.

Prior to the rally the Brookes car was featured at the Motor Show and then taken to Wales for pre-rally testing by Brookes and the team. A week prior to the start further testing occurred on the Silverstone Rally School Circuit to finalise minor modifications and adjustments.

Russell, with some persuasive talking, managed to obtain from Rover manufacturer endorsement as a works driver in the F2 Cup, which gave him an 'A' seeded position and an early start number of 24. It also meant that the car had to run on 'control fuel', charged at £10 a gallon; with an average of 12 to 13mpg, this was going to prove to become very expensive!

Sunday Stages		
SS1 Ferodo Park	2.61 miles	Open parkland, twisty tarmac interspersed with wide bends, hairpin and a chicane incorporating the famous Knutsford Mere bend
SS2 Tatton Park	4.27 miles	Tarmac and loose surface with a section through a wooded area
SS3 Chatsworth	6.53 miles	Fast open roads with twisty hill sections, tricky hairpin bends, two spectacular water splashes and a jump
SS4 Clumber Hill	5.70 miles	Cars competing in the Millers Oils RAC International Historic Rally had to attempt the Stage twice. The Stage comprised fast tarmac roads through National Trust parkland, tight corners and forest roads on the south side of the park
SS5/SS6 Jamo Donnington 1 & 2 Circuit	4 miles	Used both the circuit and variable width gravel roads, narrow in places with tricky corners. Stage used twice. Starting at 30 second intervals. Cars on the Millers Oils International Historic Rally also attempted the Stage twice
SS7 Harewood Hill	1.86 miles	The National Hillclimb course. The Stage started on a loose level surface then downhill on a narrow and tricky loose-surfaced track, finishing with the smooth tarmac hairpins of the hillclimb course

Russell Brookes and Neil Wilson, along with members of the support team, prior to the start of what was to be a gruelling rally. (Courtesy Autosport)

The Mini always attracted a vast amount of spectator support at every service halt. (Donald Farr Collection)

Whilst the service crew checked out the car prior to the start, Russell even had time to read the paper ... (Donald Farr Collection)

With less than a fortnight to the start of the rally, Mini Sport offered to field the service crew. (Courtesy Mini Sport)

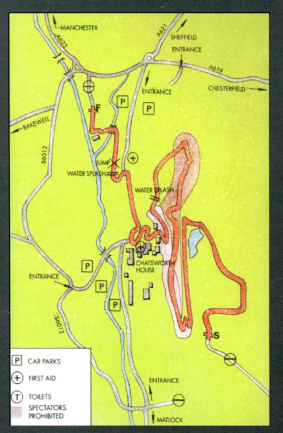

Stage 3 in the grounds of Chatsworth House, a distance of 6.53 miles. The section through the woods was very narrow and out of bounds to spectators. (Network Q RAC Official programme, courtesy 1994 RAC Motorsports Association Ltd)

Tyre change and continuous changing of the front ball joints. In the end it proved quicker to change the complete hub assembly. (Courtesy Mini Sport)

Pre-arranged service points were sited along the route generally just prior to a Stage. (Donald Farr Collection)

Monday Stages

Stage	Distance	Description
SS8 Hamsterley	16.86 miles	The first of the forest stages. Generally a good surface on both fast and twisty sections. On the high ground early morning mist and ice was expected. At the end of the Stage was the Hamsterely ford
SS9 Shepherdshield	7.67 miles	The first and shortest of the three Kielder stages which ran in daylight mainly on fast straights but with some sharp bends
SS10 Pundershaw	28.18 miles	The longest Stage of the rally over the Kielder roads, a very fast, curving route with deep ditches
SS11 Chirdonhead	10.58 miles	Mainly fast roads; well surfaced but with soft, unforgiving verges, especially when wet
SS12 Wauchope	8.80 miles	The only Stage on this year's event that was totally in Scotland, using high and fast tracks over the moors
SS13 Kershope	19.55 miles	Starting in Scotland and finishing in England. The roads were mainly fast and rugged with a very twisty opening section along the riverside, and numerous deceptive long, bumpy straights
SS14 Grizedale West	17.33 miles	One of the toughest stages of the rally; virtually a series of continuous bends with numerous junctions and crests
SS15 Grizedale East	4.85 miles	A very twisty and deceptive route

Crossing a ford. (Courtesy Mini Sport)

Service crew in action; essential throughout any rally. (Courtesy Mini Sport)

Stage 14, Grizedale West, length 17.33 miles: one of the toughest Stages of the rally with continuous bends, numerous junctions and crests. Stage 15, Grizedale East, length 4.85 miles was equally twisty and deceptive. The letters in red blocks indicate spectator vantage points. (Network Q RAC Official programme, courtesy 1994 RAC Motorsports Association Ltd)

Tuesday Stages		
SS16 Dyfnant 1	13.46 miles	Consisted of fast open roads with long flowing corners and several tight sections. This region does experience early morning adverse weather conditions
SS17 Sweetlamb Hafren	18.00 miles	Long and testing Stage along flowing forest roads, also using Sweetlamb tracks with two watersplashes and the Hafren forest
SS18 Brechfa	20.29 miles	Abandoned due to accident
SS19 Trawscoed	22.76 miles	A tough and uncompromising Stage which used tracks in the Gorlech valley together with some high mountain roads
SS20 Cryhan	3.88 miles	The last of the west Welsh stages which incorporated twisty roads with unseen, sharp corners and junctions
SS21 Hafren	20.53 miles	A long and testing Stage along flowing forest roads
SS22 Dyfnant 2	13.46 miles	Mainly fast open roads with long flowing corners but several tight sections

Stage Commanders were officially responsible for the overall running of a designated Stage, and were given an official rally plaque, of which only 29 were distributed by the RAC. (Bryan Purves Collection)

Sweetlamb Hafren Special Stage 17 consisted of 18 miles through forest and then into Sweetlamb bowl and the water splashes. (Network Q RAC Official programme, courtesy 1994 RAC Motorsports Association Ltd)

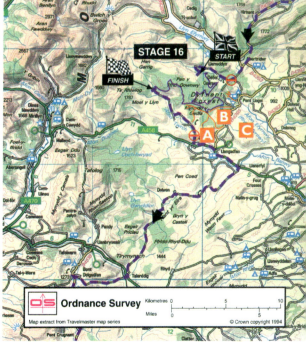

A total of 178 cars departed from Chester in heavy rain on Sunday morning to cover 29 competitive stages over the three-day period. The early morning heavy rain, plus a considerable amount of standing water, made driving conditions extremely slippery.

On the opening Stage Brookes lost time when a primary fuel pump failed on the Mini. Will Hoy, the British touring car driver, made a spectacular exit from the event

Wednesday Stages		
SS23 Pantperthog	9.41 miles	A difficult Stage on narrow, twisty and hilly roads often affected by mist and rain
SS24 Dyfi	14.57 miles	Wide sweeping corners and an excellent road surface but with some difficult tight hairpins
SS25 Gartheiniog	14.04 miles	Good surface but with some very deceptive bends
SS26 Penmachno South	8.31 miles	A mixture of some very fast unclassified roads, steep hills, tight hairpins and fearsome drops
SS27 Penmachno North	6.25 miles	Similar to the previous Stage but faster with fewer hairpins and fast corners
SS28 Clocaenog West	3.75 miles	A short Stage of twisty roads and deep ditches
SS29 Clocaenog East	12.04 miles	Good firm roads which were extremely slippery when wet. Some long straights but with deceptive crests combined with sharp junctions

Changing brake pads proved essential. (Donald Farr Collection)

when, driving his Toyota along a straight gravel section and over a series of fast bumps, he misjudged a corner and drove straight into a tree on SS3, all in front of the television cameras! As Hoy said: "We were pitched off the road into lots of trees so I chose one. We hit it at 70-80mph." Also on the same Chatsworth Stage Steve Wedgbury, driving a Skoda, badly damaged its front nearside and rear axle by hitting a boulder, thereby losing his lead in the Group 'N' 1300cc Class.

Rover Cooper positions at the end of SS6 were: Wills/Brown 85th, Brookes/Wilson 119th, Godwin/Wyer 144th, Johnson/ Flynn 145th, Moore/Lucas 160th, and Plant/Plant 162nd.

The rally on the second day moved to muddy country roads in northern England with nineteen of the original crews failing to restart from Harrogate. The survivors faced a hard day, comprising eight stages over 113.82 competitive miles passing through the Kielder Forest (the largest man-made forest in Europe, with over 150,000 trees originally planted in the late 1800s), the Scottish borders and the Lake District, finishing back in Chester. Russell Brookes said that he found the Monday stages hard going in his Mini. "I'm sliding all over the place" he declared, whilst co-driver Neil Wilson added: "It's different – for a start, we're much lower down."

The final two Stages. (Network Q RAC Official programme, courtesy 1994 RAC Motorsports Association Ltd)

Tough going and hard on the suspension. The tally of damaged wheels on the event amounted to 18 with no punctures, using tyres developed by Dunlop. L54 CVP also got through two sump guards in two days. (Courtesy Mini Sport)

A tough rally. Mini Sport supplied its new, 4–pot billet aluminium front brake calipers for the car. (Courtesy Mini Sport)

Rover Cooper positions at the end of SS15, Grizedale East, were: Wills/Brown 88th; Brookes/Wilson 90th; Johnson/Flynn 113th; Plant/Plant 123rd; Moore/Lucas 124th, and Godwin/Wyer 132nd.

The next day took the rally into the Welsh forests with the competitors encountering mud which was generally soft on the top and hard underneath; driving conditions were becoming more of a problem for the cars that were running further down the field.

On SS18, Brechfa, a 27 year old male spectator was airlifted to hospital with a broken leg, having been struck by one of the leading cars, number 38, a Ford driven by South African Jan Habig. "It's very upsetting, we were off the road a bit but not by much." said Douglas Judd, Habig's co-driver. The Stage was then abandoned and all the cars that had yet to compete were given the same time as the slowest

driver. The cars were sent straight to SS19 which caused massive traffic jams due to the enormous spectator following.

On day three only 131 crews departed from Chester to cover the seven stages over a total of 112.21 miles scheduled for the Welsh forests, before returning to Chester to an overnight halt. SS22 was found by many to be extremely difficult with descriptions such as: "... very very tricky," "... quick and very frightening", "... paralysing."

By now Russell Brookes seemed to be questioning the wisdom of his decision to compete again in a Mini. "You realise how small they are when you pull alongside an Escort and all you can see is the lettering on the side-walls ... and the rocks look bigger!"

Brookes also experienced a mysterious oil leak which was eventually traced to a bolt that had fallen out of the gearbox casing. Fuel pump problems were also

Racing through one of the Welsh Stages to finish 6th in Class and 72nd overall. (Courtesy Mini Sport)

responsible for what ultimately became slow progress.

Results at the end of day 3 were: Brookes/Wilson 75th; Wills/Brown 87th; Moore/Lucas 103rd; Plant/Plant 103rd, and Godwin/Wyer 110th.

On the final day 109 cars departed from Chester with 69 crews having retired during the first three days. The crews were to experience very slippery stages, once again through mid and north Wales, covering 68.37 competitive miles with seven stages. On the first Stage, SS23, Carlos Sainz encountered two large logs in his driving path that had not been there earlier when Colin McRae had driven through ... Luckily, this inexcusable behaviour lost Sainz only a couple of seconds. Whilst lying second

overall he then drove a little too wide on SS24, Dyfi, into a sweeping right-hand bend, dropped the rear into a ditch, spun softly and got bogged down in the mud, which eventually led to his retirement.

In the meantime a further drama evolved with the communications plane losing one of its two engines, being forced to make an emergency landing at a local airfield. The aircraft had been carrying the radio and telephone repeater equipment for the majority of the top teams with the exception of Toyota.

Five Minis completed the rally with Brookes and Wilson finishing 6th in class, and with the last place Mini of Trevor Godwin and David Wyer finishing 97 overall, almost 3.5 hours behind winner Colin McRae. "Our manager, Tom Seal, issued us with team orders that we must, at all costs, retain our last place in the classification positions," said Trevor.

Final Mini classifications				
69th	Wills/ Brown	Group 'N'	Car no 148	Class 3:4 7:19:46
72nd	Brookes/ Wilson	Group 'A'	Car no 24	Class 5:6 7:22:45
91st	Moore/ Lucas	Group 'N'	Car no 192	Class 1:12 8:16:03
93rd	Plant/Plant	Group 'N'	Car no 193	Class 1:128:19:14
97th	Godwin/ Wyer	Group 'A'	Car no 184	Class 5:10 8:43:25

Retirements

Car no 96 Northall/Joy on SS03
Car no 175 Johnson/Flyn Group 'N' Class 1:12 on SS17 with broken differential

Brookes and Wilson were classified as one of the twenty-two 'Selected Entries' for the Network Q RAC Rally, featuring in this event amongst the top teams in the world.

Network Q RAC Rally media/support statistics	
Total television viewers	188,596,000
Readership of accredited publications	83,500,000
BBC2 viewers	26,000,000
Other UK channels	14,947,000
Live spectators	2,100,000
TV coverage worldwide	27,154 minutes
TV coverage UK	965 minutes
BBC2 TV coverage	261 minutes
Media attending the event	762 persons
Accredited TV personnel	198 persons
TV cameras	65
Countries taking TV coverage	79
Countries with media attending	26

- 60 rally rescue ambulances
- 50 doctors
- 50 St John ambulances
- 1 helicopter
- 12 fire tenders

One slip! (Bryan Purves Collection)

A Network Q RAC Rally Finisher's Award. (Bryan Purves Collection)

RALLYE MONTE CARLO 1995

Date; 21-27th January 1995
Distance: 2617km including 547km
 over 21 Special Stages
Surface: asphalt occasionally
 covered with snow or ice
Participants: 199 teams started and 83
 finished

All competitors experienced wet weather on the first Leg, but, as the rally progressed, the roads began to dry out, although a light covering of snow and ice was experienced on the latter stages of the event.

Two Minis were entered for this rally: car number 197, the private entry of Michael and Robert Plant in Group 'N' Class 1, and car number 32, registration 389 BHY 95, a Rover France entry in Group 'A', Class 5, driven by Jean-Claude Andruet and Michele 'Biche' Petit. Jean-Claude was originally a member of the Renault Alpine factory team in 1968, soon to meet up with 'Biche', whereupon the duo rallied together for many years, winning the 1972 Rallye Solitude and the 1973 Rallye Monte Carlo, on both occasions driving a 'works' Renault Alpine A110 1800cc.

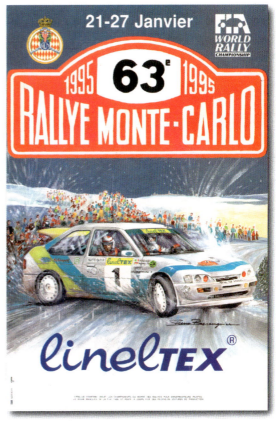

Artist: Pierre Bereuguir.
(Tim Brenchley Collection)

The Rover France entry was built with the full support of Philippe Chevalier's garage in Valence, France. The car was built to Group 'A' specification based upon a left-hand drive Rover Monte Carlo model variant. It featured only minor rose-jointed modifications to the suspension, along with relatively minor engine modifications, which was then mated with a close ratio straight cut gearbox. Minator 5in x 12in wheels were used throughout the rally, shod with appropriate Michelin rally tyres.

A virtually standard-looking engine compartment with the addition of a non-original air filter. (Bryan Purves Collection)

Rose joints were fitted to the lower suspension arms. (Bryan Purves Collection)

Motordrive of Manchester supplied the seats. Note the additional strengthening of the roll cage to the B-post. The car retained original trim panels. (Bryan Purves Collection)

The basis of the car was one of the limited edition, left-hand drive Rover Monte Carlo models. (Bryan Purves Collection)

The Custom Cages roll cage was fully welded-in, with a bowed lower dashboard tube. The navigator had a foot-operated horn button fitted to the top right-hand side of the toe-board. (Bryan Purves Collection)

A Tarcal bias brake, manual operating lever was situated within easy reach of the driver's right hand. Note where the roll cage has been welded with literally no supports to take any compressive load underneath the seat pan. (Bryan Purves Collection)

On the starting ramp ready for departure after the Concentration Run. (Courtesy Maurice Louche)

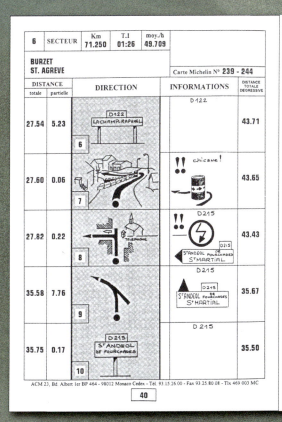
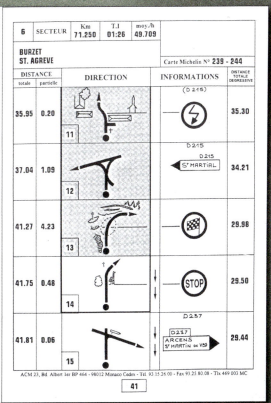

Pages from the Burzet/St Agreve secteur. All of the distances set out in the Carnet d'Itineraire were calculated using a 'Terratrip'. (This example belonged to car number 32.) (Courtesy Maurice Louche)

French supporters were always there to offer encouragement.
(Courtesy Maurice Louche)

Roof damage sustained when the car was put on its side. The scrutineer's pass was generally fixed to the outside of the car. (Bryan Purves Collection)

Jean-Claude Andruet in the driving seat, having just damaged the front A-post, gutter, front wing, door mirror, left-hand door and handle, and changing the shape of the upper door closure panel, plus bending the rear radius arm. (Ian Moore Collection)

The rally plate issued to all Rallye officials. (Bryan Purves Collection)

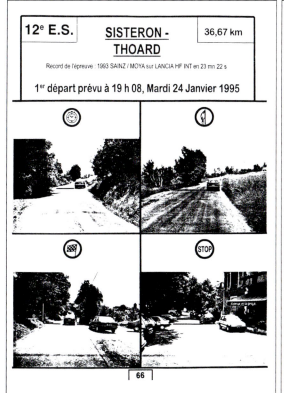

12e E.S.	SISTERON - THOARD	36,67 km

Record de l'épreuve : 1993 SAINZ / MOYA sur LANCIA HF INT en 23 mn 22 s

1er départ prévu à 19 h 08, Mardi 24 Janvier 1995

23	SECTEUR	Km 53.340	T.I 01:36	moy./h 33.338	

SISTERON
DIGNE LES BAINS (entrée)   Carte Michelin N° **245**

DISTANCE totale	DISTANCE partielle	DIRECTION	INFORMATIONS	DISTANCE TOTALE DEGRESSIVE
0.00	0.00	**1**	(D3)	53.34
4.72	4.72	**2**	D 3 — St GENIEZ AUTHON	48.62
6.63	1.91	**3**	D 3 — St GENIEZ AUTHON	46.71
11.43	4.80	**4**	CHARDAVON	41.91
13.56	2.13	**5**	St GENIEZ — D 3	39.78

ACM 23, Bd. Albert 1er BP 464 - 98012 Monaco Cedex - Tél. 93.15.26.00 - Fax 93.25.80.08 - Tlx 469 003 MC

The start of the 36.67km Sisteron/Thoad secteur as set out in the Carnet d'Itineraire. (This example belonged to car number 32.) (Ian Moore Collection)

The Concentration Run started from five European cities: Bad Homburg, Lausanne, Monte Carlo, Reims and Torino all with an average distance of 922km and converging at Valence.

Leg 1 Valence-St Agreve-Valence
416.22km with 6 stages over 171.71km

Leg 2 Valence-Serres-Dignes-les Bains
526.24km with 6 stages over 167.34km

Leg 3 Dignes-les-Bains-Monte Carlo
268.55km with 3 stages over 59.09km

Leg 4 Monte Carlo-Monte Carlo
474.07km with 6 stages over 148.66km

The French car failed to finish due to

suspension failure on the offside rear which occurred on Special Stage 11.

Drivers who retire during the final Leg – the 'Etape Finale' of the Rallye Monte Carlo – are always officially classified in the results. This year there was a total of 131 classified drivers.

A bent left-hand rear radius arm caused steering problems. (Bryan Purves Collection)

THE RACING SCENE AT THE NÜRBURGRING

U ndoubtedly the most scenic race and the finest racetrack in the world – and the most dangerous! This world-famous racetrack is situated in the west of Germany, deep in the Eifel Mountains close to the Ardennes Forest and adjacent to Luxembourg. The history of the circuit stems back to before World War 1 when the Kaiser watched a motor race in which the French cars continually thrashed the German opposition. It was brought to the Kaiser's attention that Germany did not have a proper car race or test track and facilities, to which his immediate reaction was that one must be built! Over the following eighteen months 1500 German workers were employed to produce what is possibly the best racing circuit in the world. Finally opened in 1927, originally the circuit comprised three loops: the 14 mile Nordschleife; the five mile Sudschleife, and the third loop which, together, resulted in an 18 mile lap.

When Nicki Lauda was involved in an horrific accident there in 1976, the circuit was decreed no longer safe for international racing. Then, in 1982, the

Der Nürburgring.

Sudschleife circuit was torn up and a new Grand Prix circuit constructed in its place, built so as to link with the Nordschleife loop.

Currently, the Nürburgring comprises the Nordscheife circuit, which is 20.8 kilometres in length, and the Grand Prix, Formula 1 circuit which adds a further 4.5 kilometres. It is, it has to be said, the most frightening, most awesome, and most picturesque motor racing circuit in the world with its 176 bends, 76 corners on the Nordscheife, and further 11 corners on the Grand Prix circuit.

The 'Ring' is approximately 1500 feet above sea level and varies in altitude by nearly 1000 feet. There are approximately 48 changes in asphalt where the track has been resurfaced over the years, all of them with different rates of adhesion as some are abrasive while others are as slippery as ice.

The reason for adding the modern track to the length of the 24 Hour and 6 Hour Races was that it gave the opportunity for drivers who had encountered a problem whilst on the long circuit, to peel off and double-back into the pit lane without risk of becoming stranded somewhere out on the circuit.

Another point to bear in mind is that when racing at this circuit, due to its location in the mountains and length, drivers can experience clear blue skies on one part of the circuit and rain in another.

This 24 Hour Race is acknowledged by

An aerial view of the Formula 1 circuit, which, until the mid-1990s, was the home of the German Grand Prix. (Bryan Purves Collection)

all those involved in the world of racing as the biggest and toughest race in the world. It usually has an entry of at least 200 cars every year but, according to the ONS Track Permit (the official classification of the racing permit for the event), a maximum of just 180 cars are permitted to race at any one time, and – in this event – in three starting groups comprising a maximum of 60 cars per group starting 3 minutes apart. Should cars not meet the practice time criteria, they are not permitted to take part in the event. The fastest qualifier in practice is given the choice of starting on the right or the left of the grid. Such a popular event always attracts an estimated gate of at least 150,000 spectators.

ADAC 1995 International Nürburgring 24 Hour Race
Date: 16-17th June 1995

John Brigden and Jeremy Coulter decided just weeks before this event that they would submit an entry for the 24 Hour Race using the Russell Brookes' Network Q RAC rally car, registration number L54 CVP.

A team of skilled enthusiasts and experts was brought together in order to produce a fully prepared race car. Bill Richards was brought in to build an engine that would last the 24 Hour Race. Peter Cook of Southern Carburettors and Injection was responsible for setting up the power output of the engine. Nick Chalkley, Mike Askew and Simon Skelton were also part of the team.

L to R: Tony Dron, Jeremy Coulter, Simon Skelton, Peter Cook, Nick Chalkley, Mini World Editor Mike Askew, John Brigden in red overall, and Bill Richard kneeling. (Bill Richards Collection)

The drivers were to be Jeremy Coulter, John Brigden, and Tony Dron, who would take spells at the wheel, especially during the night.

Nick's and Simon's main job initially was to prepare the car for the race, which meant converting a rally car into a race car. All of the additional rally underbody protection had to be removed, as well as conventional rally components. A new front sub-frame was fitted and numerous rally-damaged parts replaced. Peter Cook developed a new 'map' for the engine ECU more suited for racing, setting up the car on his rolling road. Working to very fine timing, the car was eventually ready for transportation to the Nürburgring.

Before the first qualifying session on the Friday, several changes were made to the car in the pits as the driveshafts and CV joints were replaced, along with the steering wheel and driver's seat. Then, after a couple of laps, in overcast and showery conditions, Tony Dron came in and reported that there was a problem with the rear

Tony Dron prior to the start of the Nürburgring 24 Hour race. At 6 feet 5 inches tall, he still managed to fit into and drive a Mini! (Courtesy Mini World)

tyres rubbing the wheelarches. It was discovered that this continual rubbing had worn a groove in the tyre tread. In order to overcome this problem, an anti-roll bar was fitted to the rear of the car, and the suspension raised by 5mm in order to compensate for the weight of fuel at the start of the race, all of which was helpful. Another problem was also discovered: incorrect brake pads had been supplied which meant that the ventilated front discs and four-pot callipers had to be replaced with standard Mini Cooper units, albeit with carbon metallic pads on the front and competition linings on the rear.

Dron's initial qualifying time put the car 81st on the grid, but then the track dried out and a subsequent 12 minute 14 second lap placed the car on the 74th penultimate row of the start grid, with 147 cars in front. (The cars at the front of the grid had driven the circuit in under 9 minutes.)

After just one hour out on the circuit Dron brought the car into the pits with the engine overheating and running at 95F, along with vibration problems which were attributed to a tyre. The front grille and lamp bar were removed in an attempt to increase air flow through the front of the car. The cause of the vibration problem was not discovered. Thirteen minutes later Dron was passing the pits with a thumbs-up sign: engine temperature had dropped to below 90F and the engine was pulling the right revs; the replacement tyres had worn-in and the vibration had disappeared. All was well.

Being the first driver Tony Dron had been allocated the first ten laps, but after the fifth lap the engine began to cut out which necessitated switching over to the second fuel pump. On the ninth lap the car came to a halt for 12 minutes and the pit crew naturally began to panic. Twenty-two minutes later it arrived back at the pits with what Tony thought was fuel pump problems again, only to discover that the fuel level was too low. From then on the car was pitted every eight laps as opposed to every ten. At 6.45pm it was changeover time when John Brigden took over the driving seat just as rain started to fall, so out he went on 'wet' tyres.

At 02.44 hours in the black of night and following a routine fuel stop, the car arrived back in the pits after having completed just one lap with only a quarter tank of fuel remaining. There was no obvious fuel leak so Peter Cook considered that the ECU mapping could possibly require re-adjustment; no, that was all correct. Eventually the problem was discovered to be a missing O-ring on the

With the removal of the front grille it was then a case of refuel and back on the track. (Bill Richards Collection)

A pit stop with tyre change and refuel.
(Bill Richards Collection)

Driving in the dark and trying to remember the driving line on a long circuit requires considerable concentration. (Bryan Purves Collection)

fuel filler neck which meant that petrol was being thrown out on right-hand bends. A replacement O-ring was not available so the filler was wrapped in tape and the car returned to the race.

Eventually the missing O-ring was found on the pit floor near to where the car pulled in for refuelling. By now, after 12 hours of hard driving on both a rain-soaked and

*Driving through the night is a different experience to daytime racing.
(Bryan Purves Collection)*

dry track and numerous tyre changes, the car was starting to show signs of tiring. John Brigden reported that it was becoming increasingly difficult to engage second gear, the throttle cable was becoming rather stiff, and the pit crew had to push-start the car away from every pit stop.

By early morning it was obvious that many of the top teams had not survived the night, with both BMW and Volvo off the leader board. The Mini, having covered over 1000 miles, was brought in for a necessary oil change; removing one of the throttle springs cured the heavy throttle problem. By early afternoon noises could be heard coming from the differential, and a considerable amount of backlash could be felt,

which meant that the car was becoming increasingly difficult to drive. John Brigden was sent out to nurse the car around the track with the ultimate aim of finishing the race around 14.00 hours. Brigden was signalled for a pit stop for an engine oil change to reduce the risk of metal fragments suspended in the oil circulating the engine, in an attempt to prolong its life.

When the Mini pulled into the pits for its quick service the heavens opened and cars were dashing in for a change of tyres

Driver change, refuel, clean windscreen, and back on the track. (Donald Farr Collection)

Bill Richards in white T-shirt with (L to R): Tony Dron, Jeremy Coulter and John Brigden.
(Bill Richards Collection)

for the wet conditions. This meant that the Mini's closest rival, the Fiat Cinquecento, in front from the start of the race, now had a reduced lead time.

At 14.02 Tony Dron drove the Mini over the finish line to the Chequered Flag and applause of the watching crowd in the grandstand opposite, 31 laps behind the winner. The final position was 92nd overall out of 180 starters, and 9th in Class ahead of the Fiat Cinquecento, having completed 98 laps of a race in which 122 cars finished. The fastest lap was 12 minutes 17 seconds which equated to a 76mph average speed.

The final winners were Ravaglia, Duez and Burgstaller, driving a BMW 320i, finished with 129 penalty points. The Mini team finished with 160 points.

Tony Dron waves his hand with delight, having finished the 24 Hour Race.
(Courtesy Mini World)

Visit us on the web – www.velocebooks.com
New book news • Gift vouchers • Details all books in print • Special offers

NETWORK Q
RAC RALLY 1995

Date: 19-22nd November 1995
Total mileage: 1445 miles starting and finishing in Chester
Stages: 28 timed Stages over 317.45 miles
Surface: tarmac, gravel, snow and mud
Participants: 199

This year the Network Q RAC Rally again started and finished in the historic walled Roman city of Chester. It was the final round of the 8-event FIA World Rally Championship, and set the scene for a dramatic finale to a closely fought season with both Driver's and Manufacturer's titles to be decided. With unpredictable weather conditions the norm during this event, drivers had to be capable of coping with a vast range of temperatures and track conditions.

Keith Bird, with Tony Graham navigating, had the pleasure of once again competing in the ex-Makinen/Easter car loaned to them by Keith Dodd of Mini Spares. The car was entered in the Group A/5 class with start number 148.

The FIA made a change in the World Rally Championship regulations pertaining to the length of a Stage. Previously, a maximum Stage length of 20.5 miles was permitted but for 1995 this was extended to 37 miles between official service points. SS9 Kielder Forest-Pundershaw was the first new length Stage of the series, consisting of 37 miles on the gravel roads of Europe's largest man-made forest. Also this year Fred Gallagher took over from Malcolm

(Bryan Purves Collection)

NETWORK Q

RAC RALLY

WORLD RALLY CHAMPIONSHIP

19-23 November

M'RAE SV1

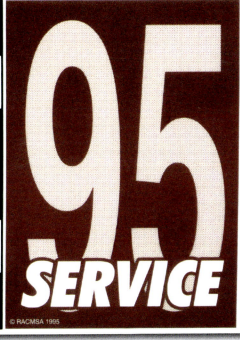

2 CHESTER RACE COURSE

5 SCRUTINEERING

95 SERVICE

© RACMSA 1995

contact with the numerous straw bales and brightly-painted logs placed by estate authorities to prevent 'ditch hooking'. On the Saturday prior to the rally a shoot had taken place at the park which had driven almost all of the region's feathered population into the area of the Stage, with a number of crews reporting 'bagging' the birds.

Stage 2 Beechdale Chatsworth: A 5.26 mile Stage around the Duke of Devonshire's estate, including a jump and

Neill as the new Clerk of the Course, Malcolm retiring from the post after 11 years.

With Chester the start of Leg 1, rally action began at SS1, a 4.94 mile Stage at Ferodo Tatton Park on open parkland with fast winding roads interspersed with wide bends, hairpins, and a chicane. It was here that over a dozen crews slid broadside and reported damage after coming into

MONTEBERG 1995
NAGEZIEN

NETWORK Q RALLY
PASSED SCRUTINEERING
1995
WORLD RALLY CHAMPIONSHIP

Spectator Information

NETWORK Q
RAC RALLY

19-22 November 1995

DAY 2

DAY 1

11
10
12
9
8
13
14

LEEDS

7

**HALT LEEDS
SUNDAY 19**

CHESTER

1

6
2
3

DAY 4

26
25 27 28

15

24
22 23

16

21

4
5

**RALLY HQ CHESTER
START/FINISH
HALT MONDAY 20
HALT TUESDAY 21**

*Spectator
information.
(Courtesy Rally
Sport magazine)*

DAY 3

20
18 19

17

DAY 1
Sunday November 19
Chester (08.15) — Leeds (18.35)
Special Stages 1-7
28.7 Miles

DAY 2
Monday November 20
Leeds (05.00) — Chester (21.45)
Special Stages 8-14
118.3 Miles

DAY 3
Tuesday November 21
Chester (05.00) — Chester (20.20)
Special Stages 15-21
106.6 Miles

DAY 4
Wednesday November 22
Chester (05.00) — Chester (15.00)
Special Stages 22-28
65.0 Miles

cars starting at 30 second intervals.

Stage 6 Rother Valley: flat country park of 2.56 miles.

Stage 7 Leeds: a mixture of tarmac and loose gravel surfaces through the park with a fast start and twisty route through the spectator area, culminating with short fast sections to the finish.

Day two, Leg 2 did not get off to a very good start when a spectator, situated near the end of the first all-forest Stage of the rally (SS8) collapsed with a heart attack and died by the roadside, delaying the start of the Stage and causing the rally to run 11 minutes late throughout the day. The 16.92 mile Hamsterley Stage featured both fast and twisty sections with parts of the high ground often affected by early morning ice and mist. Towards the end of the Stage is the famous Hamsterely Ford which is always a popular spectator area.

The rally then moved on to Stage 9 – Pundershaw – the longest Stage of the World Championship covering the classic open Kielder roads, and a supreme test of man and machine, driving on a fast curving route with deep ditches each side, over a distance of 36.61 miles.

Stage 10 Broomylinn: a distance of 11.45 miles driving an essentially circular route through a wooded area.

Stage 11 Wauchope: 8.80 miles; the

two water splashes. Another rally story: the service crew for Rover Mini Cooper number 189, driven by Trevor Godwin and David Wyer, was held up on its way to the pre-arranged Chatsworth rendezvous by a Victorian Stagecoach occupying the full width of the road.

Stage 3 Clumber Park: 5.11 miles over mainly tarmac surfaces. The fastest Stage of the rally incorporated many tight corners and a bridge.

Stages 4 and 5: each of 3.85 miles using both the Donnington tarmac race circuit and off-track gravel surfaces. Narrow in places with tricky corners. A jump also included. The Stage was used twice with

only Stage totally in Scotland, using high, fast tracks over the moors.

Stage 12 Kershope: 22.54 miles. The Stage started in Scotland and finished in England, covering fast, rugged roads with a very twisty open section along the riverside, and through forest sections with bumpy straights to the finish.

Stage 13 Grizedale West: 17.39 miles. A winding, testing route with virtually continuous bends making it one of the toughest Stages of the rally, along with deceptive crests and firebreaks. When 100 cars had passed through this penultimate Stage the rally was stopped as one spectator had collapsed and died near to the Stage finish and another had fallen off a wall and broken a Leg. The rally rescue services and a helicopter were both called to the scene.

Stage 14 Grizedale East: 4.73 miles encompassing a twisty and deceptive route with the Leg finishing at Chester Racecourse.

During the night heavy rain had fallen, continuing through to the morning start of Leg 3, and the first Stage of the day.

Stage 15 Dyfnant: 13.46 miles. Inclement weather overnight made driving very difficult, with a deepening layer of treacherous mud throughout the Stage; a scenario which persisted through to SS18, where weather conditions turned to dense fog.

Stage 16 was to the infamous Sweetlamb Hafren with 15.84 miles of testing, flowing forest roads passing through the Sweetlamb bowl, including two watersplashes.

The rain finally gave way to blue skies after dense fog through which navigators had to work entirely from their pace notes. On the following 20.27 mile Brechfa Stage 17, under-tyre conditions remained hazardous as the road hugged the hillside in a series of long sweeping bends combined with numerous sharp bends.

Three miles north east of Brechfa was the 22.82 mile SS18 at Trawscoed, an uncompromising Stage which tested crews to their limits. Then came the 10.97 mile Stage 19 Crychan Forest leading on to Stage 20 through the 5.64 mile Cefn Forest, returning to Sweetlamb for Stage 21 which consisted of a 17.9 mile route slightly modified from the former Stage 16, but still including the two watersplashes. The cars then returned to Chester for the overnight halt.

On the final day, after heavy rain had again fallen throughout the night, there were 106 starters out of the original 196 which had originally departed from Chester on the first day. The first Stage 22 – Pantperthog – was a 9.58 mile serpentine type of route leading on to Stage 23, Dyfi, a complete contrast with 14.62 miles of excellent road surface through the Dyfi Forest.

Stage 24 Gartheiniog: 9.16 miles that followed on from the previous stage, incorporating numerous deceptively tight bends.

Stage 25 Penmachno South: 8.36 miles with a mixture of very fast roads, steep hills, tight hairpins and fearsome drops, which then led directly on to Stage 26, Penmachno North, 6.28 miles of road with fast corners.

Stage 27 Clocaenog West: 3.75 miles of twisty roads and copious deep ditches, followed by Stage 28, Clocaenog East, 12.05 miles of good, firm road with long straights and deceptive crests eventually leading on to the finish in Chester.

Final Mini classifications				
73rd	David Johnson/ John Flynn	Group 'N'	Car no 184	Class N/1a
75th	Trevor Godwin/ David Wyer	Group 'A'	Car no 189	Class A/5a2
95th	Michael Plant/ Marina Francks	Group 'N'	Car no 193	ClassN/1a
Retirements				
Keith Bird/Tony Graham	Car no 148	Group 'A'	Class A/5a2	On SS12 with broken driveshaft
Daniel Harper/Les Reger	Car no 147	Group 'A'	Class A/5a2	On RS08 with gearbox failure
Robert Plant/Jason Austin	Car no 199	Group 'A'	Class A/5a2	On RS22 with hole in gearbox casing
Andrea Hall/ Gill Cotton	Car no.202	Group 'A'	Class A/5a2	Mechanical failure

An estimated 2,500,000 spectators lined the route of the rally, with 77,260 paying spectators at the six prescribed venues on Leg 1.

The world rally scene was now gaining prominence in the eyes of the general public, as evidenced by the media figures released for the Network Q RAC Rally. In the United Kingdom the rally was listened to by 382,556,000 people on 162 radio stations and watched by 62,435,000 television viewers, with magazine and newspaper reports read by 335,004,000 enthusiasts.

British television totalled 96 broadcasts with coverage of 9 hours, 12 minutes.

14,300,000 viewers watched the BBC2 *Top Gear Rally Report* and the BBC2 Christmas Day programme attracted 21 per cent of the total viewing audience.

Coverage in the UK written media – twenty of the best-selling British newspapers – amounted to 544 photographs and 10,680 column centimetres. The national newspress derived 62 per cent value, 18 per cent from regional newspapers and 20 per cent from specialist magazines.

Throughout 71 countries around the world an estimated 2,149,652,000 people watched the rally on television, with a further 507,906,000 individuals reading magazine reports.

RALLYE MONTE CARLO 1996

Date: 20-25th January 1996
Surface: tarmac
Concentration Run: 928 kilometres
Stage miles: 370

Why, it must be asked, should Rover enter the Rallye Monte Carlo again in 1996, thirty years after Timo Makinen's works Mini-Cooper S, GRX 555D, was disqualified for what can only be regarded a laughable infringement of the lighting regulations? It seemed that Tony Dron and Alistair Douglas were going to drive a Mini Cooper, D555 GRX, in the 1996 rally to set the record straight ...

The Minis that took part in this event – as in previous entries that decade – were not radically different to the 1960s cars, the most notable changes being 12 inch wheels, fuel injection, and larger front disc brakes. The sub-frames were now rubber-mounted and the engine had been moved forward by 0.75 inches.

Why was the diminutive Mini considered for such an event when the modern competition was far superior? For Rover and the car the answer was obvious from

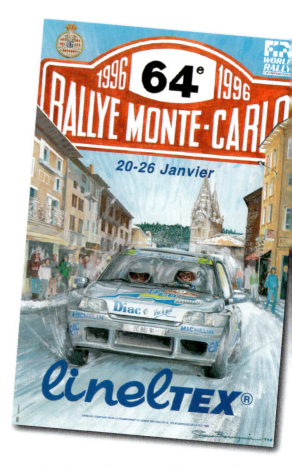

Artist: Pierre Bereuguir. (Tim Brenchley Collection)

The sporty Abarth Fiat Cinquecento, modern competitor of the Mini. (Martin Holmes)

to assemble a team for the 1996 Monte Carlo Rally. Rover Heritage was responsible for the entry and a proportion of its funding. It was decided to use the Rover Cooper, chassis number SAXXNNDYCBD071, which Russell Brookes had driven in the 1994 RAC Rally, and which then went on to be raced in the ADAC Nürburgring 24 Hour event of 1995.

Responsibility for building and preparation of the engine for the BMH car once again rested in the capable hands of Bill Richards Racing of Ashford, Kent. The power unit was 1293cc with a Weber Alpha fuel injection system capable of reving to 8000rpm if necessary, although maximum power of 93bhp was achieved at 6000rpm. A five-speed gearbox had been homologated but was never used, and the reliable Jack Knight four-speed dog box was used in preference, a 4.666:1 final drive ratio giving a top speed of 92mph with a limited slip differential. 12 inch wheels were fitted with snow tyres, or 13 inch wheels with low profile competition rubber subject to driving conditions. Overall car build was entrusted to Barretts of Canterbury, which had to ensure that weight conformed to Group 'A' regulations (a minimum of 790kg).

John Brigden of Brigden Associates and formerly of BCM Ltd, was the person responsible for compilation of all information and details for the project. In turn, Ian Phillipson was the Service Co-ordinator, responsible for route planning, details of which would be distributed to all involved personel at the team's scheduled meeting place in Valence, France, at the end of

a commercial point of view: the Mini was a current mainstream product with sales exceeding 20,000 units per year, over 8000 of which were exported to Japan. 10 per cent of sales were Mini Coopers, and aftermarket parts sales were booming. But the main reason for participating in the 1996 rally was to promote Rover Group's best-kept secret: BMH – British Motor Heritage – which was based at Faringdon in Oxfordshire.

British Motor Heritage now had a multi-million pound turnover, and every Rover dealership throughout the world had access to this resource, which no other manufacturer could offer. Since purchasing the Rover Group BMW had been very supportive of this facility, and taking part in the rally was a way of promoting remanufactured parts and considered a sound commercial venture.

Rover saw the Fiat Cinquecento as a direct threat to Mini sales. In the 1300cc Group 'A' category of this rally there were to be two Mini entrants; that of Tony Dron/Alistair Douglas and the second car the ex-Makinen/Easter Mini, now owned by Mini Spares and driven as a private entry by Keith Bird and Robert Dyson. Also entered was a Suzuki Swift, three Peugeots, and 23 Fiat Cinquecentos, the latter specially-developed sporting Abarth models.

During the latter part of 1995, Brian Cameron, MD at Rover Heritage, began

Tony Dron at Gaydon with the 1996 Rallye Monte Carlo Mini. (Courtesy Rover Group)

The co-driver's toe-board. (Peter J Fox)

Relays and fuses were mounted on the dashboard for easy access. (Peter J Fox)

the first day's Concentration Run. The driver for this event was due to be Tony Dron – who drove the car in the 24 Hour Nürburgring Race of 1995 – alongside

Craig Thorley navigating, but, due to unforeseen circumstances, Alistair Douglas had to substitute.

In the meantime the Bird/Dyson team

The ATL fuel cell made especially to fit in the boot with minimal room for the spare wheel. (Peter J Fox)

had driven through thick fog to Dover when Keith realised that he had forgotten his driving licence, and had to drive to Lincoln and back before the could make the crossing to France. Both crews then spent four days prior to the start of the rally undertaking a recce of the route to establish appropriate notes, pace notes and information for the event.

The first part of the Rallye Monte Carlo was always a Concentration Run with cars starting from a choice of venues; either Bad Hombourg, Lausanne, Turin, Reims or Monaco, with all cars congregating in Valence for the rally

Tony Dron with Alistair Douglas navigating.
(Bill Richards Collection)

	MARQUE - TYPE		N° Compétition
PUBLICITE	64e RALLYE MONTE-CARLO	WORLD RALLY	113

	MARQUE - TYPE	Coéquipier
	ROVER MINI COOPER	
	Immatriculation	
	D55 SGRX	
	Couleur - toit	
	red / white	
M. DRON	N° Châssis	M. THORLEY Douglas
Prénom: TONY	SAXXNNDyCBD071746	Prénom: CRAIG Alistair
VILLE DE DÉPART	PROMOTION	Catégorie	Classe
BAD HOMBOURG		A	5

The car passport which, on all international rallies, must be attached to the inside of the left-hand rear window (Bill Richards Collection)

proper from Monday. The Minis of Bird and Dyson and Dron and Douglas both started from Bad Hombourg just north of Frankfurt in Germany, principally because of the support received from Rover Germany. The scrutineering was relatively uneventful, with only minor gripes about advertising on the rear side windows on the Mini Spares-entered car, and there was a good-natured and peaceful protest by the German Green party at the start of the rally. Eventually, both cars started the Concentration Run in the evening, taking them along the Rhine and into France with the first overnight stop at Nancy. The route then progressed via the Vosges mountains on through Dijon towards Valence, a distance of just under 1000km.

Once in France the roads – and especially the junctions – were crowded with enthusiastic spectators; the car of Bird and Dyson was running just in front of French driver, Francois Delacour, who was obviously a great favourite with them.

The afternoon arrival and rendezvous with their service crews was the last real opportunity to thoroughly check the cars in preparation of the competitive part of the rally. A team meeting of all 12 personnel involved with the BCM team was called by John Brigden, and included Bill Richards whose main responsibility was maintaining the engine; Andy Williams and Nick Chalkley were also present with specific responsibilities. John Brigden gave what can only be called a speech to all present: "The Monte Carlo Rally is the most prestigious round of the World Rally Championship, and of enormous significance to any owner of a Rover vehicle and to Rover Group itself. At all costs the Mini rally car must make it to the end of the event; the team must commit 100 per cent to ensure that this happens. The entry is also of major significance because

The Bird/Dyson Mini Spares-sponsored car being pushed into the scrutineering hall, where they were told to remove a sponsorship logo on the left-hand side rear window as it was blocking the crew details. (Courtesy Keith Bird)

The Bird/Dyson car having completed scrutineering. (Courtesy Keith Bird)

1996 is the 30th anniversary of the infamous disqualification of GRX 555D. Our vehicle this year will be carrying the registration number D555 GRX, kindly donated by the DVLA for the occasion. It is also important that all crew be made aware that 167 cars

are entered on the 1996 Monte, but only the top 100 will be allowed to start the fourth and final Leg."

The BMH 'chase' car was a Mini Mayfair, registration number N679 TOK, loaned from the Rover pool car section of the company and driven by Dave Paveley and Nigel Bowle, whose job it was to report to the team the weather notes for the Stages in order that the correct choice of tyres could be made for each. On day one the first car was due to depart at 10.00am with minute intervals between each car. Bird/Dyson had a start time of 11.51am and the Dron/Douglas car two minutes after that.

Prior to the start of the first Leg of the rally, Valence-St Agreve-Valence, a total distance of 389.24km with six Stages over 150.62km, it was considered that some modification should be made to G555 GRX in order that the studded snow tyres would not foul the wheelarches. Time was at a premium with only a 15 minute window of opportunity. With the copious use of an angle grinder the rear radius arms were appropriately modified and the ECU changed to try and eliminate the intermittent misfire; this was not helpful as the car then refused to start so the original

Keith Bird and Robert Dyson leaving the starting ramp. (Courtesy Keith Bird)

*The rally began in wet and driving snow.
(Donald Farr Collection)*

A roadside service. The Barretts van in the background is the same as that used for servicing Paddy Hopkirk's car in 1994. On this event it was Service Unit B.
(Bill Richards Collection)

unit was refitted. The front brake pads were changed to try and improve braking efficiency (the car was already fitted with four pot callipers and ventilated discs) and it was then ready for the event.

By now both sets of crews had established a 'language of notes' which was tested out on the recce several days before. There were seven grades of corner with 7 denoting flat out and 1 the slowest above hairpin, elaborating further with comments such as 300 Right 6 into Left 4 immediate hairpin Left.

Bird and Dyson had a nasty experience half a mile from the end of Stage 2 when, on a wet road bordered with snow, they rounded a sharp bend onto a narrow bridge to

find the road covered with snow courtesy of French fans anxious to see some action. The car came to a sudden halt, wrecking the nearside front corner. As Robert Dyson put it: "The management's words echoed loudly in our ears ..." The service crew at the end of the Stage patched up the car in order to get it to the end where the entire front corner was replaced. Due to lost time a 'dash' had to be made to the next

Servicing along the route.
(Bill Richards Collection)

Keith Bird and Robert Dyson in the ex-Makinen/Easter 1994 car. (Martin Holmes)

A page from the Carnet d'Itineraire from which all the navigators have to work. The rally was split into road sections, which generally started with a competitive Stage. There was an exact time in which to complete the section but the competitive Stage had be driven as quickly as possible, and servicing was only allowed in the non-competitive element, hence a lower average speed. This is the start of Leg 1, Stage 3, Burzet to St Martial, a distance of 60.57km, which should be driven in 1.20 hours at an average speed of 45.42kph. The first car left the Control at 12.41 hours. (This example belongs to car number 113.) (Bill Richards Collection)

stage – Burzet – reached with just a minute to spare, A 30 minute cost in penalty points placed the pair almost last overall. Only later in the event was the full extent of the damage discovered: a bent steering rack and twisted front sub-frame moving

4	SECTEUR	Km 60.570	T.I 01:20	moy./h 45.428	

BURZET ST AGREVE — Carte IGN Nº **111**

DISTANCE totale	DISTANCE particlle	DIRECTION	INFORMATIONS	DISTANCE TOTALE DEGRESSIVE
0.00	0.00	1		60.57
5.92	5.92	2	(D 215) PEREYRES	54.65
9.70	3.78	3		50.87
16.93	7.23	4	(D 215)	43.64
17.00	0.07	5	!!! CHICANE	43.57

ACM 23, Bd. Albert 1er BP 464 - 98012 Monaco Cedex - Tel. 93.15.26.00 - Fax 93.25.80.08 - Tlx 469 003 MC

35

A faulty master switch caused engine misfiring. (Bill Richards Collection)

the floor inside the passenger footwell. The service crew worked diligently to keep the car running. The adjustable tie bar helped but eventually ran out of thread, so was removed and the threads shortened. At longer service stops a body jack was used to push the sub-frame and passenger floor forward. The accident had affected the geometry of the car, and the nearside front wheel bearing kept wearing out, so the chase car crew had to change the front hubs on the road sections. When all the spare hubs had been used the main service crew built replacements and passed them back to the chase car.

The following Stages for the Dron car were difficult to drive, melting snow making driving very slippery and the engine constantly misfiring under load to the extent that the car eventually stopped altogether. The cause, a faulty master switch which was quickly replaced by the Mini Spares service team supporting the Keith Bird and Robert Dyson Mini. Tony Dron had no alternative but to put his foot flat to the floor in order to meet the section time which he managed with just 9 seconds in hand to avoid exclusion from the remainder of the rally.

The next morning on the section to

Service crew transport was issued with a Rallye plate appropriate to the car it was supporting. (Bryan Purves Collection)

Replacing a front ball joint.
(Bill Richards Collection)

the first competitive Stage 7 (St Jean en Royans) the decision was taken to change the brakes on the Bird/Dyson car. This, however, took a lot longer than anticipated and meant yet another 'dash' to the start. Whilst driving through a built-up area, they were stopped by a policeman who pointed out in no uncertain terms that they were driving at well over twice the speed limit: needs must when the devil drives! Keith and Robert had been delayed a further 5 minutes, eventually reaching the start of the stage with 9 seconds in hand. They were running last on the road and the concern was that the controls would be closed upon arrival. Looking in the rear view mirror after they had departed, they saw the controls being packed away ...

In the meantime Dron and Douglas departed from Digne at 8.07am but within 16km the front left wheel came off the car, wrecking the ball joint. Luckily, this happened on a road section and not during a competitive stage. One of Keith Bird's service crews stopped and quickly jacked the car whilst Alistair retrieved the wheel, their own service crew summoned on the radio at the same time. A replacement ball joint was fitted in record time to avoid road penalties. By now the four-pot callipers and ventilated discs on the Dron/Douglas car were proving all but useless so were replaced with standard parts.

The next Leg was the famous Sisteron Stage, possibly one of the most famous in world rallying with fast corners, sheer drops and rocky streams. Panic set in when the news was received that Simon and service crew 2 had been arrested and were not allowed to continue, though the reason for this was not known. The weather had begun to turn nasty with rain at the lower level changing to snow at the higher altitude. The service crew was due to meet the BMH rally car at the end of the Sisteron Stage, a 15 minute journey in torrential rain and total darkness. In the meantime Bird and Dyson were experiencing problems with the engine cutting out and losing time, although their main priority was to qualify in the top 100 for the night mountain loop.

The crew in the management vehicle went to see what had happened to Simon in the service van, discovering that all that he had done was to cross a solid white line in order to pass a slow-moving convoy of traffic as he was about to enter the service area. As a result service crew 1 had to complete the service at the start of the Stage, then dash to the end via a long road section to meet the car upon arrival. They arrived just in time to see the rally car approaching from a distance.

The next Stage was Digne-les-Baines to

Keith Bird and Robert Dyson passing through the Col de Joux SS3.
(Courtesy Peter Barker)

Roadside servicing outside a Mini motocross circuit on the outskirts of the village of
Monti. (Bill Richards Collection)

It is vital to service the rally car as well as the support vehicles and, in this case, the chase car, which was a new vehicle supplied by Rover and driven by Dave Paveley. Consider the registration number of the chase car, N679TOK, and see how the registration number featured later in the year. A good rally story ... At the end of the lane was a small cottage, whose owners had two Minis which required replacement wheel bearings. After ensuring that the rally and chase cars were serviced and safely on their way, the owners invited the service crew to partake in a freshly cooked meal, in exchange for the bearings that they needed, plus other sundry parts. (Bill Richards Collection)

Tony Dron feeling confident and ready for the next stage. (Bill Richards Collection)

Due to an accident towards the end of Stage 2, the Bird/Dyson service crew had to work diligently throughout the remainder of the rally to keep the car running.

Monte Carlo, over a distance of 289.78km. Two Stages covering 31.40km were cancelled as a result of a spectator having rolled his car in the middle of the Stage just prior to the road being closed to the public. The following Stages – 13, 14 and 15 – were by now relatively clear of snow in contrast to the road sections where the teams encountered heavy snowfall.

After an anxious wait for the results to be published in Monte Carlo, especially for the Mini Spares crew, Tony Dron and Alistair Douglas, along with Keith Bird and Robert Dyson, were placed 83rd and 100th respectively, which ensured that both cars qualified in the top 100 to take part in the last night Leg of Monte to Monte; 430km with 5 Stages over 31.40km. Partway through the event, Dron was classified as last until the team identified an organiser error of 1 hour 40 minutes, which meant that they were not disqualified.

The Col de Turini Stage is always a favourite with spectators.
(Bryan Purves Collection)

The start time was 12.23am on the Thursday morning, with everyone in the team confident that, providing Tony Dron could keep the car driving in a forward direction, he would reach the finish. The only car in front was a Suzuki Swift which had leap-frogged the Mini when they were replacing the master switch. Unfortunately, this maintenance time incurred road penalties.

The recce crews set out to check out Stages 18 and 19 as the first two Stages of the leg – the famous Col de Turini (16) and St Sauveur sur Tinlee (17) – were known to have snow. The Dron car had been previously prepared with studded tyres ready for the steep, snow-covered climb. Now, because of the communication problems of making contact with the rally car, the service crews and the recce teams decided to check out Stages 18 and 19 in reverse, then drive back to the arranged service area situated between 17 and 18 in order to relay the information. Due to ice and snow it had become impossible for the service vans to meet up with the rally car to refuel prior to Stage 20.

At 6.20am the Dron/Douglas car appeared with a large dent in the rear passenger side. There was no chance to explain as time lost on the road section had to be made up so refuelling time was discounted. What had actually happened was that, upon exiting Stage 19 whilst heading for the refuelling rendezvous, the pair went too quickly around a right-hand corner, unexpectedly encountering snow on the road, whereupon the car twitched and slid into a Peugeot that had already gone off into a snow-covered ditch. The snow was getting deeper and with the rally car on wet tyres it was decided to pull the car into the side of the road and fit the two spare studded wheels and tyres. A very sound decision as many cars were struggling at this Stage.

Bill Richards straightening the rear quarter after sliding into the Peugeot. (Bill Richards Collection)

The short twisty Stage above Monaco. After a surprise blizzard, the Minis were virtually undriveable on the pure white roads. (Bryan Purves Collection)

"Scuse me garkon"
(Bill Richards Collection)

attendance, blocking the road. Now there was just the one remaining short, twisty stage above Monaco and the finish.

Upon arrival in Monte Carlo the Dron/Douglas team had achieved 67th overall and 2nd in Class. It was then that the organising body decided to combine the smaller cubic capacity classes with the 23 Fiat Cinquecentos, in so doing relegating the Mini to 12th in Class. However, the fact remains that the Rover Mini Cooper was technically the second Group 'A' car up to 1300cc to complete and finish the rally. Dyson and Bird in their Rover Mini finished 85th overall and 16th in Class. The two Minis were the only British survivors on the rally.

Car number 113 made the time control in good time, only to be informed that a spectator on Stage 20 had fallen off a wall and medical crews were in

Dron and Douglas on the finishing ramp at Monte Carlo at the end of a very tough rally.
(Courtesy Peter Barker)

L to R: Robert Dyson, Gary Hall, Jonathon Scully, John Marsh, Ben Bird, Ian Chamberlain and Keith Bird. (Courtesy Keith Bird)

On the harbourside at Monte Carlo, a cheeky Fiat Cinquecento parked directly in front. (Donald Farr Collection

The 1996 Finisher's Award. (Courtesy Keith Bird)

Outside the Royal Palace in Monaco with the WRC winners in the background. (Bill Richards Collection)

Concentration Run 928km
Leg 1 Valence-St Agreve-Valence
389.24km with 6 stages over 150.62km
Leg 2 Valence-Serres-Digne les Baines
531.97km with 6 stages over 172.50km
Leg 3 Digne les Baines-Monte Carlo
289.78km with 2 stages over 31.40km
Leg 4 Monte Carlo-Monte Carlo
430.36km with 5 stages over 108.14km

A plate from the Rallye Monte Carlo. (Bryan Purves Collection)

*Tony Dron and Alistair Douglas.
(Bill Richards Collection)*

*After the Rallye Monte Carlo, D555 GRX
featured with Stephen Smith's replica of
L33 EJB on the 1996 Lord Mayor's Parade.
(Donald Farr Collection)*

With Barretts of Canterbury now wanting to terminate its involvement with rally Minis, and D555 GRX having competed in three major events, the decision was made to sell the car, which was purchased jointly by Donald Farr and Dave Tippett, more about which follows in chapter 14.

BMH DEVELOPMENT PROGRAMME 1996

In 1996 British Motor Heritage obtained two new production Rover Cooper LE35 bodies (numbers 2 B205 021926A and 2 B205 021924A), and contracted John and Mike Southall of Enterprise Garage and Racing, Oldbury, Birmingham, to fully modify them with a view to racing the cars during the forthcoming 1996 season. The ultimate aim was to produce what was ultimately classified as the lightweight Rover Mini body, part number HMP141031.

The idea behind these two cars was to use them for testing and general experimentation to develop products based around the Mini, and to re-establish what would become the new Special Tuning Department, plus supply tuning parts to the general public. The project progressed extremely quickly due to the enthusiasm and dedication of all concerned, and thoughts turned to entering two cars in the 1996 Nürburgring 6 Hour and 24 Hour Races, which would act as proving grounds for Group 'A' parts.

Into the bodyshells was welded a full roll cage manufactured by Tarcal in T45, 41/30mm diameter, USA specification, high tensile chrome molybdenum steel tubing,

making the shell a completely 'solid' and safe unit. The cage itself was also welded to the sheet steel of the body; the tubing welded in such a manner that it protruded through into the front crossmember, eight-point floor mounting, and through the rear bulkhead into the boot, where an internal boot structure was welded to the shock absorber turrets directly behind the rear bulkhead, providing a substantial mounting for the seat belt shoulder straps. A member ran directly horizontal on the lower edge of the dashboard with further diagonals bracing the roof, door openings and rear quarters. Total weight of the roll cage was 31 kilograms.

Regarding the weight of the cars, Brian Cameron asked Dave Bloomfield, who worked at BMH, if it would be possible to manufacture doors, bonnet and boot panels in aluminium for the two Minis but, unfortunately, this never happened.

The two LE35 cars were built to the same level of detail, painted Almond Green, and developed to full Group 'A' racing specification with the aim of getting the most out of a Mini in terms of power and handling. Engine build was sub-contracted to Bill Richards Racing of Ashford, Kent, where both cars were fitted with six-speed gearboxes as built and supplied by Dave Hirons of Tran-X. The front disc brakes were especially designed and made by Bob Green of BG Developments Ltd, purely for these two cars using CP3228 calipers and 280mm diameter x 22.9mm thick discs, along with specially designed and manufactured bells and mounts. It's interesting to note that, during the Nürburgring event, the disc pads did not have to be replaced. The rear shock absorber mount design took into account that coilover shock absorbers might eventually be fitted.

The Tran-X gearbox casing is easily identifiable. Only two of these gearboxes have been located! The limited slip differential was built by Quaife of Sevenoaks, Kent. (Tim Brenchley Collection)

A sketch of the possible construction of the rear wheelarch in order to accept coil-over shock absorbers. (Courtesy Mike Southall)

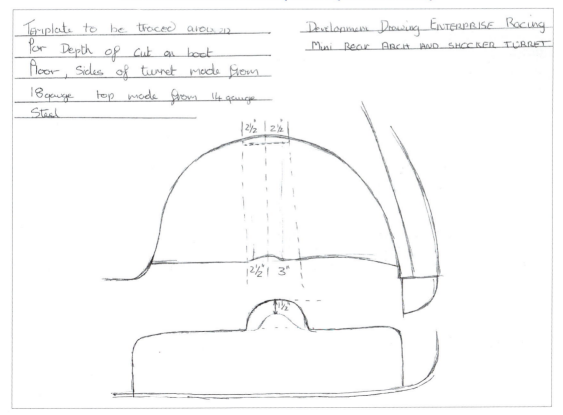

The sketch now became a reality.
(Bryan Purves Collection)

The roll cage structure within the boot
was linked directly to the top of the shock
absorber turret. The harness anchorage
was on the uppermost horizontal bar.
(Bryan Purves Collection)

The rear of the roll cage passed through
the rear firewall to the shock absorber
turrets. (Bryan Purves Collection)

The front of the roll cage passed through
the front bulkhead and was then
welded to the front scuttle crossmember.
(Bryan Purves Collection)

The majority of Mini body panels are
pressed from 20swg steel, the bulkhead
from 16 and 18swg, front sub-frame
from 13 gauge and rear from 16 and 18
gauge. (Bryan Purves Collection)

A fully welded-in roll cage was fitted to both of the cars. (Bryan Purves Collection)

Adjustable rose jointed engine steady tie bar with a specially designed bracket on the bulkhead. (Bryan Purves Collection)

A toothed belt drive was used for the water pump and alternator, but wear on the alloy pulleys proved troublesome. (Courtesy Mini World)

Group 'A' Mini parts list (race) per car		
Part number	**Description**	**Qty**
HMP141031	Bodyshell, cage & seam welded	1
	Tarcal welded-in roll cage 41/30 USA spec including certificate	1
	Wheelarch extensions	1
HMP141261	FIA homolgated 6-speed dog gearbox	1
HMP141296	Twin point engine 106bhp@6100rpm	1

Part number	Description	Qty
HMP141264	Six-speed gear control rod kit	1
	Weber Alpha pre-programmable fuel injection/ ignition control unit	1
HMP141065	Group 'A' o/s driveshaft	1
HMP141066	Group 'A' n/s driveshaft	1
HMP141278	Flange output shaft	2
HMP141279	Joint, output shaft	
HMP141068	Engine stabiliser kit	1
HMP141002	Front sub-frame, strengthened, for ARB	1
HMP141003	Rear sub-frame, strengthened, for ARB	1
HMP141123	Group 'A' sub-frame clevis	1
HMP141124	Group 'A' sub-frame clevis washer	1
HMP141004	Group 'A' Front anti-roll bar	1
HMP141109	Group 'A' rear anti-roll bar	1
HMP141008	Rose-jointed adj lower arm o/s	1
HMP141009	Rose-jointed adj lower arm n/s	1
HMP141120	Group 'A' adj tie bar kit for 008/009	1
	Momo Competition suede s/wheel	1
HMP141016	Group 'A' steering rack	1
HMP141017	Steering rack rose-joints	1
HMP141129	Conical safety washers	1
HMP141018	Group 'A' steering arms	2
HMP141130	Steering arm reducer sleeves	2
STR 1085	Spax front damper	2
STR 1086	Spax rear damper	2
NAM7163	Radius arm	1
NAM7162	Radius arm	1
GSJ166	Ball joint	2
GCV1013	Outer CV joint	2
GCV1102	Inner CV joint	2
GSV1053	Boot kit	2
HMP141303	Hi-lo kit	1
HMP141046	Fuel tank 80 litres	1
HMP141048	Fuel tank cover 80 litres	1
	Mocal 3" Fuel filler cap	1
HMP141050	Fuel hose kit Group 'A'	1
HMP141051	High capacity fuel pump	2

Part number	Description	Qty
HMP141052	Fuel filter	1
HMP141053	Fuel pump bracket	1
HMP141067	Radiator	1
HMP141163	Top mount	1
HMP141164	Bottom mount	1
HMP141165	Electric water pump	1
HMP141166	Pump bracket	1
HMP141182	Bolt set	1
HMP141167	Silicon top hose	1
HMP141168	Silicon rad/pump hose	1
HMP141169	Silicon pump/water pump hose	1
HMP141170	Silicon heater hose	1
HMP141181	Thermostat set	1
HMP141082	Group 'A' o/s front calliper	1
HMP141083	Group 'A' n/s front calliper	1
HMP141086	Group 'A' front discs	2
HMP141087	Group 'A' front disc bells	2
HMP141089	Group 'A' disc bell bolts	8
HMP141088	Group 'A' calliper mounts	2
HMP141199	L/H brake cooling duct	1
HMP141200	R/H brake cooling duct	1
HMP141092	Bias pedal box	1
HMP141093	Reservoir	3
HMP141094	Adj cable	1
HMP141095	Adj cable bracket	1
HMP141096	Reservoir bracket	3
HMP141097	Hydraulic handbrake kit	1
HMP141201	Handbrake bracket	1
HMP141203	Brake hose kit	1
HMP141099	Group 'A' carbon brake pads	1
HMP141027	Carbon door panels	2
HMP141028	Carbon ¼ panels	2
HMP141029	Carbon parcel shelf	1
HMP141305	Recaro Profi SP-G, GRF bucket seat	1
HMP141037	Seat frame set	1
HMP190199	6-point harness	1
HMP190210	Shoulder pads	1

Part number	Description	Qty
C-AJJ4016	Competition spring hooks (stainless steel)	2
HMP141030	Competition alloy door handle set	1
HMP141032	Drivers floor panel alloy anodised	1
HMP141148	Drivers clutch footrest alloy anodised	1
HMP141149	Throttle pedal extension alloy anodised	1
HMP141150	Clutch/brake pedal extensions	2
HMP141080	Front screen retainers	4
HMP141081	Rear screen retainers	4
HMP141137	Group 'A' front shock top mount L-H	1
HMP141138	Group 'A' front shock top mount R-H	1
HMP141151	Fire extinguisher manual 1.5kg	1
	Plumbed-in fire extinguisher	1
ST8131-038	STACK gauge display system	1
ST533	Shroud shift light – white	1
ST546	STACK lap timer	1
ST670	Inductive proximity sensor	1
	5g accelerometer	1
ST890 U	Network interface	1
ST800 PCNIU	Network interface	1
HMP141153	Wiring loom set Group 'A' or Gp N	1
HMP141079	¼ glass modified	2
HMP141196	Group 'A' battery box GRP	1
HMP141010	Front hub o/s standard	1
HMP141011	Front hub n/s standard	1
HMP141126	Rose-joint tie bar Group 'A'	1
GHK1140	Front wheel bearings standard	2
RUC10005	Front drive flange standard	2
HMP141069	Alternator fast road, race or rally	1
HMP141183	Oil breather tank fast road, race or rally	1
HMP141184	Oil breather tank filter fast road, race or rally	1
HMP141185	Oil breather hose set fast road, race or rally	1
HMP141186	Clutch housing breather adapter fast road	1
HMP141187	Oil cooler, various sizes	1
HMP141188	Oil hose set for HMP141187 MSB	1
HMP141189	Oil filter/block adapter	1
HMP141190	Remote filter assembly	1
HMP141191	Oil filter for remote assembly	1

Part number	Description	Qty
HMP141014	Group 'A' hub Mini o/s	1
HMP141015	Group 'A' hub Mini n/s	1
HMP 141300	Gold 5in x 13in 5.60kg wheels	6
HMP 141300	Silver 5in x 13in 5.60kg wheels	6
	45 degree wheel nuts	16
	Intercom	1
	Door light	2
	Bonnet pins	1
	Boot pins	1
	Pip pins	2
	Momo Sport gear knob	1
	Panex D ring fasteners	4
	Heated front screen	1
	Heated rear screen	1
	Relays	6
	Illuminating fuses	12
HMP141058	Lamp pod (4 lamp arrangement)	1
PA 801 WE	PIAA drive lens	2
PA 803 WE	PIAA spot lens	2
H4 1359E	Bulbs	4
PMTG 555	Mounting kit	4
HMP141044	Switch and fuse set	1
HMP141060	Lamp pod loom	1

(For stainless steel parts, nuts, bolts, screws, washers, brake hoses, unions, etc., see Appendix 6.)

In March 1996 the estimated cost for full development of the car to VK specification was £36,750, plus vat at 17.5 per cent, which included the engine, engine management

Enterprise Racing made two lamp pods in aluminium for both cars to take the PIAA lamps. The pods were designed so as not to impinge upon the driver's forward visibility, so the unit had to sit as low as possible on the leading edge of the bonnet. (Bryan Purves Collection)

MODIFICATION TO STD FRONT WHEEL HUB FOR TAPER BEARING KIT WITH HEAT
TREATED SPACER. AND BLUE PRINTING REQUIRED FOR INCREASED RELIABILITY
SET UP ON FREE ISSUE HUB CASTING.
                                      20   PLUS BEARING SET

GROUP A DRIVE SHAFT GRADE A   CHANGE AT 1500 STAGE MILES
                                                            80
GROUP B DRIVE SHAFT GRADE B   CHANGE AT 1000 STAGE MILES
                                                            65

JOINT CV   150

JOINT PLUNGE   95

PLEASE NOTE AT TODAYS DATE THE JOINTS ARE PRESENTING A PROBLEM
BUT WE CAN OBTAIN 29 OFF NEW ALLEGRO JOINTS PRICE UNKNOWN.
HOWEVER A DESIGN IS BEING EVALUATED IN THIS AREA .

TRAN-X ARE HAPPY TO LET ROVER PURCHASE JOINTS AT THEIR MUCH MORE
FAVOURABLE PRICES .

IT SHOULD BE UNDERSTOOD THAT THE DISPARITY BETWEEN PRICE OF SIX
SPEED CWG GEAR BOX AND A FOUR SPEED SYNCRO KIT SPECIAL TUNING RATIOS
IS THE DIFFERENCE OF 450-500 KITS PER ANNUM AND SYNCRO VERSUS DOG
ENGAGEMENT.

A section taken from the instructions sent to Enterprise Racing relating to the life expectancy of the different grades of driveshaft. (Courtesy Enterprise Racing)

Panex 'D' ring fasteners held closed the rear quarter windows, making for quick access. (Courtesy Corgi Classics)

system, 6-speed sequential gearbox, roll cage bucket seats, fuel cell, brake system with balance bar and AP racing callipers, wiring loom, with a separate engine loom, modified sub-frames, heated screens, STACK instruments, adjustable rear camber and track and modified dashboard.

The estimated Tran-X cost for both the tooling and casting of the various casings appropriate to the manufacture of the six-speed gearboxes was £7500. The cost to manufacture an initial six experimental gearboxes was estimated to be £24,000 and a compatible sequential gear change £10,000.

On 21st November 1996 Tran-X Gears wrote to BMH to advise that the manufactured Group 'A' driveshafts, classified as Grade A, should be changed at 1500 Stage miles, whilst the Grade B variety should be changed at 1000 Stage miles.

The wiring loom construction and all the electrical installation was undertaken by

A fully functional dashboard designed so that every control and switch was directly to hand. A Stack display instrument was also fitted with a speedometer reading taken off the right rear hub, sending electrical impulses to the dashboard display. The entire layout was mounted in a Kevlar panel. These dashes were fitted to the two Enterprise-built Minis, and used for racing at the Nürburgring. (Courtesy Mini World)

Max Mosam, head of electronics with the company responsible for the preparation of the Mitsubishi rally cars. The installation was undertaken at the Enterprise Racing workshops. James Lister of West Bromwich made the brake hoses, and Bob Green of B G Developments machined the brake callipers and hub units for the Group 'A' cars to be used in conjunction with A P Racing discs. (Refer to Appendix 7.)

The hydraulic handbrake utilised an A P Racing CP2623 master cylinder with a travel to cut-off of between 0.68mm and 1.09mm. This was then linked to the alloy handbrake lever via a clevis. The pushrod was supplied threaded as standard and provided an easy method of adjustment.

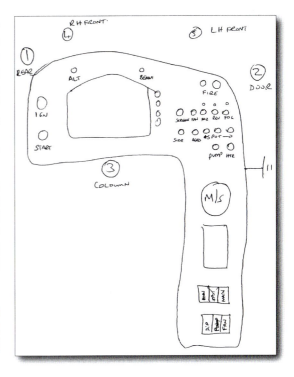

Max Mosam's basic wiring plan viewed from the back of the dashboard. (Courtesy Max Mosam)

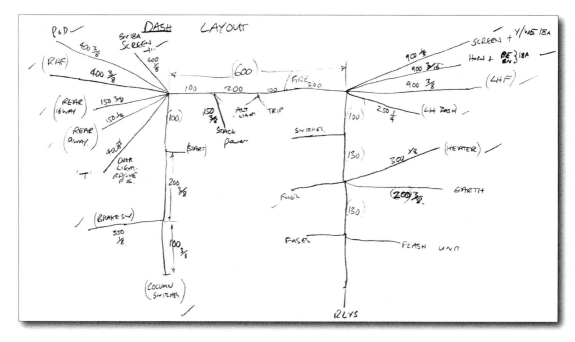

Max Mosam's freehand sketch of the dashboard wiring, including the individual lengths of each wire. Dated 14/6/96. (Courtesy Max Mosam)

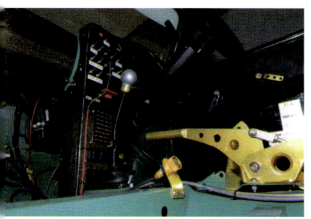

The very sophisticated dashboard with the bias brake control within easy reach of the driver's left hand, and just to the left of the alloy hydraulic handbrake. (Courtesy Mini World)

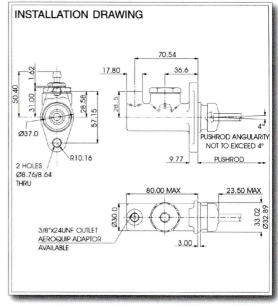

The installation drawing for the CP2623 Compact Master Cylinder, which was used for both brake and handbrake systems. (Courtesy AP Racing)

The two cars were duly entered for their first competitive event at the Nürburgring circuit where they were to compete in the 1996 ADAC 24 Hour Race and later in the year the 6 Hour Race.

Once the cars had been built they were

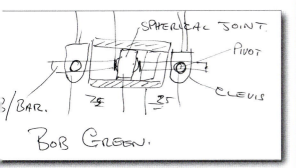

The bias brake system designed by Bob Green of B G Developments Ltd. (Courtesy Bob Green)

Twin master cylinders and bias brake system, controlled from within the car. (Courtesy Mini World)

taken to the Curborough Sprint Circuit on 15th May 1996 for testing and suspension set-up. Opposite are the handwritten notes made by Mike Southall on this occasion.

The ADAC 1996 International Nürburgring 24 Hour Race Date: 14-16th June 1996

BMH's entry in this international 24 hour race was carefully timed to coincide with the launch of the new Mini Cooper model in Germany, where it enjoyed a huge and enthusiastic following. Brewing up for a PR battle at this race meeting was the six-car team entry of the technologically modern Fiat Cinquecento versus the time-served design and engineering of the Mini.

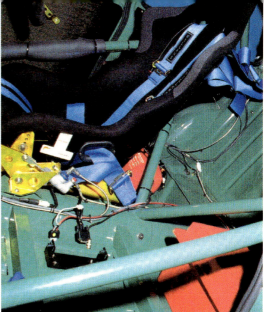

Internally the cars were very spartan. The plumbed-in fire extinguisher was positioned directly behind the driver's seat. The battery was contained in a sealed fibreglass box on the left-hand side. (Courtesy Mini World)

GROUP A MINI

SET UP DATA FOR CURBOROUGH 15ᵗʰ MAY

FRONT TRACK ___20" IN___ REAR TRACK 1°45′ OUT

TYRE PRESSURES   F : 26 PSI
                    R : 26 PSI

FRONT CAMBER

L. 3.0°   R. 3.0°

REAR CAMBER

L. 1.4°   R 1.4°

FRONT CASTOR

L. 5.0°   R. 5.0°

RIDE HEIGHT (TO SEAM)

F. 260 MM   R. 275 MM

Suspension and steering geometry set-up details from Curborough, 15th May 1996. (Courtesy Mike Southall)

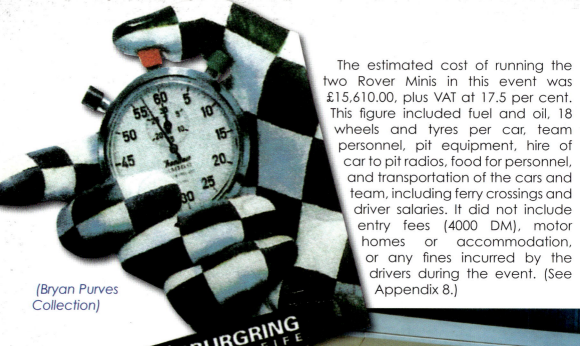

The estimated cost of running the two Rover Minis in this event was £15,610.00, plus VAT at 17.5 per cent. This figure included fuel and oil, 18 wheels and tyres per car, team personnel, pit equipment, hire of car to pit radios, food for personnel, and transportation of the cars and team, including ferry crossings and driver salaries. It did not include entry fees (4000 DM), motor homes or accommodation, or any fines incurred by the drivers during the event. (See Appendix 8.)

(Bryan Purves Collection)

The two Rover cars were, to all intents and purposes, a works-based team, with both cars built and prepared under the auspices of BMH, the Rover satellite dedicated to producing products and parts which would keep older BMC, Rover and Leyland cars on the road and track. The Nürburgring races were intended from the beginning to be used as development exercises in preparation for the 1997 Rallye Monte Carlo, with the ultimate aim of claiming a class victory.

Tony Dron considering his shared drive in car number 87. The team used the McLaren pits at the 'ring with the Rover hospitality suite directly above. (Courtesy Corgi Classics)

Jim Wirtz and Bill Richards at work on the engine. (Courtesy Corgi Classics)

Darren Povey attending to the brakes on car number 87 with car number 88 in the background. (Courtesy Corgi Classics)

The two cars, drivers and team. The green distinguishing discs on the right-hand side of the sun stripes indicated the composition of the race starting groups. (Courtesy Corgi Classics)

A final check on the right-hand front wheel. (Courtesy Corgi Classics)

The pre-race preparation virtually completed. (Courtesy Corgi Classics)

similar situation evolved with participants like the powerful BMW, Audi, and Cosworth Escorts.

The British Motor Heritage two-car entry was in Class 5, the FIA Group 'A' Touring Car, the only British entry out of 16 with a maximum capacity of 1400cc. In total, no fewer than 218 participants – with a total of 35 different classifications, including the various engine divisions – had entered although, in the event, just 180 cars were permitted to take part.

To qualify to race in the 24 Hour event

This year's race was limited to saloon cars only in an attempt to make the event safer by not having the powerful 935 Porsche Turbos coming across the slower group 'N' cars which had proved highly dangerous in previous years. Even so, a

Two Rover Cooper 35 Minis were entered in the ADAC Nürburgring 24 Hour Race, carrying consecutive race numbers 87 and 88. (Bill Richards Collection)

Engines built by Bill Richards Racing. (Courtesy Richard Franklin)

the cars had to undertake a two-lap qualifier just prior to the event. With this in mind – and because there were 218 entries – the qualifying session was scheduled to take at least 4 hours, which gave the first batch of cars the added advantage of a chance to make any necessary modifications. Luckily, for this session the track had remained dry.

The engines for the BMH cars had been built by Bill Richards Racing, and incorporated a EN40B crankshaft, 35.6mm. long stem valves, copper cylinder head gaskets, forged 'S' rockers, heavy-duty rocker shaft, grey diaphragm, 3.9:1 semi-helical limited slip differential gear set and Verto clutch. The engines also sported Marelli Weber electronic fuel injection, six-speed gearboxes by

Large 4-pot calipers operated on vented discs. Rose jointed suspension and steering, and beautifully designed linkage was used on the anti-roll bar. (Courtesy Richard Franklin)

Front anti-roll bar. (Courtesy Richard Franklin)

Tran-X, Koni shock absorbers, rose-jointed suspension parts, and AP brakes on the front, and ran on 165 x 13 inch Dunlop slicks. Insufficient time had been available to run-in the engines or set them up on the rolling road prior to the race.

Car number 87 was driven by the all-British crew of Tony Dron, Paul Taft, Steven Warburton and John Brigden, and finished 82nd overall. Car number 88 was driven by an Anglo-German team comprising Michael Hess (whose local H & H Autohaus Rover company was part-sponsoring the team), along with former Fiesta champion, Thomas Beyer, Mark Hales from *Car and Car Conversions* magazine, and Joachim Weber, who ran a driving school at the circuit. It finished 98th overall.

Drivers were given a rev limit of 7000rpm in anticipation of the length and time of racing, using speed rather than force in order to avoid the gnash from the dogs in the straight cut six-speed boxes.

Car number 88 developed a chronic misfire with just three miles to go to the pits during Friday practice. The electronic timing eye for the ignition had come loose but, with careful application of Loctite, the problem was soon resolved.

Car 87 was not without problems on practice day either. Following repeated removal of the air filter assembly to access the exhaust manifold, four washers passed through the engine, damaging valves and seats. The small valve 'A' specification cylinder head was removed from the spare engine and fitted to the car. There's a lesson to be learnt here: always ensure that air cleaner bolts are locked in place when fitting them!

The race itself traditionally starts with the cars released in timed grid order in three waves from behind a pace car, each wave 30 seconds apart. Michael Hess was the first driver in Car 88 but, by the time he had reached turn three, something in the engine or transmission had locked solid. He managed to glide off the circuit and persuaded the organisers (Michael was local to the circuit) to tow him back to the pits. Under normal circumstances this would have resulted in exclusion from the race,

Paul Taft making his way back to the pits, controlling the throttle with a length of baling twine. (Courtesy Richard Franklin)

Hard-pressed on the top of the Karrausel banked hairpin bend. (Courtesy Richard Franklin)

but we are talking about a Mini Cooper, something special in Germany!

Meanwhile, Paul Taft appeared back in the pits in Car number 87 controlling the throttle with a piece of baling twine as the cable had broken. This was quickly repaired and he was soon on his way again, recording a lap time of 11 minutes 30 seconds.

Just after the second lap into the race, Car 88 had the engine seize. The car was recovered to the pits to discover that the fuelling map was not correctly adjusted; the mixture was too rich which resulted in overheating of the main bearings caused by dilution of the oil with fuel, also increasing the fluid within the gearbox by over a litre. It was decided that an engine change was necessary if the car was to continue racing.

With great enthusiasm the pit crew took on the challenge of building Car 88 a replacement engine from the spare parts that had been brought to the meeting as back-up. After a four hour panic, finally, by 9.00pm. the car was back on the track with Mark Hales in the driving seat. At just around 10.00pm it was back in the pits with another

A night pit stop with the driver remaining seated in the car! By this time the left-hand front wheelarch extension was missing. (Courtesy Richard Franklin)

problem – an oil leak in a union – which was quickly repaired. By 11.00pm, and with the moon hidden behind the clouds, the car was again on the racing line although at least 5 hours behind schedule.

Bill Richards and Jim Wirtz working hard assembling the engine to replace the damaged unit. (Bill Richards Collection)

Racing continued throughout the night, the pit crew changing the engine and transmission whilst others raced on. What an atmosphere!
(Courtesy Car and Car Conversions)

Bill Richards under the bonnet of car 87 with Tony Dron in the driving seat. (Courtesy Richard Franklin)

It's lonely during the night but after 24 hours it seems even lonelier! The long drag up the Bergwerk to Klostertal hill. (Courtesy Richard Franklin)

Car number 88, driven by Hess, Beyer, Hales and Weber finished 89th overall. (Courtesy Corgi Classics)

Both cars ran through the night without further problems with the exception of a collapsed wheel bearing on Car 88, which was easily remedied. It was then decided that the cars really should finish together with Taft and Hales driving. The pits held out a sign – SLOW DOWN – to inform the drivers that they did not wish the two cars to pass the pits before 4pm, and then have to drive another lap. This did not happen and, on the following lap, some 2000 marshals and hundreds of spectators leapt over the barriers, waving Union Jacks and cheering and hooting when they saw the two Minis approaching. To quote Mark Hales: "It could have even been Silverstone at the end of the British Grand Prix."

Given the growing enthusiasm within the company, and with the forthcoming Rallye Monte Carlo in mind, Brian Cameron informed Enterprise Racing that two numbers had been reserved from Rover's allocation of registrations issued by the DVLA. It was suggested that Enterprise Racing should forward the appropriate paperwork in order that the registration numbers could be assigned for the Monte cars ...

Engine setup was undertaken by Southern Carburettors and Injection on a rolling road, the only satisfactory way that the maximum potential of the engines could be established using the Weber Alpha engine management system. The car on the rollers was number 88 which raced in the Nürburgring 24 Hour event. (Refer to Appendix 9 for the rolling road read-out for both cars.) (Courtesy Richard Franklin)

A full and thorough checkover has to be carried out on a car prior to any race. Note the rear anti-roll bar. (Courtesy Richard Franklin)

Hard cornering ... (Courtesy Richard Franklin)

DEUTSCHER

LANGSTREC...

... and a tight driving line. (Courtesy Richard Franklin)

The winning team. Car number 409. (Courtesy Richard Franklin)

Tony Dron and Paul Taft after receiving their second place trophies. (Courtesy Richard Franklin)

The 1996 Nürburgring 6 Hour Race
Date: 17th August 1996

In the 6 Hour Nürburgring Race meeting on 17th August 1996, both cars retained their build to Group 'A' specification. Car number 88 (in the 24 hour race) now became car number 409, and was driven by Jo Weber, Michael Hess and Thomas Beyer, finishing first in class.

Car number 408 (previously 87) was driven by Tony Dron and Paul Taft, who came second in the 1400cc class.

Both engines were built by Bill Richards with the brief to construct them to the "ultimate spec". Two new bare cylinder heads were supplied by Rover, and both engines were to run on the Weber Alpha management system, single point injection and six-speed gearboxes. At the same time that the order to Bill Richards Racing was submitted, a request was made for a third engine to be built using a supplied used test power unit, to be kept as a spare.

During the race the cars are reported to have topped 111mph on the straights.

FURTHER DEVELOPMENT & TESTING

H aving now completed the Nürburgring races further development and testing was undertaken with the cars often seen at Rover's test track at Gaydon, Warwickshire and also using Curborough Sprint Circuit which was only some 25 miles from the Enterprise Racing workshops. As with most manufacturers the cars were to be developed by associated companies, in this case by BMH and Rover Sport. The idea was to develop a package

Development of the cars continued with testing at Pershore Airfield, Evesham. (Courtesy Richard Franklin)

of BMH branded parts that would work together. It is a known fact that it is not practically possible to construct a real rally car by converting a road car and by obtaining parts on an adhoc basis. The build of a competitive car has to be done from the ground-up.

During July 1996 there had been discussion between Enterprise Racing and

Brian Cameron concerning the future 1997 Rallye Monte Carlo. Serious consideration had been given to a possible entry in this event of two Group 'A' cars and four Group 'N' cars. As Enterprise Racing was solely responsible for the build of the BMH/Rover cars, it would need time to undertake such a project, especially as a team of eight staff was concentrating on the current cars. Unfortunately, the idea went no further.

One important factor that did emerge from testing at Gaydon and Curborough, and the idea of entering these cars for international rallies, was that clearance between tyres and wheelarches was not sufficient. Both front and rear body arches had to be carefully cut and hand-beaten to raise the profiles quite considerably; this is evident when studying the position of the front repeater light in relation to the wheelarch extension of the Tour of Mull rally car. This modification was later reproduced as the Sport-Pack body.

In August 1996 in a letter to Enterprise Racing, Tony Dron put on paper his thoughts about driving the car at the Nürburgring: "… it's the gearing that needs our attention if lap times are to be reduced. We have a six-speed gearbox but, as we are only using the top four gears, we are not getting any benefit from it. Second is too low even at Wehrseifen.

"The critical sections are the long straights, especially the 2.5km climb from Bergwerk to Klostertal. We come out of Bergwerk at 6400rpm in third, changed to fourth in due course and watched the revs climb; if fifth is engaged once they reach 7000rpm, the revs drop away in the higher gear instantly. Even if you hang on to 7500rpm in fourth, the same thing happens. The quick way up the hill with the current ratios is to stay in fourth, flat out at 7500rpm.

"The ratios are far too widely spaced; first and second are too low for a race car, whilst top is a cruising gear which never gave us more than 7500rpm briefly, downhill at the Foxhole.

"We need gears that bring us out of Bergwerk, pulling about 6800rpm in second … sixth gear would probably only be used toward Schwedenkreuz, the Foxhole, and on the main straight. It should be chosen to reach 7900rpm where we are now pulling 7500rpm. I believe that 7900rpm or 8000rpm is a satisfactory limit for long distance events … slogging up hills for long spells at 7500rpm in an intermediate gear … is possibly an engine killer … how much damage did missed gears do to the engine? We all had difficulty with the selection of fifth and sixth gears so that must be improved if we want to achieve reliability."

Tony's constructive criticism was necessary for the team in order to move forward and further develop the power unit, with entry in the Rallye Monte Carlo in everybody's mind.

Regarding homologation for the Rallye Monte Carlo, knowing that the current dash would not be acceptable – but also that it played an important role in efficiency – Mark Powell produced the adjacent sketch of a dash which was eventually used in the Group 'A' car. The Monte Group 'N' car had to keep the production dash.

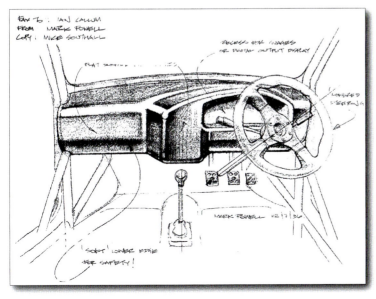

Mark Powell produced the dashboard design for the proposed Monte cars. (Courtesy Mike Southall)

The next event for testing purposes was intended to be the upcoming Tour of Mull Rally, but a decision had not yet been made on engine specification for this car. Swiftune Racing was contacted and asked to supply specifications for both a Kit Car (VK) rally engine and a Clubman 1293 rally engine, along with dyno read outs and prices. The specifications were as follows:

Mini Kit Car Rally engine:
1275cc 'works' specification short stroke, 76mm EN40B forged crankshaft with 73.5mm pistons, lightweight steel Carrillo con-rods, steel main caps with four-bolt centre cap, steel camshaft, lightened cam followers, steel vernier timing chain set, heavy-duty oil pump, belt drive water pump kit, Cooper 'S' damper, ultra light steel flywheel and steel billet pressure plate, clutch diaphragm, paddle plate, 45mm throttle body. Alloy rocker cover with breather system, 1.5 roller rocker set, full rally specification cylinder head. Engine output 140bhp@8200rpm. 102lb/ft@6000rpm. Retail price plus labour £8222 plus VAT at 17.5 per cent.

Mini Clubman Rally engine:
1293cc using forged EN40B 81.3mm crankshaft with lightened and stress relieved A+ con-rods fitted with ARP big end bolts. Centre main strap and radiused standard main caps. A power output of 130-135bhp@7500rpm. 102lb/ft@5500rpm. Retail price plus labour £7207 plus VAT at 17.5 per cent.

The Rover Group authorisation for the vehicle to be delivered to Enterprise Racing, from where the registration was then transferred to the Tour of Mull rally car. (Refer to Appendix 10.) (Courtesy Mike Southall)

The 27th Philips Tour of Mull Rally
Date: 18-20th October 1996

Having competed in both Nürburgring races, upon return to the Enterprise Racing workshops, Brian Cameron and John Brigden took the decision to show the world that the Mini could live up to the fine achievements of the 1960s 'works' cars by submitting a factory-entered team for the Rallye Monte Carlo.

As a test bed to the Rallye Monte Carlo, the car used to race at Nürburgring (number 87 and 408) was further developed to virtually Kit Car (VK) specification with an engine built by Swiftune, and then entered in the 27th Philips Tour of Mull Rally/ *Motoring News* Rally/EARS Championship on 18-20th October 1996. Neither of the cars built to date were road registered

The debut of the new era of 'works' rally cars, which were initially tested at Gaydon on Friday 11th October 1996. (Courtesy Richard Franklin)

so the registration number N679 TOK was used. This registration number had been allocated to a Rover Group pool car which had already been used as a chase car on the 1996 Rallye Monte Carlo. Authorisation for use of vehicle was given to Enterprise Racing on 1st March 1996 by the Rover Group, Vehicle Ops Department, Longbridge.

The Tour of Mull Rally car received the number 50 and retained its Almond Green livery and chequered roof, plus Sport-Pack wheelarches. This time the car was driven by Dave Paveley with Andy Bull (a Rover employee) navigating. Given the future racing and rallying proposals envisaged for the company, it was decided that the vehicle would be used as a 'test bed' to try and produce a car that could conceivably be competing on the world rally stage in the forthcoming year. BMH's goal was to try and get the most out of a Mini in terms of handling and power

output, and this was the debut of a brand new Mini rally car.

British Motor Heritage was enthusiastic about the possibility of entering a Group 'A' twin point car in the Rallye Monte Carlo in January 1997. Brian Cameron, who was also competing in the Tour of Mull Rally in a Rover 220T, intended this event to be used primarily for testing purposes, where the new Michelin tyres, heavy-duty transmission driveshafts, and a new six-speed gearbox would be put to the test. The front wheelarches were raised to the extent that the side repeater lights were tight against the upper edge of the wheelarch extensions. Keeping the weight down and being within the limit is such an important aspect when building a rally car that the internals of the front wing repeater lights were never fitted or wired-up. (These repeater lights are now a mandatory requirement for the current British Ministry of Transport tests.)

For promotional reasons the car was to be upgraded to the 1997 Cooper Sport-Pack specification, but was to retain all appropriate Group 'A' components where applicable. It would then form the basis upon which BMH submitted the application for homologation for rallying in 1997.

For the Monte Carlo event the engine was built by Swiftune Racing and fitted with a multi-point injection system and throttle body. The engine achieved a

The larger Sport Pack arches have now been fitted. Note the front jacking point at the lower rear corner of the arch. Michelin TA20 tyres were fitted to the early version of the Sport Pack wheel. (Courtesy Richard Franklin)

The KV-developed car prior to the start of the Philips Tour of Mull Rally. (Courtesy Richard Franklin)

On the starting ramp of what was to become an interesting event. (Courtesy Richard Franklin)

Dave Paveley and Andy Bull on the 1996 Tour of Mull Rally. Jaggy Bunnet, in the island publication, Mull Murmour, made quite a point: "By the way, have a good look at Paveley's Mini. This wee beastie is reputed to have 145bhp and a 6-speed sequential gearbox, and the whole device is reckoned to weigh 8cwt". (Courtesy Speedsport)

The car now featured a central towing eye by modification of the front valance. (Courtesy Speedsport)

dynamometer output reading of 136bhp at a maximum rev limit of 8200rpm. This represented a huge increase in power in comparison to the 107bhp of the previous version of the single-point engine; the aim was to improve torque as opposed to top end speed. The cost of this engine (number 2701096) and management system totalled £7800.

It was anticipated that a fully sequential gearbox would be developed in conjunction with the Tran-X six-speed unit, and Michelin TA00 tyres to be fitted to either 6 x 13 inch or 5 x 13 inch wheel rims. Other options were to include a revised front anti-roll bar. What, in effect, was happening was testing of what could possibly be used within the Kit Car regulations of the WRC. (See Appendix 11.)

With this increase in engine power and output now being transmitted through the wheels, stronger and larger driveshafts were considered in order to assist in combating torque steer. What was evolving was the specification eventually homologated for the 1997 Rallye Monte Carlo.

To quote driver Dave Paveley:

Paveley and Bull landing after one of the numerous 'yumps' encountered on the rally. (Courtesy Speedsport)

(Courtesy Speedsport)

(Courtesy Speedsport)

"Scrutineering before most rallies is usually a pretty mundane affair, that is unless you are perceived to be the first 'works' Mini Cooper S driver in nearly 30 years. One gentleman, in his mid-60s asked me to stand next to the Mini for a photo, and explained that this was to be framed and mounted, with the caption 'The luckiest man in the world.'"

The Tour of Mull Rally started at 19.00 hours on the Friday evening from the car park in Tobermory, the first leg finishing at 02.45 on Saturday morning. The afternoon section began at 12.40 and finished at 15.35, with the crews allowed just a few hours' rest before the final run through the darkness, starting at 20.45. The BMH car did not complete the first part of the event due to damage to the radiator fan blades, and so the entry was withdrawn, which gave a window of opportunity to spend time repairing and checking over the car prior to the Trophy event the following day.

The first stage of the Saturday afternoon Trophy Rally was a gruelling 8-mile section on mainly single track mountain roads, full

The BMH car being put through its paces evaluating the full potential of the kit car. (Courtesy Speedsport)

Having completed the Philips Tour of Mull Rally, the car accompanied 33EJB on the Mini Cooper Register float at the 1996 Lord Mayor's Parade in London on Saturday 9th November 1996. (Donald Farr Collection)

of blind crests. Pulling away with the new power unit installed in the car meant that engine revs had to be around 6000rpm, with a quick change at 8400rpm to engage second gear in the straight cut six-speed gearbox.

Unfortunately, the team had to withdraw at the end of SS11 due to body damage to the car and with a total of 24.56 accrued time penalty points, which meant that it did not take part in the second leg event, the Saturday Night Trophy Rally.

As Paveley said: "The rally was invaluable as a proving/testing ground and gave us the opportunity to test various anti-roll bar settings, damper rates and tyre pressures."

Daniel Harper of *Mini Sport* won the prestigious award for The Best Prepared and Presented Car of the Event.

The Mini Cooper was back!

The 1996 Children in Need Appeal

On Friday 22nd November 1996, having completed The Tour of Mull Rally, Dave Paveley and Russell Monaghan undertook the challenge to drive around the UK mainland in the BMH Rover Cooper in the rally car. The intention was to raise as much money as possible for the 1996 Children in Need Appeal, at the same time visiting 33 branches of the Rover network.

Rover offered a prize of a weekend break in Monte Carlo, with up to £1500 spending money, to the sponsor that correctly guessed the time it would take

Dave Paveley ready to take on the challenge of raising money for the BBC Children in Need appeal. (Courtesy Richard Franklin)

The poster advertising the challenge, along with the major sponsors. (Courtesy Dave Paveley)

to complete the drive, excluding rest halts, fuel stops and mechanical failure.

Unfortunately, due to mechanical failure of N679 TOK during the Tour of Mull Rally, a substitute Mini Cooper, with appropriate logos, was used. *The Sun* newspaper became involved and the team appeared on various local television news programmes.

Completing the challenge in just four days, in what were atrocious weather conditions, Dave and Russell raised £20,000 for the appeal.

The cars were repainted red and white directly over the original Almond Green. (Bryan Purves Collection)

Return to the works

In late November 1996 the two cars were returned to the workshop after being fully tested in the two races at the Nürburgring circuit and the Phillips Tour of Mull Rally. The team felt they had achieved a satisfactory level in development of the cars. The next stage in the competitive calendar was to apply for entry in the 1997 Rallye Monte Carlo.

It was decided to completely strip the cars to bare shells and respray them in the traditional BMC works rally colours of Red with a White roof, prior to a total rebuild. The chequered roof of the race cars was removed and replaced with a similar version, this time with the middle black square directly in the centre and above the

The underside of the bodyshell being repainted. (Bryan Purves Collection)

front windscreen. The cars were then registered with the DVLA on 14th January 1997 with consecutive registration numbers: P245 WFH and P246 WFH (the latter car was previously N679 TOK). P245 WFH was built to FIA Group 'A' specification whilst at the Curborough Sprint Circuit. As a personal favour Dave Paveley invited Gwyndaf Evans, who, in 1996, won the British Rally Championship, to bring along his overalls, have a drive and pass opinion about the cars, and confirm Dave's set-up.

Without realising it, these were the last 'works' Mini Coopers to be built and associated with the forthcoming Rallye Monte Carlo, which was due to start in Monaco on Sunday 19th January 1997. The Group 'A' car, number 156, was to be driven by Tony Dron with navigator Alistair Douglas, and the Group 'N', number 222,

P246 WFH was to become a Group 'N' car. Swiftune Racing was commissioned to undertake both the Group 'A' and 'N' engine builds.

On the 11th, 12th and 13th December 1996, without it being public knowledge (to avoid the motoring press), the cars were once again taken for a private testing session

Whilst the Group 'N' car was nearing completion, it was discovered that the regulations did not permit the car to have sill stands. As they were already fitted they had to be ground flush with the sill and covered to prevent use during the rally. (Courtesy Richard Franklin)

by Dave Paveley with Andy Bull on the maps and clocks.

It was BMH's intention that the Rallye Monte Carlo would be the first of a series of International rally events to be contested, as illustrated in the following BMH document. Unfortunately, this never became a reality.

The draft costs of the proposed events that British Motor Heritage envisaged for the Minis in 1997 to 1999. (Courtesy BMH)

Event Costs - Draft

		1997			1998			1999		
Focus on	6 cars	Monte Carlo Rally	100,000 30th anniversary of 1967 win							
Europe	2 cars	Tulip	15,000 2nd overall 1967							
	2 cars	Corsica	45,000 Entered in 1967							
	2 cars	1000 Lakes	25,000 1st 1967							
	2 cars	Nurburgring	18,000							
	2 cars	Circuit of Ireland	8,000 1st 1967							
Europe				2 cars	Monte Carlo	45,000 3rd 1968				
and Further				2 cars	Australia	30,000				
				2 cars	New Zealand	30,000				
				2 cars	Tulip	15,000 3rd 1988				
				2 cars	Ypres	15,000				
				2 cars	Nurburgring	18,000				
RoW							2 cars	Monte Carlo	45,000	
							2 cars	Safari	60,000	
							2 cars	RAC Rally	30,000 1st 1965	
							2 cars	Sebring	30,000 Class 1st 1967	
							2 cars	Nurburgring	18,000	
							2 cars	Acropolis	30,000 1st 1967	
Car costs		92,000			46,000			92,000		
Maintenance		42,000			42,000			42,000		
TOTAL		345,000			241,000			347,000		
Sponsorship income:	TBA									

RALLYE MONTE CARLO 1997

Group 'A' specification Rallye Monte Carlo

Registration number: P245 WFH
Date of registration: 14th January 1997
Engine number: 2781296. Built by Swiftune (December 1996). Twin-point injection
VIN number: SAXBMHC97A1100101
Body number: B 205 021926A

In preparation for the Rallye Monte Carlo, the Group 'N' car had front and rear anti-roll bars removed. P245 WFH remained as a Group 'A' specification vehicle and was fitted with the twin-point ignition system taken directly from the Tour of Mull rally car. Specification of the engine and engine bay was such that it really did not conform to Group 'A' regulations for the event, so in order to prevent interested 'admirers' opening the bonnet whilst the car was parked in Parc Ferme the service crew wired the bonnet in a permanently closed position.

Group 'A' cars may be modified by adding approved parts such as engine and gearboxes, provided that more than 5000 of these parts have been manufactured. (See Appendix 10.)

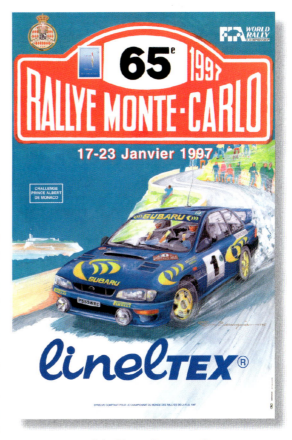

Artist: Pierre Bereuguir.
(Tim Brenchley Collection)

Rally entry number 156 on full power. (Tim Brenchley Collection)

Group 'A' Mini parts list (rally)
Specific Group 'A' rally parts fitted to the car, over and above race car specification, are as follows:

Part number	Description	Qty	*
	Sport-Pack lightened wheelarch extensions	1	N
HMP141297	Group 'A' rally engine 106bhp	1	
	Weber Alpha management system	1	
HMP141067	Radiator aluminium	1	
HMP141163	Alloy radiator top mount	1	
HMP141164	Alloy radiator bottom mount	1	
HMP141046	Fuel tank 45 litres	1	N
HMP141049	Fuel tank cover 45 litres	1	N
	Mocal 3" fuel filler cap	1	N
HMP141169	Silicon water pump hose	1	N
HMP141170	Silicon heater hose	1	N
HMP141305	Recaro Profi SP-G, GRF bucket seat	1	N
HMP141037	Seat frame set	1	N
HMP190199	6 point harness	1	N
HMP 190210	Shoulder pads	1	N
HMP141197	Duralamin towing eye front	1	N
HMP141198	Duralamin towing eye rear	1	N

Part number	Description	Qty	*
HMP141151	Fire extinguisher manual 1.5kg	1	N
HMP141078	Heated front screen	1	N
	Heated rear screen	1	N
	Heavy-duty front bump stops	1	N
HMP141193	Alloy sump guard 8kg	1	N
HMP141194	L/H fuel pump guard alloy anodised	1	N
HMP141195	R/H fuel pump guard alloy anodised	1	N
	Trip meter Terratrip 202	1	N
	Intercom	1	N
	Sparco front mud flaps	4	
	Avanti 18 inch navigators light	1	N
	Maserati air horns	1	N
MBD1200	Mintex C-Tech brake pads front		
	1144 fast road	1	
	1155 forest	1	
	1166 tarmac/race	1	
MLR5	Mintex C-Tech brake shoes rear	1	
	Sport-Pack 6 x 13 inch alloy wheels	5	N
HMP141301	KN 5 x 13 inch gold alloy wheels	1	N
HMP141301	KN 5 x 13 inch silver alloy wheels	5	N
	Michelin TA00 soft compound tyres	5	N
	Michelin TA20 medium compound tyres	5	N
	Michelin G50 studded snow tyres	5	N
HMP141020	AVO front shock absorbers	2	
HMP141019	AVO rear shock absorbers	2	
	Navigator's floor panel anodised alloy	1	

*'N' indicates parts that were also used on the Group 'N' Rallye Monte Carlo car. Refer to Appendices 12 and 13 for details of FIA homologated gearbox, final drive ratios and cylinder head porting.

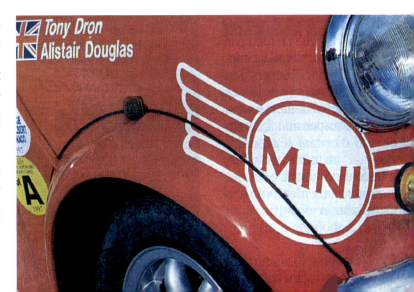

Sport Pack wheelarch extensions were fitted to modified front wings. (Tim Brenchley Collection)

The Group 'A' engine bay. The engine used for the Rallye Monte Carlo was changed for the Swiftune racing engine number 2980597 (May 1977) and used for racing in the 24 Hour Nürbrugring meeting. Only on this car was the bulkhead cut away to form a cold air box. A 170 amp Black Knight alternator was fitted which was manufactured by John Bevan Motorsport of Daventry. Only three of these units were ever built.
(Courtesy Richard Franklin)

The left-hand rose jointed engine top steady bar was fitted to both Group 'A' and 'N' cars. (Tim Brenchley Collection)

A rose jointed engine steady bar was also fitted to the bell-housing end of the engine. The BG Developments pedal box was now vertically mounted.
(Tim Brenchley Collection)

The use of aluminium Minifin brake drums on the rear was only permitted for Group 'A' cars. (Tim Brenchley Collection)

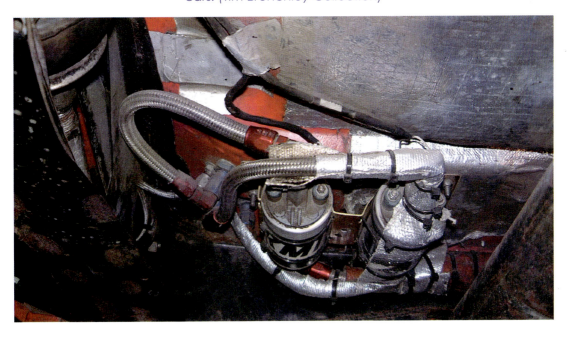

The twin fuel pumps were mounted under the rear left-hand side boot floor on a special anodised aluminium-mounting cradle. The underside of the boot floor was externally lined with a heatproof panel. (Tim Brenchley Collection)

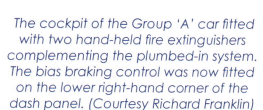

The cockpit of the Group 'A' car fitted with two hand-held fire extinguishers complementing the plumbed-in system. The bias braking control was now fitted on the lower right-hand corner of the dash panel. (Courtesy Richard Franklin)

On the right-hand side, fuel was fed from the ATL fuel cell in the boot to the pumps. The exhaust was fitted as tight to the body as practically possible and solidly mounted. (Tim Brenchley Collection)

The Group 'A' car in the foreground, the spare wheel fitted snugly in the boot with the 45-litre fuel cell. (Courtesy Richard Franklin)

The electrical installation from the back of the dashboard used on the Rallye Monte Carlo Group 'A' car and the two 1996 and 1997 Nürburgring cars. (Bryan Purves Collection)

Group 'N' specification Rallye Monte Carlo

In order to enter any rally championship, an FIA Group 'N' car has to conform to specific criteria, as the car should be essentially a road-going production vehicle. A Group 'A' car may be modified to greater extent but, in the case of a Mini, the cubic capacity of the Group 'A' engine may only be increased to 1293cc, whereas the Group 'N' (for Normal) car must remain as 1275cc with little more modification than beefed-up suspension and safety equipmentwith. Study the comparison between the two Groups and it quickly becomes apparent what can be modified.

Manufacturers are allowed to make modifications within the specific Group 'A' and 'N' constraints, and these are classified as 'Extensions'. A maximum of ten sensible mods are permitted when a car is presented for its very first event, within the classification used in the assembly of the car. Rally teams are cautious about using these Extensions, as there is a catch; under FIA regulations five of them have a shelf life of just one year and, if not used within this period, are lost forever. Now, in order to prolong the life of a rally car that is three years old, a further five Extensions are awarded.

Registration number: P246 WFH
Date of registration: 14th January 1997
Engine number: BMHE97N1100202 (on registration document V5)
Replacement engine; built by Swiftune No. 2771296 (December 1996). Twin-point injection, blueprinted
Rover MEMS injection control system
VIN number: SAXBMHC97N1100102
Body number: B205 021928A

Group 'N' Mini parts list (rally)
Specific Group 'A' race parts were removed and the appropriate Group 'N' parts fitted, as listed in the following table with the parts catalogued in the Group 'A' Mini parts list (rally):

Part number	Description		Qty	*
HMP141296	Group 'N' rally engine 85bhp		1	
HMP141289	Cylinder head Janspeed		1	
CAM 622	Rocker cover		1	
	Gearbox		1	
	Quick shift gear change lever		1	
	Thermostatically controlled radiator fan		1	
	Front mounted radiator		1	
	Heavy duty front tie rods		2	
	Relays		6	
	Illuminating fuses		24	
	Sparco front mud flaps		2	
	Switched light above drivers door		1	
MLB37	Mintex C-Tech brake pads front			
		1144 fast road	1	
		1155 tarmac/forest	1	
MLR5	Mintex C-Tech brake shoes rear		1	

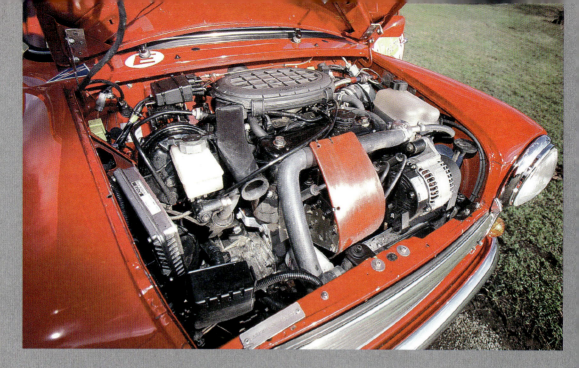

The Group 'N' engine. For the Monte it was compulsory for both Group 'N' and 'A' cars to have bonnet hinges to replace the bonnet pins fitted for racing at the Nürburgring. (Courtesy Les Kolczak)

The boot hinges were modified for easy removal by replacing the pivot pins with Pip pins. (Bryan Purves Collection)

For the Rallye Monte Carlo both Group 'A' and 'N' cars were fitted with a 45-litre fuel cell, which were volume balled down to 35-litre capacity. The picture shows P246WFH utilising a specially made funnel. (Courtesy Enchappement)

The boot of P245WFH fitted with the 45-litre fuel cell. After the Monte the cells were exchanged for 80-litre versions. (Courtesy British Motor Heritage)

The internal roof light fitted to the Group 'N' car. (Bryan Purves Collection)

The original specification placed with ATL for the supply of two fuel cells suitable for the 1997 Rallye Monte Carlo cars. Serial number 829553 was fitted to the Group 'N' car and 829554 was fitted to the Group 'A' car. (Refer to Appendix 14.) (Courtesy Aero Tec Laboratories Inc)

AERO TEC LABORATORIES INC

QUOTATION

Address:
ENTERPRISE RACING
95-101 BROADWELL ROAD
OLDBURY
WEST MIDLANDS
B69 4BL

No:1985-km-96
(Please indicate this No. when ordering)
Page: 1   of   1
Date:31-7-96
Your Reference No:
Your enquiry dated:31-7-96
Name: MIKE SOUTHALL

For the attention of: MIKE SOUTHALL   Salesman:KEVIN MOLLOY

QTY	DESCRIPTION
	Offer valid ONLY for goods described
1	CUSTOM FUEL CELL TO FIT CUSTOMER SUPPLIED MINI (CAPACITY 45 LITRES). FUEL CELL TO BE CONSTRUCTED USING ATL 694-B NYLON REINFORCED MATERIAL IN ACCORDANCE WITH FIA/FT3/SPEC MATERIAL.
	FUEL CELL TO INCLUDE:-
	- INTERNAL FOAM BAFFLING.
	- 6"x 10" NUT RING/COVER PLATE ASSEMBLE
	- FUEL LEVEL GAUGE
	- LOW LEVEL WARNING LIGHT
	- INTERNAL COLLECTOR AREA IN SUMP WITH ONE WAY FLAP VALVES.
	- -6 AN FUEL OUTLET IN SUMP AREA
	- -6 AN FUEL RETURN
	- -6 AN ROLLOVER VENT CHECK VALVE ON COVER PLATE
	- ATL FLUSH FILLER CAP (TF427)
ADDL	ADDITIONAL FUEL CELLS TO ABOVE SPEC.
	FUEL CELLS ARE FOR HYDROCARBON FUELS ONLY.
	A 50% DEPOSIT (PLUS VAT) IS REQUIRED BEFORE WE COMMENCE MANUFACTURE OF ANY CUSTOM CELL. THE BALANCE IS TO BE PAID BEFORE DESPATCH OF GOODS.

PRICES EXCLUDE VAT AND FREIGHT CHARGES.
Terms: SEE ABOVE
Delivery date: 2 - 3 WEEKS FROM RECEIPT OF DEPOSIT
Courier: TBA
Quote valid: 30 DAYS

40 CLARKE ROAD, MOUNT FARM ESTATE, BLETCHLEY, MILTON KEYNES, M9
TEL: (01908) 270590 FAX: (01908) 270591 INTERNATIONAL CODE

INSPEC.

SHOP ORDER NO: 5339 1
DUE DATE: YESTERDAY

ATL
QUALITY CONTROL
INSPECTION SHOP FOLLOWER

CUSTOMER: ENTERPRISE RACING   TEMPLATE NO:
DRAWING NO: CAD FILE NAME:
MATERIAL: 694-B   FOAM: YELLOW
QUANTITY: TWO   TECHNICIAN: S.D.
INSTRUCTIONS: SEE KEVIN FOR DETAILS + USE FOAM THAT IS ALREADY CUT.

ITEM NO	INSPECTION	DATE	RESULT	TECHN.	INSP.
1	TEMPLATE DIMS	?	✓	B.	* ?
2	MATERIAL TYPE	15/12/16	694-B	✓	
3	ROLL NO.	15/12/16	4651	✓	
4	MATERIAL ORIENTATION	15/12/16	✓	✓	
5	TEMPLATE ORIENTATION	15/12/16	✓	✓	
6	NIPPLE CHECK				*
7	SEAM CHECK	16/12/16	INSIDE PET(MANUAL)	✓	G.D.
8	SEAM COAT INSIDE	17/12/16	✓	✓	*KM
9	SEALED,FINISHED OUT	19/12/96	✓	✓	
10	INTERNAL FITTINGS	19/12/96	✓	✓	G.C.
11	FOAM DIMS,RELIEVED	19/12/96	✓	✓	* KM
12	1st PRESSURE TEST	20/12/96	✓	✓	
13	CORNERS	20/12/96	✓	✓	
14	FINAL COAT	23/12/96	✓	✓	
15	STENCIL	23/12/96	✓	✓	
16	SERIAL NO.	23/12/96	829553/554	✓	
17	FINAL PRESSURE TEST	24/12/96	✓		*
18	DIMENSION/VIS.CHECK				*
19	EXTRA HARDWARE/ACC.				
20	PACKING(SHIPPING)				

DOCUMENT   COMPLETE :

*An aluminium lightweight hydraulic handbrake was fitted to Group 'A' and 'N' cars.
It was purely a handbrake as there wasn't a ratchet for parking purposes.
(Bryan Purves Collection)*

*Both of the cars were fitted with Group 'A' solid subframe mounts.
(Bryan Purves Collection)*

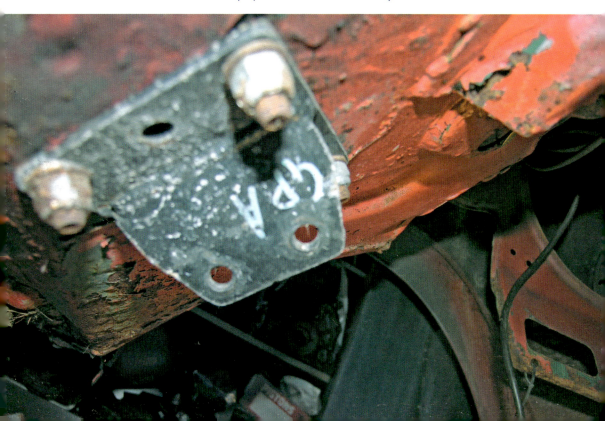

Whilst testing and setting up the cars prior to the Rallye Monte Carlo, it was found that the offset of the Rover Sport-Pack 13 inch x 6 inch wheels was incorrect for the cars, and not very beneficial to handling. In order to overcome this problem on the event the wheels on the Group 'N' car were surreptitiously replaced with Minator KN alloys after scrutineering was completed and before the start of the rally. Several sets of wheels and tyres were carried in the support vehicles and, for ease of identification, wheel sets were either in a gold or silver finish. All wheels were fitted with the appropriate tyres and then marked accordingly, identifying their axle on the car. Upon this occasion the silver wheels were fitted with snow tyres and the gold with tarmac tyres. (See Appendix 16.)

The Group 'N' Rallye Monte Carlo-prepared car. (Courtesy Les Kolczak)

All the wheels were assigned to an axle and coded accordingly, and, as many tyres are directional, this is important when fitting. All the wheels and tyres were balanced as a complete unit and also to each hub. A very simple and essential exercise, but when time is at a premium this is important in the event of a complete tyre change. As a general rule, all tyres should be inflated to 35psi, as it is easier to let the pressure out than to have to pump up the tyres, especially when running against the clock. (Courtesy Piranha Models)

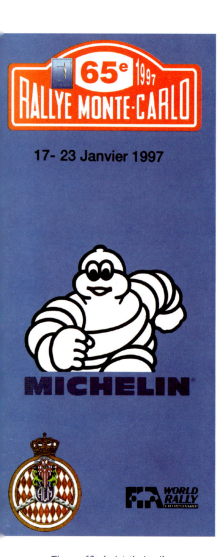

17- 23 Janvier 1997

MICHELIN

WORLD RALLY CHAMPIONSHIP

The official Michelin map
issued to all competitors
and their service crews.
(Bryan Purves Collection)

The rally plaque issued to
members of the media
covering the event.
(Bryan Purves Collection)

1997 Rallye Monte Carlo statistics

Date: 18-23rd January 1997
Distance: 1704.9 kilometres
Total SS/EC: 410.04 kilometres
Total entrants: 141 – 69 Group 'A'; 72 Group 'N'
118 cars entered the 'Challenge Prince Albert De Monaco'
Starters: 23+118

Constructors/cars:			
Peugeot	23	Rover	5
Ford	23	Lancia	4
Renault	21	Volkswagen	3
Fiat	16	Citroën	3
Mitsubishi	7	Mazda	3
Opel	7	Honda	3
Subaru	6	Skoda	2
Suzuki	6	Seat	2
Toyota	5	Proton	1
Nissan	1		

Nations/participants:			
France	67	Sweden	2
Germany	20	Austria	2
Italy	17	Poland	1
Spain	5	Holland	1
UK	4	Croatia	1
Finland	3	Luxembourg	1
Switzerland	3	Norway	1
Denmark	3	Jersey	1
Monaco	3	Greece	1
Belgium	2	Bulgaria	1
Russia	1	Japan	1

One of the oldest and most prestigious events in the rally calendar, it was in 1911 that the first Rallye Monte Carlo occurred; ever since drivers and navigators have strived to add their names to the list of winners of this world-famous rally, which is also one of the most difficult.

Winter brings to this asphalt-surfaced rally an unpredictable mix of road conditions: snow, ice, rain and dry weather can be experienced in this quickly-changing environment. Crews need to be all-round performers, with a good knowledge of the route and climatic changes but, above all, have the ability to make the best use of the available tyres to meet prevailing conditions.

As an introduction to this far-famed rally, 1997 is particularly relevant, and was also the 700th anniversary of The House of Grimaldi, as noted on the top left-hand side of the rally plate (a brief history of the family is outlined in Appendix 15). 1997 was the start of a new era in WRC rallying, with main homologated Group 'A' car differences being that a manufacturer was required to build only 20 units to the same specification, although 2500 road cars must also have been built. It was also permissible to add a turbocharger to a normally aspirated engine. Two-wheel drive systems could be replaced with four-wheel drive, and the chassis could be modified to take larger wheels, extra air intakes and better aerodynamics. The engine power of a 'VK' world rally car was no greater than that of a Group 'A' car, but with suspension and aerodynamic improvements they were expected to be a lot quicker.

A Group 'A' car specification was based on the homologated specification. For WRC cars twenty kits of parts were permitted to transform a road car into full specification, legal for the championship WRC car.

Besides specific build requirements the Rallye Monte Carlo this year had a revised

Rally enthusiasts expressed in paint on the roads their dismay about the effects of FIA rule changes for the Monte.
(Bryan Purves Collection)

65e RALLYE AUTOMOBILE MONTE-CARLO

17 AU 23 JANVIER 1997

ANNEXE VI

ITINÉRAIRES

CHALLENGE
"PRINCE ALBERT DE MONACO"

format. The rally started and finished with a new stage on the streets of the Monaco waterfront, using some of the roads that make up the Formula 1 circuit. The last time this kind of rally action was seen in Monaco was in 1964, when the event had three full days on the mountain roads in the hinterland of Southern France. Again this year the famous Monte night stages were omitted. Purists amongst us might also regret the disappearance after this year's event of the format whereby drivers would start from numerous European towns; stages in the Ardeche (Burzet, Antraigues) and Vercors (St Jean-en-Royan) were also omitted.

The World Rally Championship (WRC) round of the 65eme Rallye Automobile Monte Carlo had another event running parallel with it which enabled non-WRC contenders who were non-FIA seeded drivers to compete on the same stages as the top manufacturer teams. This special event was called 'The Challenge Prince Albert de Monaco' and classified as 'epreuve comptant pour le classement amateur' (counting toward the classification of amateur status).

The Monte Carlo Rally is the first round of the FIA World Rally Championship for both manufacturers and drivers. It will always be the 'Rally of Superlatives' and the best known in the world. Best described as an endurance event conducted at sprint speeds, it is also the most expensive event to enter due to the vast number of tyres required to cover all eventualities of terrain and climatic conditions.

This year five Minis were entered for the event, two in Group 'A' and three in Group 'N' (thirty years prior the 'works' Minis had achieved their hat trick in this, the most prestigious rally in the world). One Group 'A' was from the UK and the second from France, whilst the three Group 'N' cars were from the UK, Italy and Japan. Prior to the start of the rally all contestants had to undertake what was essentially a main road Concentration Run from a selected start venue of either Bad Hombourg in Germany, Reims in France, or Torino in Italy, terminating in Monaco from where the main event would start. The two British entrants had elected to start from Bad Hombourg with Tony Dron and Alistair Douglas driving the Group 'A' and Dave Paveley and Andy Bull the Group 'N' car. This meant that the cars had to cover 1245.1 kilometres in the 'ideal time' of 21 hours 16 minutes to the 'proper' start of the event. The rally itself then comprised nine legs with eighteen special stages covering a further 1697.41 kilometres during the five-day period.

Unfortunately, the Dron and Douglas

The rally plate carried by the teams responsible for media transmission. (Bryan Purves Collection)

Tony Dron being interviewed at the scrutineering post in Bad Hombourg prior to the start of the Concentration Run to Monte Carlo. (Courtesy Corgi Classics)

On the Concentration Run to Monte Carlo. (Courtesy Piranha Models)

The basic map that was given to all teams, denoting the Concentration Runs to Monaco from either Bad Hombourg, Reims or Torino. (Courtesy Cartographie Michelin. Cartes Nos 244 et 245. 15e edition 1/200 000)

car encountered problems on the Concentration Run to Monte Carlo, which began when they were running short of time, driving the car hard with the engine revving to around 8500rpm in sixth gear. The car developed a misfire on one cylinder. The problem seemed to be caused by the alternator adjustment bracket having worked loose, allowing the alternator belt to jump off the pulley. This then affected the ECU by not supplying adequate electrical power, and hence the ignition system would not operate to the required degree.

The service crew eventually arrived, replacing the missing bolt and investigating the engine misfire. A compression test was carried out, which revealed that the compression was down on number three cylinder; subsequent examination revealed that a valve was stuck. This was eased back and the engine restarted to the noise of what proved to be the valve head banging around in the cylinder bore, having broken off the valve stem. This was the end of the rally for car number 156 as there just wasn't enough time to make the required repairs.

The car was taken to the Rover dealership in Valence where Phillipe Chevalier, the owner, helped Nick Swift to remove the cylinder head. In the meantime, arrangements were made for a replacement cylinder head to be flown from Heathrow airport directly to Lyon. For some reason the head was not despatched on the outgoing flight which was due to arrive at 6.00am, but instead arrived on the next flight at 7.00am. Nick had waited patiently in the car park at the airport, having been up all night. Eventually, the head was fitted and the car was up and running again.

By this time essentials such as maps, ear defenders and intercom had been removed from the car. Nick

Tony Dron with 'thumbs down' prior to coming to an unforeseen halt due to engine problems. (Courtesy Piranha Models)

A rally plate pin badge issued to personnel responsible for assistance during the event. (Tim Brenchley Collection)

The Group 'A' cylinder head with damage to number three combustion chamber. (Courtesy Richard Franklin)

The service crew rally plate. (Bryan Purves Collection)

had the task of driving the car to Monte Carlo and, in order to reduce the noise, Nick had no alternative but to stuff a sock in each ear!

The other Group 'A' car of the French team, number 153, driven by Claudia Peroni and Liliana Armand, completed the Concentration Run without any problems. The three Group 'N' cars all made it to the start. Paveley and Bull talked their way through the autoroute pay booths as they had no French francs with which to pay the tolls. With just 120 kilometres to the end of the Concentration Run, the clutch master cylinder of Paveley's car began to leak, leaving him no choice but to drive without a clutch. Prior to entering Parc Ferme they replenished the reservoir and trusted to luck that they would have pedal for the start the next morning.

Unfortunately, Tony Dron and Alistair Douglas had to retire with a broken valve. Both Group 'A' and 'N' cars had identifiable bonnets as the PIAA spot lamps were pre-set to the drivers' requirements. The PA 801 lamps were on the outside of the pod with the PA803 in the centre. The Group 'A' car had white stripes with the lamp pod fitted whilst the Group 'N' was the reverse. The spare bonnets were transported in the service crew vehicles. (Courtesy Piranha Models)

Sunday morning the three Group 'N' cars were lined up, with the Rover Japan car (number 219) of Yasou Kusakabe and Osam Morikawa in front of Dave Paveley and Andy Bull (number 222) and, finally, the Rover France

Monte Carlo and the scene around the harbour, which formed part of the initial Special Stage of the 65eme Rallye Monte Carlo. (Courtesy Richard Franklin)

car (number 223) of Frederic Vie and Lionel Curat. This year the rally started with timed laps of the Monaco harbour, and then a run up to Valence ready for the special stage the following morning.

Paveley's and Bull's intention was to complete the timed laps and then change the master cylinder en route to Valence, which should take only a few minutes.

However, all their careful planning went wrong.

Special Stage 1 (SS1) road circuit around the harbour should have been completed by 15.00 hours. With this in mind, the service crew had set up ready to accept car 222 on the roadside outside Monaco. The organisers had forgotten to take into account the time allowed for each

Final connections being made after replacement of the clutch master cylinder.
(Courtesy Richard Franklin)

The navigator's map of SS1, a 2.80 kilometre circuit which was the initial Special Stage of the rally before heading out through the tunnel on a 381.45 kilometre drive towards Valence for the night halt. The 'ideal time' for the leg was 8 hours and 55 minutes. (Courtesy 65e Monte Carlo Itineraires)

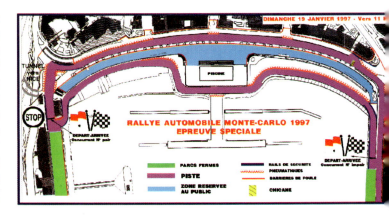

car to undertake a recce lap, however, so the start times were, in effect, non-applicable. The British Rover Cooper car did not start SS1 until 17.30 hours. By 18.00 hours Paveley and Bull were on their way to Valence, stopping only for the service crew to replace the master cylinder. Even with the delay they were the fastest car in class on SS1.

The teams woke on Monday morning ready for the Valance start to be greeted with continual rain, which resulted in slippery road surfaces for the majority of the day. Dave and Andy expressed deep concern that there was not enough clearance between the rear tyres and the wheelarches as the tyres were sometimes fouling and locking up. As the cars were getting to the point when they were going to be using snow tyres with a higher profile, the

The service crew hard at work with general servicing and replacement of rear shock absorbers, anticipating that, by achieving greater clearance of the rear tyres, this would help eliminate bodywork rubbing on hard cornering. Independent Insurance of Edenbridge, Kent, one of the major sponsors of the two cars, went into liquidation in May 2001. (Courtesy Richard Franklin)

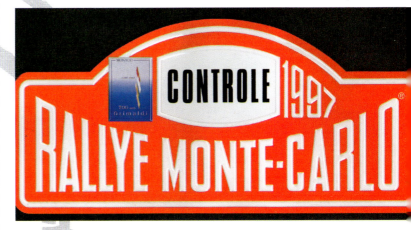

Rallye plate issued to personnel operating the en route controles. (Bryan Purves Collection)

Hard cornering meant that some serious thought had to be given to how to raise the suspension, or, alternatively, modify the rear wheelarches to help prevent the rear tyres from cutting up. When the car was being driven during daylight hours the bonnet featured white stripes with British Motor Heritage lettering. (Courtesy Richard Franklin)

pair could foresee further complications with tyre clearance. Matt Weinberg attempted to resolve the problem with a pair of tin-snips and a 3lb lump hammer, achieving 5-6mm additional clearance which, on some of the later stages, was still not enough.

Monday saw the retirement of the Italian Group 'N' car – number 153, driven by Claudia Peroni and Liliana Armand – due to gearbox failure. With the British Group 'A' car now no longer a contender, the British Motor Heritage support crew evaluated the situation that confronted it. A decision was taken to remove all Group 'A' spares from the support vehicles, put them into storage, and re-route to ensure that the Paveley/Bull car had the maximum

support throughout the remainder of the event.

With the clutch cylinder replaced on that car, a further problem arose with second gear becoming difficult to select. This had to be lived with as the time that it would take to replace a gearbox would exceed their maximum permitted lateness.

Dave had decided to run on cut slicks after hearing that SS5 was expected to be clear of snow and ice, but possibly with some surface water. This stage did not give any provision for the crews to change tyres, so the rubber selected prior to the start had to see them through to the end of this group of stages. Also, it should be remembered that any recce work is generally carried out well in advance of the rally car actually being driven along the route; conditions can change very quickly, snow may fall, and a number of cars will already have driven that road, possibly compacting snow to sheet ice. Road conditions were also made more difficult for the drivers by spectators throwing snow on otherwise clear corners.

The Japanese driver, Yasuo, offered his thoughts on how the British team should progress, given the problems it faced. Yasuo, who was due to leave the control just prior to Dave and Andy, felt that they should be running on studded 'wets' as he was. Following the Japanese car several minutes later, the Paveley/ Bull decision on which tyres to run was justified, as the first tricky corner on the stage saw the Japanese Mini parked against the far-side of a stone bridge, with the front wheel folded under the bodywork, steering damage resulting in debris and bodywork all over the entrance to the bridge. Studded tyres on damp tarmac are also a problem, it seems ...

The British crew was encountering throttle problems. With the throttle

Public support for the Paveley/Bull Mini was continuous throughout the event. (Courtesy Richard Franklin)

stuck open, and having to negotiate compacted snow driving on cut slicks, something was bound to happen – and did: the Mini hit a snow bank created by French spectators shovelling snow in the path of the rally cars. Fortunately, the cushioning effect of the snow saved the car from damage and they finished without losing too much time. Progressing along this stage they observed another unfortunate situation; the Italian car parked up with what was later discovered to be mechanical problems; retirement was the only option. The Group 'N' crew had expected SS5 to be a clear stage with possible damp tarmac in places; instead it found the last 3 kilometres were covered in snow, which continued through into SS6.

Despite all these incidents, at the end of the day there still remained two of the original Mini entries, both strong contenders. Overnight snow had fallen to the west of Valence, which later in the day turned to slush. The roads were initially wet in the valleys, turning to snow and ice higher on the sides of the mountains, and then endless rain.

Dave and Andy started with a throttle cable change at the first service halt, which resolved the sticking throttle problem. Thankfully, the change into second gear did not get any worse during the day. But on SS9, a lack of traction on one corner meant Dave and Andy found themselves straddling a snow bank. Fortunately, spectators assisted and pushed them back onto the stage, but not before the French Mini had pulled out a time difference between them. The remainder of the day continued without incident.

Wednesday saw the final push to the finish in Monte Carlo. Starting out from Gap, tyre choice was now critical, with the Minis running near to the end of the pack. The highest point en route was some 1650 metres above sea level so there was a guarantee of heavy snow. The ice note crew had driven the route several hours before the Minis were due to leave, and again 100 plus cars passed along this route in advance of the Minis.

Sliding on the snow and ice heading towards a snow bank. (Courtesy Aymani Foto Racing)

The snow retreated to the higher peaks and heavy rain began to fall, the cars having to contend with a combination of snow and slush for a distance of 4 kilometres on the Sisteron to Thoard stage, prior to the 36 kilometre test.

Dave and Andy stuck in the snow with enthusiastic French rally supporters helping to get the car back on the road – after the French Mini had passed! (Courtesy Aymani Foto Racing)

Conditions during the day improved, and for cars at the latter end of the race tyre changing was not so important. The Rover France Mini finished 52nd overall, 56 minutes 41 seconds behind the winner. The Rover Heritage Mini of Dave and Andy followed seven places behind, with just 8 minutes 32 seconds separating the two cars. A very commendable

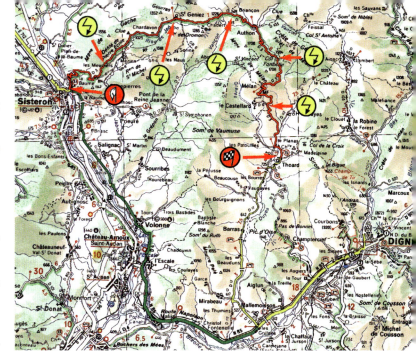

Special Stage 13, Sisteron to Thoad. Total distance 36.67 kilometres. Crews had to drive the Stage and arrive at the control in Digne Les Bains in the ideal time of 1 hour 29 minutes. (Courtesy 65e Monte Carlo Itineraires)

achievement by the UK team, finishing 59th overall, 4th in Class, and also awarded the Top Overseas Finishers in Group 'N' up to 1300cc.

Like all international rallies, besides the cars that are directly competing in the event, the back-up team and recce cars are so important. For this rally the recce car was a Rover Group company vehicle, a red and white Mini Cooper 1.3i, registration number M963 PJW, which was crewed by John Flynne and Dave Johnson.

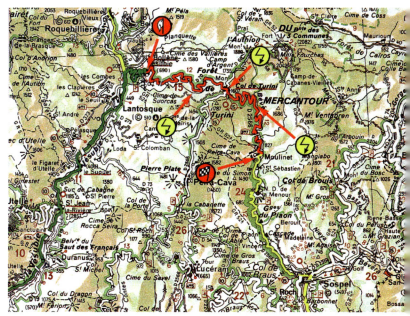

The final Special Stage and the climax of rally driving through the famous Col de Turini with the final drive down to the Monte Carlo harbourside. The staggered black arrows on yellow backing indicate a marshals' post. (Courtesy 65e Monte Carlo Itineraires)

Slowly working down to Monte Carlo, the snow turned to ice and then into slush, so the careful selection of tyres was important. (Courtesy Richard Franklin)

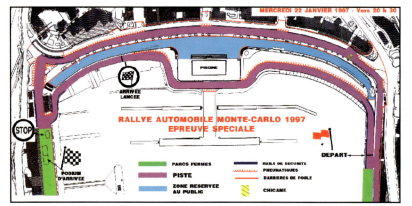

RALLYE AUTOMOBILE MONTE-CARLO 1997
EPREUVE SPECIALE

PARCS FERMES — RAILS DE SECURITE
PISTE — PNEUMATIQUES
ZONE RESERVEE AU PUBLIC — BARRIERES DE FOULE
CHICANE

The final Stage of the Rallye Monte Carlo was a timed 4.82 kilometre drive along the harbour to the finishers' podium. (Courtesy 65e Monte Carlo Itineraires)

The finishing ramp in Monte Carlo. (Courtesy Richard Franklin)

Dave Paveley and Andy Bull achieved Best Overseas Finisher in the Group 'N' 1300cc class, 4th in Class, and 59 overall. On the night sections of the rally the white striped bonnet was replaced with a fully-fitted PIAA lamp pod unit. The replacement bonnet is identifiable, as it did not have the white stripes. (Courtesy Richard Franklin)

Thanks must go to the service crews that gave full support throughout the rally.
(Courtesy Richard Franklin)

During the early part of 1996 David Paveley, along with motoring photographer, Richard Franklin, were approached by British Motor Heritage to become involved with the driving and recording of future company motoring exploits. David did the driving whilst Richard had the task of making a photographic record of everything from the building of the cars to competing in the Nürburgring 24 Hour and 6 Hour Races. He also recorded the transition of the cars from racing specification to fully prepared units competing in the 1997 Rallye Monte Carlo.

L to R: Richard Franklin, David Paveley and Andy Bull.
(Courtesy Richard Franklin)

Other 'works' contenders

The 1997 Rallye Monte Carlo had an entry of no fewer than five of the latest Mini Coopers: besides the two British cars a further three were sponsored by Rover national sales companies in Japan, Italy and France.

Tom Seal, of D R Engineering Consultants, Coventry, was given the responsibility of overseeing the construction of two cars for Rover Japan and Rover France. Quotations were sent to Roy Ford at Rover Sport, Cowley, Oxford, who sanctioned the projects, with Rover supplying direct off the Longbridge production line a new Rover Sport-Pack car, and Rover France supplying a very low mileage, French registered example of the same model. Trevor Godwin of Coventry Automotive agreed to undertake the build of the two units. Overall build cost for each of the Group 'N' Japanese and French cars amounted to £22,576.45 per car. A spares package was put together and delivered to Monte Carlo at a cost of £2402.8p.

Both cars were welded where it was considered appropriate along with additional spot welds around door apertures, and Safety Devices manufactured from 38mm diameter, CDS 2 BS980 steel tubing the bolt-in roll cages (with a wall thickness of 2.6mm) that were fitted in both.

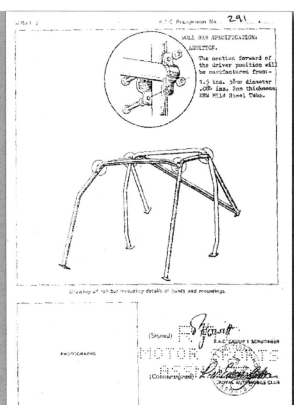

The Safety Devices amendments to the design appropriate to the two cars and homologated on 13th December 1996. (Courtesy FIA 1996 Homologation Papers)

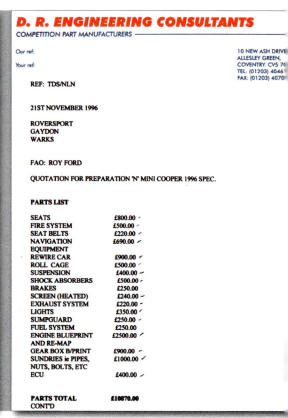

The quote sent to Ray Ford at Rover for the build of the Group 'N' Mini Cooper (Courtesy Tom Seal)

PREPARATION LIST

PAINT WORK, STICKERS ETC   £1200.00

STRIP CAR TO BARE SHELL REMOVE ALL SOUNDING DEADNING, PLUMB ALL PIPES INSIDE CAR, INSTALL ROLL CAGE, INSTALL FIRE SAFETY SYSTEMS, TRIM CAR TO GROUP 'N' SPECIFICATION, OVERHAUL FRONT AND REAR SUSPENSIONS, REBUILD, ADJUST RIDE HEIGHTS TO SUIT, MODIFY FRONT SUBFRAME TO ACCEPT SUMPGUARD AND OTHER GROUP 'N' AUTHORISED PROTECTION, MODIFY REAR SUBFRAME TO GROUP 'N' AUTHORISED PROTECTION, REMOVE WIRING HARNESS FOR REWIRE, MAKE AND FIT AUXILARY LIGHTS, REFIT ENGINE AND GEARBOX ASSY., MODIFY COOLING SYSTEM AS REQUIRED, IE; HEATER ETC. INITIAL ROAD AND ROLLING ROAD TESTS PRIOR TO DELIVERY FOR TESTING WITH DRIVERS.

 COST   £7144.00

GRAND OVERALL COST - £19,214.00

THE ABOVE QUOTE IS BASED ON A COMPLETE CAR BEING DELIVERED TO US BY 30/11/96. COMPLETE CAR AS ABOVE SPEC TO BE DELIVERED TO YOU BY 31/12/96. THE ABOVE SPECIFICATION IS INTENDED TO ACHIEVE THE LOWEST POSSIBLE TOTAL CAR WEIGHT FOR GROUP 'N'.

THIS DOES NOT INCLUDE A TYRE BUDGET OR SPARES BUDGET.

BEST REGARDS

TOM.

P.S. CAN I HAVE BOXING DAY OFF AS WELL AS CHRISTMAS DAY.

Can I have Boxing Day off as well as Christmas Day? (Courtesy Tom Seal)

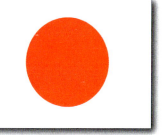

Rover Japan
Driver: Yasuo Kusakabe
Navigator: Osam Morikawa
Car number: 219
Group 'N'
Registration number: 757 BVV 95
The Group 'N' Rover car crashed out on the morning of Monday 20th January, damaging the front wing and steering, resulting in retirement.

The standard engine bay as supplied direct from Longbridge. (Courtesy Trevor Godwin)

With the engine removed there was good access to the bulkhead.
(Courtesy Trevor Godwin)

Repositioning and location of wiring and fuel lines was made easy.
(Courtesy Trevor Godwin)

The engine reinstalled with numerous minor amendments made to the body.
(Courtesy Trevor Godwin)

The interior remained basically standard with the addition of rally seats and a roll cage. Dropping the glove box lid revealed the fuse board. (Courtesy Ronnie White)

The French Group 'N' car in front of the Japanese entry, which also carried a French number plate. (Courtesy Trevor Godwin)

The Rover Japan car ran under French number plates. The official Rallye logo was affixed to the rear screen. (Courtesy Ronnie White)

The intercom control unit and additional lighting was cable-tied to the roll cage. (Courtesy Ronnie White)

Crash damage resulted in steering problems and retirement on Monday 20th January. (Courtesy Richard Franklin)

The Japanese entry as it is today. (Courtesy Ronnie White)

Rover France

Driver: Frederic Vie
Navigator: Lionel Curat
Car number: 223
Group 'N'
Registration number: 572 BTX 95

The car finished a respectable 52nd in the Challenge Prince Albert de Monaco just 56 minutes and 41 seconds behind the overall winner and in front of British car number 222.

The French entry being built in the Coventry Automotive workshop.
(Courtesy Trevor Godwin)

Built by Trevor Godwin and ready for the event.
(Courtesy Trevor Godwin)

The use of an 'R' clip and pin was an effective bonnet retainer.
(Courtesy Trevor Godwin)

Being a Group 'N' car the majority of the parts and interior had to remain as showroom supplied.
(Courtesy Philippe Gutierrez)

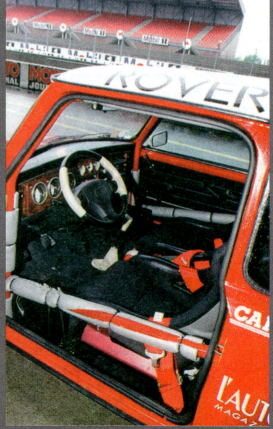

Comfortable seating is vitally important.
(Courtesy Philippe Gutierrez)

Pressing on hard during a night stage. (Courtesy Richard Franklin)

*The Rover France Group 'N' entrant being counted down at a control.
(Courtesy Enchappement)*

Very good handling in wet conditions. (Courtesy Philippe Gutiereez)

Rover Italy

Driver: Claudia Peroni
Navigator: Liliana Armand
Car number: 153
Group 'A'
Registration number: AL 555 CW

The girls started their Concentration Run from Turino, Italy, and successfully made the Monte Carlo start. Unfortunately, they had to retire from the rally with suspect gearbox problems on the first day, Monday 20th January.

The full Rover Italy support team prior to the rally. (Courtesy Rover Italy)

Claudia Peroni and Liliana Armand completely prepared for the event. (Courtesy Rover Italy)

The Italian Mini amongst the Fiat Cinquecentos waiting to check-in at a control. (Courtesy Richard Franklin)

*Full throttle and hard cornering prior to retirement due to transmission failure.
(Courtesy Rover Italy)*

Anniversary concept vehicle ACV 30

The concept car was developed by Rover and BMW to celebrate the win on the 1967 Rallye Monte Carlo. As a combined design exercise the idea was to produce a Mini super car that would be entered in current day rallies.

The car was launched at a glamorous party held in Monte Carlo directly after the end of the event, with press and dignitaries present. A selection of the 1960 'works' cars acted as a backdrop. The styling and looks of the car were greeted with enthusiasm by all present, Fred Coultas, MD of Rover Heritage, expressing good-natured doubts that the final design of the car might not actually live up to these good looks, or that the Millennium Mini may fail to live up to the looks of the prototype. It was also confirmed that the 1999 car would remain front-wheel drive with an engine developed jointly by BMW and Chrysler.

The interior was mostly aluminium, featuring a large tachometer set directly behind the steering wheel, a centre instrument pod paying tribute to that of the 1960s Minis. Bucket seats were mounted directly to an aluminium MGF floorpan. Aluminium and carbon-fibre were prolific within the interior, with a fully integrated roll cage. The door windows were fixed as the door skins were too narrow to accommodate the window regulators and channels.

An 1.8-litre overhead camshaft, 16 valve K-Series engine was fitted directly behind the front seats, giving a good balance to the feel of the car with drive going directly to the rear wheels. MGF running gear was also used.

Rover Sales and Marketing Director, Tom Purves, felt that the ACV 30: "... captures the essence of the Mini."

What was the cost of this combined

Around the Monaco harbour the ACV 30 looked and performed superbly. (Courtesy Richard Franklin)

Aluminium and carbon fibre was used extensively within the interior. (Courtesy Richard Franklin)

The car was nicely balanced with the engine in the rear and the spare wheel mounted above, possibly limiting rear view visibility. (Courtesy Mini World)

project? It was suggested that, in order to develop the concept car to this level, £500,000 would be the spend ...

Upon return to England

Upon the cars' return to England, a press day was held in February at the Curborough Sprint Circuit, where members of the press were given the opportunity to see, photograph and experience the Monte Carlo Rally cars in action around the circuit. It was also an opportunity for the team to run tests to establish tyre and suspension settings, and generally resolve any problems with the cars in the hope of participating in future events.

Journalists were able to take the navigator's seat for a ride in both Group 'A' and Group 'N' cars, with Mike Southall in the Group 'A' car and Dave Paveley behind the wheel of the Group 'N' car. In the afternoon they swapped over and with Mike in the navigator's seat of the Group 'N' car, a journalist was given the opportunity to drive the car. Having driven one lap of the circuit in reverse direction, the journalist in question became over-enthusiastic and miscalculated the corner by the finish line in relation to the speed that he was driving, rolling the car onto its roof, resulting in considerable damage. Back at the workshop the bonnet, lamp pod, lights, both front wings, nearside and offside 'A' post panels, nearside door,

The Monte Carlo Rally entrants. On the left the Group 'A' car and on the right the Group 'N' car. (Courtesy Les Kolczak)

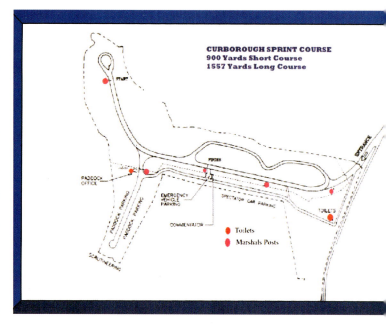

The Curborough Sprint Course. (Courtesy Shenstone and District Car Club)

Dave Paveley, on the far right, walking away from the car in which he successfully managed to complete the 1997 Monte Carlo Rally. (Courtesy Les Kolczak)

Andy Bull looks on in despair! (Courtesy Les Kolczak)

All rally cars should have duralumin windscreen clips as a matter of course, which helps prevent the windscreen from popping out! (Courtesy Les Kolczak)

front wheelarch extensions, roof panel, top section around the front windscreen, seam cover strips, door mirror and front windscreen all had to be replaced. This came at completely the wrong time as the cars were to be prepared ready for the upcoming Nürburgring 24 Hour Race.

By the time all of the work had been completed, and the damaged panels and components replaced and painted, the Nürburgring event was imminent. Only the outer body received any suggestion of top colour; the underside of the replacement wings, and 'A' post panels remained in the brown electro-phoretic primer with the Rover labels still attached.

Further exploits with P245 WFH

Given the problems that Tony Dron and Alistair Douglas experienced in the Group 'A' car on the Concentration Run to Monte Carlo, the car received the undivided attention of the service crew before being driven by Nick Swift to Monte Carlo.

From here it was taken to the Isola 2000 Ice Racing Circuit situated some 2000 metres above sea level. Author, Bryan Purves, has actually driven the circuit and proclaims it quite an experience – and somewhat scary for the first lap! The course is essentially flat with walls of snow of up to 3 metres high on each side. It was here that Tony Dron took Keith Walker, News Editor of *Car and Car Conversions* magazine, for the experience of a lifetime in a session behind the wheel of a full Group 'A' rally car, driving as fast as possible on sheet snow and ice.

What is the secret of successfully driving on this circuit? Keep the car running as

Rear undertrays provided protection for the fuel pumps. (Courtesy Piranha Models)

smoothly as possible, plan your driving line well in advance, and do not attempt to use the brakes. For the most part only the first two gears are used, dropping into third toward the end of the straight. When in trouble a little left foot braking is necessary, then quick on and off the accelerator pedal to put power to the front wheels, which will pull the car back on course.

After preparation, ready to start. (Courtesy Piranha Models)

The Group 'A' car on the Isola 2000 ice racing circuit. Studded tyres are standard equipment for ice racing. (Courtesy Car and Car Conversions)

AGBO Rally Sunday 23rd March 1997

The AGBO Rally – 'AGBO' derived from the initials of Sir Alfred George Beech Owen, founder and Chairman of the Rubery Owen Engineering Organization which was closely linked by its sponsorship to the BRM (British Racing Motors) Formula 1 team of the 1960s and '70s – was originally a *Motoring News* championship round. In 1996, it was resurrected as a one-day stage event organised by the Owen Motoring Club.

Avoiding any publicity, Dave Paveley and Andy Bull took one of the BMH cars, which carried the registration number P246 WFH, to the Weston Park Rally near Shifnal, Shropshire. The venue was a country estate with single track tarmac roadways within the grounds. The stage was quite twisty and made up of primarily 90 degree left- and right-hand bends and tight chicanes. Across the centre of the venue was a long straight incorporating a gentle kink, allowing competitors to attain a good speed. Although strategically placed cattle grids in the middle of blind bends proved unsettling to many competitors. There was an off-road surface leading to a water splash, which usually has a depth of six to eight inches of water running through it. Then into a fast corner on the far side of the estate, lined with several log piles on the outside of a fast bend, followed by an abundance of hay bales and several cattle grids.

The car that Dave and Andy took to the event was the Group 'A' car that Tony Dron and Alistair Douglas drove in the 1997 Rallye Monte Carlo. Driver and navigator names were changed, along with the number plates and day bonnet which were taken from the Group 'N' Monte car.

The car was running exceptionally well after returning from the Rallye Monte Carlo. (Courtesy Richard Franklin)

The car ran well considering that no real technical modifications had been made to its rear suspension. Good times were achieved on Stage 1, with Dave and Andy maintaining a good 11th place. On Stage 2 the clutch master cylinder developed a problem, losing pressure and causing the team to limp back to service for a replacement part to be fitted. As the event developed Dave and Andy managed to make their way up to 5th place overall, but, whilst nearing the final control, oscillation caused the car to lose traction with the result that the back of the car leapt into the air before rolling.

The weather had been somewhat inclement, making driving slippery. (Courtesy Richard Franklin)

The car was quickly removed from the venue and returned to BMH, avoiding any publicity.

The Nürburgring 24 Hour promotional poster (Bryan Purves Collection)

ADAC Jubiläumsangebot! Wochenendkarte inkl. Fahrerlager DM 68,– Karten nur im Vorverkauf!

Kinder bis 12 Jahre Eintritt frei. Jugendliche von 13 bis 17 Jahre zahlen 50% des Eintrittspreises; Behinderte ebenfalls. Keine Gruppenermäßigung.

ADAC Jugendmitglieder sowie ADAC Jugend Clubmitglieder erhalten gegen Vorlage ihrer Clubkarte am Nürburgring eine Freikarte inkl. Fahrerlager. Bei schriftlichen Bestellungen bitte Mitgliedsnummer angeben!

NÜRBURGRING
NORDSCHLEIFE

25. Internationales ADAC

24 h-RENNEN

6. bis 8. Juni 1997

Tageskasse:
Fahrerlagerkarte pro Tag, DM 20,-
Freitag Fahrerlagerkarte, DM 20,-
Samstagskarte 7. Juni '97, DM 38,-
Sonntagskarte 8. Juni '97, DM 28,-
Wochenendkarte 6. bis 8. Juni '97, DM 50,-
Telefon 02 21 / 47 27 47

ADAC 500 km Rennen für historische Fahrzeuge

VOLVO

1997 celebrated the 70th anniversary of the famous circuit (Bryan Purves Collection)

suitable for just the driver. The following additional parts were also supplemented:

Group 'A' Mini parts list (Race)	
Description	**Qty**
Alloy sump guard 3kg	1
Roof light	1
Camlock fasteners 2600 series	4
Tinted laminate rear quarter windows	2
Tinted laminate rear screen	1

The cars received new livery for the 24 Hour Race, keeping the chequered roof panel but with the addition of a centrally-mounted light above the front windscreen. (Bryan Purves Collection)

The ADAC 1997 international Nürburgring 24 Hour Race

1997 was a very significant year as it was the 70th anniversary of the first race at the Nordschleife/Nürburgring racing circuit.

Once again, British Motor Heritage cars were being prepared to race at the circuit. Having completed the 1997 Rallye Monte Carlo, the two cars were modified to 1996 race specification, the smaller fuel cells replaced by 80 litre units. Anti-roll bars were again fitted front and rear, and the navigator's seat removed, along with all additional lighting. Body logos were removed with the exception of the chequered roof. The Michelin Bibendum logos on the roofs were very carefully peeled off.

The cars were stripped of all rally equipment and fittings, making them

The Group 'N' Monte car had its engine replaced with a new full Group 'A' engine, this time built by Bill Richards Racing and running a six-speed gearbox.

The Group 'A' car retained its Swiftune engine, the fully blueprinted unit featuring a standard crankshaft that had been cross-drilled and wedged. It was fitted

The closure panel was cut out to provide easy access to the alternator. The Swiftune engine ran on single point injection. (Courtesy Ken Ayris)

with a 296F camshaft, ultra-light flywheel, Weber Alpha ignition and twin-point injection. The engine was fully balanced and achieved

The revised, fully-adjustable anti-roll bar was fitted to the Group 'A' car. The specially manufactured linkage was made by Enterprise Racing in EN19 chromilibrium steel, Rockwell hardness C. Scale 35 was used for the round link bar. (Tim Brenchley Collection)

120bhp. The engine was complemented by a Tran-X six-speed gearbox.

A third car made up the race team, and was entered by Rover Deutschland Gmbh. This was essentially a road-going vehicle with a race-prepared, blueprinted engine, and power output of 100bhp.

After the 24 Hour Race the two BMH cars were returned to British Motor Heritage, Witney, where they remained untouched until the Group 'A' car was loaned to Martin Kernahan and Simon Ayris in the spring of 1998 to compete in the WRC 34 Rallye Catalunya.

The 3 kilogram duralumin sump guard fitted to both Group 'A' race cars for the 1997 Nürburgring 24 Hour Race. (Tim Brenchley Collection)

Daylight hours in the 24 Hour Race, running without a sump guard. (Tim Brenchley Collection)

The German entry for the Nürburgring 6 Hour Race. (Bryan Purves Collection)

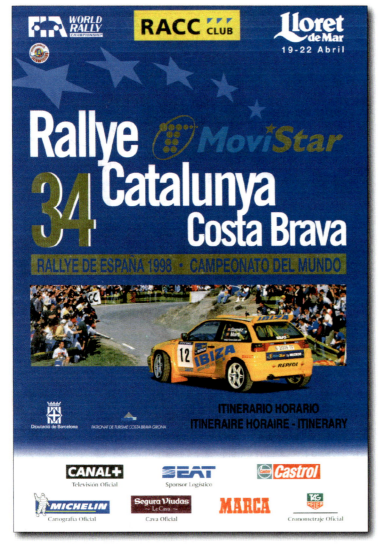

Promotional poster for the 34 Rallye Catalunya. (Tim Brenchley Collection)

Oxfordshire, and with British Motor Heritage just several minutes away, approached Brian Cameron regarding the possibility of entering one of the 'works' Group 'A' cars in Class 5 of this event.

P245 WFH was delivered to the showroom in exactly the same condition as when it took part in the 1997 Nürburgring 24 Hour Race. For several weeks it was the centre of Martin's showroom display and attracted a great amount of attention and enthusiasm from local people. Prior to the event the car was taken to the dealership workshop where the suspension was set up for rallying, as opposed to circuit racing. After much deliberation it was eventually decided that the car was in suitable condition to undertake the event, although the Swiftune engine was burning a little oil.

The car was put on display at the Witney Motor Show, and also a similar show in Oxford opened by Richard Burns, who took time to look over the car and comment.

The service crew set out with the car on a trailer drawn by a Range Rover to the start in Lloret de Mar, Spain. Scrutineering was to revolve around a local sports hall, Palau Municipal de l'Esport, where four bays were set up to individually check the 126 car entry. When the Mini (car number 74) arrived at the entrance of the hall, a wall of people pushed forward with a huge roar of enthusiasm, their noise and

World Rally Championship
34 Rallye Catalunya, Spain
Date: 19-22nd April 1998
Distance: 1471.74km
Competitive miles: 400.71km over 19 asphalt special stages
Starters: 115
Finishers: 46

Martin Kernahan and Simon Ayris thought that it would be quite a challenge to take part in the fifth round of the World Rally Championship, the Spanish 34 Rallye Catalunya at Costa Brava, which, on the WRC calender, is the first pure asphalt rally of the season.

Martin had a Rover dealership in Witney,

Spanish network provider T Movistar was one of the major rally sponsors.(Tim Brenchley Collection)

air horns drowning the commentator's microphone. The car was obviously a huge hit with the Spanish! A private entry, Rover Mini Cooper number 94, was also entered in Class 1 Group 'N' driven by Trevor Godwin and Rick Spurgeon.

All the cars had to be pushed into the scrutineering bays set up in the Palau Municipal de l'Esport. Unfortunately, the Mini was found to be underweight, as well as having bonnet pins which were not allowed on World Rally Championship events. (Courtesy Ken Ayris)

On all WRC events a Carnet de Identidad has to be permanently fixed to the inside of the rear left-hand side window. This card must contain photographs of both driver and navigator, and their licence numbers, the car rally number, Group and Class. (Courtesy Simon Ayris)

Scrutineering proved a problem with a couple of points having to be seriously addressed in order to qualify to take part in the rally: the car was underweight, and the bonnet was not allowed to be pinned; it had to be hinged. A two-hour rectification period was permitted, after which the car had to be presented for a second scrutineering session.

A quick drive down to the beach and the sills were filled with dry sand! The next problem was how to hinge the bonnet? Two of the service crew were despatched to check out a local scrapyard on the far side of Lloret. They were greeted by a hungry, very large and vocal guard dog. It was late afternoon on the Saturday and the scrapyard was closed. Moments later Martin and Simon looked at the rear lights on the Range Rover and a plan was hatched! The Range Rover rear light grille bars were quickly removed, appropriately cut and modified, and then fitted to the Mini. The 5.00pm deadline was only just met because, whilst trying to return to the scrutineering hall, the car was mobbed in the streets by members of the enthusiastic, Mini-loving Spanish public wanting to take photographs.

Clever thinking: a beach opposite the hotel meant that, by filling the sills of the car with dry sand, the required weight was achieved. (Courtesy Ken Ayris)

Simon Ayris and Martin Kernhan attach the manufactured bonnet hinges which the team fabricated from rear light grills removed from the Range Rover support vehicle. (Courtesy Ken Ayris)

The Fox FM-sponsored Group 'A' car leaving the starting ramp. Just prior to the start a young Spanish gentleman opened the door and gave the team a warm welcome, having seen the Fox FM logo on the car and recognising it as the local radio station when he was studying at Oxford University. (Courtesy Aymami Foto Racing)

Rally Catalunya-Costa Brava 1998
Leg 1 - Monday, 20 April 1998

Stage	Due Time Car 1	Name	Car XX	Location	Target Time	Road KMS	Stage KMS	Stage Miles	Road Miles	Total Miles	Ave MPH	Fuel MPG	KM	Miles	Time	MPH	Service Notes
Start	09.00 AM	Pre Start		Lloret De Mar					49	49	40						Leave Lloret By 9:00 AM
Road Section					75	79			49			4.1	78	48	120	24	
	10:15 AM	A		Manlleu	10 Mins	41	35	22	26	48		4.0	31	19	75	15	
	10:25 AM	Refuel			5 Mins												
Road Section					18	14			9		29						
SS1	10:51 AM				26	12	13	8	8		36						La Trona
SS2	11:20 AM				39	15	22	14	10		38						Alpens - Les Llosses
	11:59 AM	B		Ripoll	20 Mins	43	31	19	27	46		3.8	31	19	95	12	
	12:19 PM	Refuel			5 Mins												
Road Section					12	9			6		28						
SS3	12:39 PM				45	22	11	7	14		27						Col De Santigosa
SS4	01:27 PM				38	12	20	12	7		31						Coll De Bracons
Regroup	02:05 PM				15												
	02:20 PM	C		Manlleu	20 Mins	27	37	23	17	40		3.3	53	33	55	36	
	02:40 PM	Refuel			5 Mins												
Road Section					20	19	0	0	12		35						
SS5	03:08 PM				26	3	22	14	2		36						La Fallaca - Sant Hilari
SS6	03:37 PM				22	5	15	9	3		34						Cladells
	03:59 PM	D		Sta. Coloma De Farners	20 Mins	53	19	12	33	45		3.8	27	17	50	20	
	04:19 PM	Refuel			5 Mins												
Road Section					37	38			24		39						
SS7	05:04 PM				35	15	19	12	9		36						Sant Feliu - Tossa
	05:39 PM	E		Lloret De Mar	45 Mins	188	0	0	118	118		9.8					
	06:24 PM	Refuel			5 Mins												
Road Section					4	1			1		9						
Finish	06:33 PM																
Day 1	Totals					244	121	76	153	228							

The service schedule for Leg 1 worked out by the team prior to the event, so that everybody in the team knew exactly where they should be at specific times to service the Mini. (Courtesy Martin Kernahan)

A slight misjudgement during the early stages caused the left-hand front wing to be damaged. (Courtesy Aymami Foto Racing)

The event started badly for the Fox FM-sponsored Mini when it slid into a bank, damaging the nearside front wing. During the Leg on Stage 2 the car found itself in a ditch, this time bending the nearside rear radius arm beyond redemption. As the rally was a round of the World Rally Championship, the stages took place on 'closed roads' with police support throughout, so extricating the car was impossible until the stage had been re-opened to normal traffic. This meant that Simon and Martin had to remain with the car until the event had finished. No problem; with a local taverna to hand they enjoyed a constant flow of free sangria from rally spectators until the car could be collected.

The Godwin/Spurgeon car also had engine problems on this stage and had to withdraw from the rally.

When the car returned to the UK it remained with British Motor Heritage, Witney, until both 'works' cars were sold to Wayne Butterworth of West Pennine Motorsport in January 1999. Included in the purchase was a cache of spares for both cars, including many of the parts that had been fitted on the Mull Rally car and were removed prior to the Rallye Monte Carlo. Wayne proceeded to rebuild the now totally worn out Group 'A' engine and prepare one car for 'hire and drive' rallying. The Monte Carlo Group 'N' car parts were set aside, in the event of parts being required for P245 WFH, when the car was rallied in future.

(Opposite) L to R: Bill Hitchcock (chase car), Gary Pickard (service), Robert Hall (service), Simon Ayris (navigator), Alistair Barnes (Team Manager and chase car), Gavin Hall (chase car) and Martin Kernahan (driver). (Courtesy Ken Ayris)

The Mini was always a favourite with enthusiastic rally supporters. (Courtesy Aymami Foto Racing)

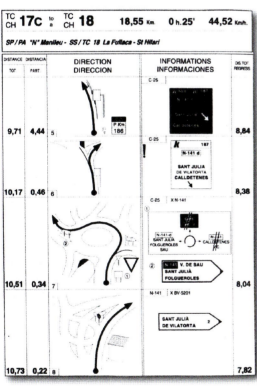

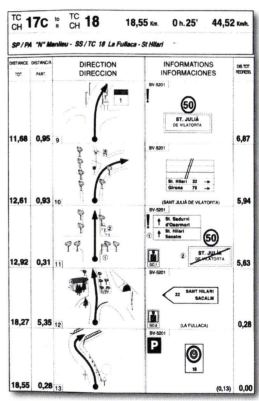

Typical pages taken from the Route Book illustrate the detail that is given to the crews prior to the event. The directions are very clearly indicated with appropriate signage and distance information. (Courtesy Martin Kernahan, car number 74)

The entire event is set out in the Route Book using 'tulips.' Note the detail that is included when competing in a WRC event: trees, buildings, junctions, road signs, and cuttings. (Courtesy Martin Kernahan, car number 74)

SEAT was the main sponsor of the rally and featured on the front cover of the souvenir programme. (Tim Brenchley Collection)

SEAT

RALLYING

World Cup Winner
FIA 2-litre World Rally
for Manufacturer
1996 1997 199

THE OFFICIAL SOUVENIR MAGAZINE OF THE SEAT JIM CLARK MEMORIAL RALLY 1999

MEET THE SEAT TEAM • THE TRUTH ABOUT RALLYING • WHERE TO CATCH THE ACTION

Mobil 1 British Rally Championship
The SEAT Jim Clark Memorial Rally
Date: 2-4th July 1999
Distance: 168 competitive miles with
27 stages
Surface: asphalt and gravel
Starters: 219

The Jim Clark Memorial Rally has been run since 1970, and in 1997 it was to become the first Special Stage rally on mainland Britain to be run on public roads, with special permission granted under an act of parliament.

The Group 'A' Rover Mini, number 76, Class A5, was entered in the Mobil 1 British Rally Championship, the SEAT Jim Clarke Memorial Rally, hired from West Pennine Motorsport and driven by Grace Owen with Ali Bohm on the maps. This was the girls' first outing in the ex-'works' Group 'A' car although, prior to this event, the pair had acquired a wealth of rally experience in a Group 'N' car, and had won a *MiniWorld* competition, which provided an experience of competing in top class rallies with a Mini. As a driving aid Grace found it beneficial to have 'left' and 'right' marked on the back of her gloves, and also on the dashboard.

1999 was the first year that this rally – Round 4 and the start of the tarmac events – featured in the Mobil 1 British Rally Championship. The opening Leg kicked off on the Friday night, followed by a longer second Leg on Saturday night through into Sunday. On the Friday the international competitors, including the Mini, were joined by the Historic and

Grace and Ali making good progress early on in the rally. (Courtesy Speedsport)

Formula 1400 event, and by competitors in the Scottish National Championships the next day.

There was a total of 76 entrants in the International class, 102 in the National entry list, and 41 in the Historic, 1400 and Land Rover classes. The international category covered a total of 168 competitive miles which included 27 Special Stages.

The car was a totally new animal with a dashboard full of fuses and instrumentation, and a completely different driving experience compared to the previous car that the girls had driven. Wayne Butterworth, proprietor of West Pennine Motorsport, spent

Always smiling … Grace Owen and Ali Bohm. Their young, smiling faces were assets when exceeding speed limits whilst recceing the event. (Peter J Fox)

Crossing a ford; always a spectacular sight. (Courtesy Speedsport)

The basic route map as supplied in the Spectators' Guide. This guide is much appreciated by the general public which supports the events. (Tim Brenchley Collection)

several weeks preparing and rebuilding the car after it was purchased from British Motor Heritage. It was hoped that the car would finish this event as, in all its previous rally outings, it had never actually finished in Group 'A' specification.

The recce was undertaken in Ali Bohm's everyday Mini Cooper. The Stages appeared to have no deceptive corners and no excessive amounts of loose surface gravel. A speed restriction of 40mph was imposed for the recce, which made it difficult to gauge how some of the jumps and crests could be driven. On one occasion the girls were cautioned by a marshal for driving at a speed of 49mph on a long, undulating straight.

Owing to the number of long straight sections, open corners – and a six-speed gearbox – it was decided to use a final drive with a ratio that would give the benefit of a top speed of around 100mph, at a sacrifice of some acceleration.

The Langton first Special Stage of the rally was, unfortunately, cancelled as a Skoda driving on a slippery road had slid off a bridge and then proceeded to go through a wall. On the second Stage the girls started with care due to the condition of the road surface, and because they

SPECTATOR INFORMATION

RALLY SCHEDULE

LEG 1 FRIDAY 2nd July

Location	Ordnance Survey Ref	First International	First National
SS1 LANGTON	778526	17:22	19:01
SS2 LANGTON	778526	17:34	19:13
SS3 BOTHWELL	680628	18:09	19:48
SS4 DUNGLASS COM.	753695	19:20	20:59
SS5 WHITSOME	856503	21:07	22:46
SS6 EDROM	787570	21:49	23:28
SS7 LANGTON	778526	23:18	0:57
SS8 LANGTON	778526	23:30	1:09
SS9 WHITEADDER DAM	664633	0:15	1:54

LEG 2 A SATURDAY 3rd July

Location	Ordnance Survey Ref	First International	First National
SS10 NISBET RHODES	787518	16:44	18:38
SS11 NISBET RHODES	787518	16:56	18:50
SS12 FOGO	789502	17:09	19:03
SS13 ECCLES	733449	17:38	19:32
SS14 BIRGHAM	798397	18:10	20:04
SS15 SWINTON	779447	18:33	20:27
SS16 LONGFORMACUS	700572	20:11	22:05
SS17 EYEMOUTH	919624	21:15	23:09
SS18 AYTON	919607	21:38	23:32

LEG 2 B SUNDAY 4th July

Location	Map Ref	First International	First National
SS19 NISBET RHODES	717518	2:23	0:48
SS20 NISBET RHODES	717518	2:35	1:00
SS21 FOGO	789502	2:48	1:13
SS22 ECCLES	733449	3:17	1:42
SS23 BIRGHAM	798397	3:49	2:14
SS24 SWINTON	779447	4:12	2:37
SS25 LONGFORMACUS	700572	5:50	4:15
SS26 EYEMOUTH	919624	6:54	5:19
SS27 AYTON	919607	7:17	5:42

SHOWGROUND

Saturday

12pm	Smiley Miley opens SEAT show
12pm	Fairground free for Happy Hour
1.30pm	Pipe band performance
1.50pm	Open the Box competition
2.00pm	Wheel changing competition
2.30pm	Aerobatic display
2.45pm	Kite display to music
3.05pm	Falconry display
3.20pm	Vintage tractors
3.35pm	Wheel changing competition
3.55pm	Karaoke competition
4.00pm	Rally restarts
4.50pm	Kite displays
5.00pm	Yes/No competition
5.15pm	Open the Box
5.30pm	Pub Quiz
5.50pm	Karaoke competition
6.00pm	Rally report
6.10pm	Yes/No competition
6.20pm	Karaoke competition
6.30pm	Pub Quiz
6.50pm	Precision driving display
7.00pm	Live rally report
7.10pm	Karaoke competition
7.20pm	Pub Quiz
7.40pm	Rally report
7.50pm	Ceilidh band first set
8.20pm	Karaoke winners showcase
8.40pm	Open the Box
8.50pm	Live rally report
9.00pm	QFX first set
9.40pm	Rally report
9.50pm	Rue and Rockets first set
10.30pm	Driver interviews
10.40pm	Ceilidh band second set
11.00pm	Rally update
11.10pm	QFX second set
11.20pm	Open the Box
11.40pm	Rue and Rockets second set
12.00pm	Fireworks

Sunday

6.00am	Hot air balloons take off
10.00am	Happy Hour in showground
10.50am	Rally report
11.00am	Kirkin Ceremony, Town Square
12.30pm	Red Devils parachute in
12.40pm	Winner announced of 'Win a SEAT Ibiza'
1.00pm	Rally Prize Giving

Please note all timing are subject to change with or without notice

Car number 76 was the only Mini in the rally! (Courtesy Speedsport)

had not really had much time to test and get the feel of the car. It was felt that ride heights and camber angles were not correct for this event.

On the Dunglass Common Special Stage 4 the girls started off at a very competitive pace, with Grace able to drive the car hard through the lanes. But on a newly asphalted section of road, whilst travelling at approximately 70mph, the car bounced very hard on a cattle grid and was thrown across the lane three times with the front wheels spinning in the air and at maximum revs in third gear. There appeared to be no obvious damage and the car was fortunately

The internals of the Tran-X six-speed gearbox. Note the stripped teeth on third gear caused by the transmitted torque that was imposed on the gear when yumping! The unit was also fitted with a limited slip differential. (Courtesy Wayne Butterworth)

still facing the direction of travel. At the service halt the Spax shock absorber settings were adjusted to help provide a smoother landing in the event of more jumps!

By the Edrom Special Stage 6 Grace was finding it difficult to get the car into gear; that and the numerous noises emanating from the car persuaded them

to pull over and watch their rivals go by. There was most definitely a mechanical problem and Wayne, at the Craigwalls Service Area, had a serious look at the transmission, discovering a twisted driveshaft. This probably happened on Stage 4 where the car must have landed on full power which twisted the driveshaft and stripped third gear of its teeth.

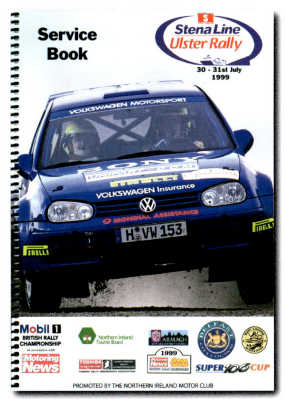

Service Book

Stena Line Ulster Rally

30 - 31st July 1999

VOLKSWAGEN MOTORSPORT

VOLKSWAGEN Insurance

H·VW 153

Mobil 1 BRITISH RALLY CHAMPIONSHIP in association with Motoring News

Northern Ireland Tourist Board

ARMAGH

BELFAST CITY COUNCIL

1999

SUPER 106 CUP

PROMOTED BY THE NORTHERN IRELAND MOTOR CLUB

The service book that was issued to all the teams, detailing service points throughout the event. (Tim Brenchley Collection)

Mobil 1 British Rally Championship
Ulster Rally, Ireland
Date: 30th and 31st July 1999
Distance: 173 competitive miles
Surface: tarmac

Grace and Ali decided once again to undertake the recce of the rally in the Mini Cooper that Ali drove as everyday transport. As purported by competitors that had previously taken part in this rally, they described it as being a lot tougher than the Jim Clarke event.

Each stage consisted of everything that could be thrown at a rally at this time of year: fast, wide sections, twisty lanes, rough terrain, gravel, and numerous bumps. There was a spectator stage consisting of every driving road condition imaginable – including a water splash – and all within a half-mile drive.

The event itself and Leg 1 started with the Mini just four seconds off the class lead, at the same time beating all of the Skoda team cars. This event, with a prize fund of £10,000 put up by Skoda, had attracted some very quick and experienced crews.

Accurate recce notes proved invaluable, moving the girls 30 places up the leader board, fighting for the lead on all seven tarmac stages of the Leg. On the next stage, unfortunately, there was a car on its roof, totally blocking the lane, holding up several of the cars. This proved unfortunate for the Rover Mini Cooper, which overheated, but the service point was within reach where the radiator received some much-needed water. This setback caused some delay, of course, which was unfortunate as the girls had made exceptional progress on the spectator Stages, beating all of the Class A5 entrants, and with a time differential of just 12 seconds behind the leader.

Seeded 94th at the start of the rally, for Grace and Ali Leg 2 started at 4am (giving just three hours' sleep) with the car now re-seeded at 48th. Within one mile of Stage 13 – a ten-mile stage – they skidded on a patch of gravel and embedded the car in a wall. With the help of the landowner, who was watching the event from behind the wall, they managed to push the car back to a safe position to inspect the damage and effect repair. The incident bent the front tie bar which Grace managed to force back into place using the jack as a hammer. Time was not on their side as it took nearly half an hour to resolve the problems caused and they had now used up their allotted lateness time of 15 minutes. Fortunately, this particular Stage did not have a maximum time limit.

The girls continued cautiously to complete the next Stage with the tie bar held precariously in place. On reaching the next service halt the West Pennine Motorsport Service Crew replaced the tie rod and sent the pair on their way.

The car did not handle at all well over the following two Stages, and it became

With Grace Owen driving and Ali Bohm expertly navigating, the ladies were doing well in the early stages of the event. (Courtesy Speedsport)

At the next service halt immediate attention was given to repair of the damaged part; here the rose jointed tie rod is adjusted. (Courtesy Mike Hally)

The information that the service crews have to adhere to at all times as published in the Service Crews' Handbook. (Tim Brenchley Collection)

A typical page taken from the Ulster Rally service crew handbook. (Tim Brenchley Collection)

SERVICE SCHEDULE AND INDEX

MAP REFERENCE / LOCATION		After Special Stage	FIRST CAR DUE TIME	SERVICE TIME (mins)	RALLY CAR MILES TO NEXT SERVICE Total/Stage	SERVICE CAR MILES TO NEXT SERVICE	PAGE
15/348 738	Alexander Hall, RUAS, Belfast	Scrutiny/ Documentation	Thur 09:00	-	25.90/ -	24.90	4/5
20/128½ 453	Banbridge,	B/F 1	Fri 14:12	10	24.69 / 17.34	12.75	7/10
29/074 295	Carnbane	2	15:27	20	39.98 / 27.87	18.40	11/13
19/877 455	Armagh	5	17:25	20	50.46 / 17.23	32.35	14/17
20/271 632	Altona, Lisburn	7	19:16	20	10.16 /1.1	8.0	18/21
15/319 725	Apollo Road, Belfast	9	20:40	30	42.69 / -	41.17	22/24
19/810 603½	Moygashel	B/F 10	Sat 05:23	10	28.45 / 21.69	4.65	27/29
19/774 606	Granville,Dungannon	11	06:53	20	41.29 / 30.58	10.05	30/32
19/664 524	Aughnacloy	14	08:48	20	36.88 / 23.44	24.21	33/35
18/445 610	Fintona	16	10:30	20	51.70 / 17.66	43.80	36/38
13/782 946	Draperstown	18	12:45	20	33.19 / 8.60	17.20	39/41
14/963½ 905½	Toome	19	13:57	10	40.13 / 8.80	41.4	32/36
15/346 772	Dargan Road, Duncrue, Belfast	20	15:13	15	4.61 / -	4.0	37/40

Unfortunately, on Special Stage 13, the car was ditched, damaging the front tie rod and track rod end.
(Courtesy Speedsport)

evident that more damage had been sustained than at first thought. Grace drove the car steadily to reach the next service halt where the West Pennine Motorsport team made a thorough inspection of the car to assess what other damage had been caused. It was bad news: a bent front sub-frame and steering rack, plus damage to all of the rose jointed arms due to the excess strain placed upon them. The front wheels were pointing in completely different directions. A decision had to be made. With just 20 minutes allowed for service it was impossible to safely repair the car to the extent that Ali and Grace could continue. There was no option but to retire after completing 16 of the 20 Stages.

Stage 16 of the Stena Line Ulster Rally, a round of the Mobil 1 British Rally Championship. Just prior to retirement with the front wheels pointing in different directions, bent sub-frame and damaged steering.
(Courtesy Speedsport)

Coasting home with damaged steering. (Courtesy Mike Hally)

Sony was the major sponsor of the Mobil 1 British Rally Championship Round 1.
(Courtesty Tim Brenchley)

Mobil 1 British Rally Championship Round 6
Manx International Rally, Isle of Man
Date: 9th-12th September 1999
Distance: Stages – 27
Starters: 71
Finishers: 34
Surface: tarmac and gravel

The Isle of Man is a small island just 30 miles long from Point of Ayr in the north to Spanish Head in the south, and can claim to have held the first motor race in Britain – the Gordon Bennett Trial – which took place in 1904.

The Manx Rally is a very prestigious event, classified as one of the top rallies in the world. The original idea began in 1962 when John Hopwood was partaking in a Veteran Car Club rally on the island. He got in touch with Leonard Bond, Tourist Board chief, about his idea, and soon found himself volunteering to organise the first event. John gathered several friends from his club, the 'Ecurie Cod Fillet', and began planning the rally. The June Effort Committee covered the ferry costs and the *Daily Mail* the printing costs.

1963 saw the debut of the 'Manx Trophy Rally', with 75 cars driven along winding island roads closed to the public. The starters included 25 local entries along with many well-known entrants from the rally scene.

The Manx Trophy Rally has now grown to become an event that encapsulates the 'Conister Trust Historical Rally', which now forms the Manx International Rally and makes up part of the British Rally Championship. The event comprises a high speed race around the towns, countryside and mountains of the Isle of Man, its miles of tarmac and dirt roads closed especially for the event.

With the support of West Pennine Motorsport, Grace Owen and Ali Bohm were in the Group 'A' Rover Cooper, entered in Class A5 though, unfortunately, the girls had to withdraw on SS5, Tynwald Mills, due to offside driveshaft becoming twisted, caused by the torque generated from the engine. This rally was the last event that P245 WPH ever entered: sadly, she never did complete an event.

The car was returned to West Pennine Motorsport in Rochdale, rebuilt to Group 'A' specification, dry stored and not used again.

Grace Owen at the wheel and Ali Bohm in command of the maps.
(Courtesy Speedsport)

The Isle of Man was very supportive
of all motorsport activity, to the
extent that a special coin was
minted. This is a 20 pence coin
illustrating two rally cars on its reverse.
(Bryan Purves Collection)

Motorsport has become
synonymous with the
Isle of Man, with all
events attracting a huge
amount of public support.
(Courtesy Speedsport)

FURTHER ACTIVITIES WITH D555 GRX

The day D555GRX was collected from British Motor Heritage in 1997.
(Donald Farr Collection)

Donald Farr and Dave Tippett were fortunate to have the opportunity to purchase D555 GRX: a chance not to be missed!

On Wednesday 6th August 1997, the pair met with John Brigden at British Motor Heritage, Witney, to collect the car, complete and as returned from the 1996 Rallye Monte Carlo.

The following weekend the car was

exhibited at Yeovil Festival of Transport, followed by a *Mini Magazine*-sponsored event, 'Mini in the Park', at Cornbury Park. Two weeks later the car was displayed at the Classic Rallycross Association Classic Car Display at Lydden Hill racing circuit in Kent. Don and his son, Matt, then took part in the Haynes Falling Leaves Classic on 21st September 1997. Within weeks of this event the car was returned to Barrett's showroom in Canterbury to be displayed during Rover's Mini Experience, a touring UK road show publicising the Mini.

Donald and Dave then took D555 GRX to the 38th birthday celebrations of the Mini at Gaydon, Warwickshire, where the car was reunited with its 1996 Monte co-driver, Alistair Douglas. On the return journey the car refused to tickover, with one cylinder down. As Bill Richards had built the original engine there was only one place to take it. The prognosis was not good, however, as a valve insert had come adrift, damaging the head and a piston. The cylinder head was replaced with a full race head which, although not allowed under Group 'A' regulations, offered more power, and also enabled the compression ratio to be lowered. A single replacement piston was also fitted.

L to R: Matt Farr, Dave Tippett and John Brigden.
(Donald Farr Collection)

The start of the Goodwood hill.
(Donald Farr Collection)

Coming around the first corner of the hill climb.
(Donald Farr Collection)

Donald and Matt Farr on Goodwood hill, rally number 159. (Donald Farr Collection)

Bill Richards analysing the problem. (Donald Farr Collection)

Dave Tippett on the Castle Combe circuit. (Donald Farr Collection)

Whilst the engine was out of the car, the Jack Knight four-speed, straight cut dog box, incorporating a Quaife limited slip differential, was replaced with a four-speed, straight cut synchromesh kit and conventional differential. The final drive ratio was changed from a 4.6:1 to 3.9:1, which gave the benefit of comfortable motorway cruising.

Following the rebuild by Bill Richards the car was displayed in the foyer of the Hinton Firs Hotel during the 1998 Mini Cooper Register Bournemouth weekend. On 29th March 1998 Don and Dave took part in the Haynes Spring Classic event.

The car was then taken to the Castle Combe Circuit where, upon exiting Quarry, the engine lost power. The car was duly recovered to Bill Richards who diagnosed a broken lead to the flywheel sensor.

Other events in 1998 in which the Mini

Donald Farr at Castle Combe.
(Donald Farr Collection)

participated included Bromley Pageant and the Footman James Retro Run to Silverstone; finally, it was displayed at the Southern Mini Day at Paddock Wood, Kent.

Silverstone 1998. (Donald Farr Collection)

In 2001 participation in the Lord Mayor's Show was arranged by Basil Wales and financed by BMW. The car has also taken part on two occasions in the 'Ideal for Mini' roads of County Cork event, following Circuit of Ireland Stages. D555 GRX's next serious appearance was as Course Opening Car for Minis to Monte 2004.

Minis to Monte 2004
Date: 26-30th September 2004
Distance: 1118.6 miles

What better way to celebrate Paddy Hopkirk's and Henry Liddon's momentous win in the 1964 Monte Carlo Rally than by running a 40th Anniversary Commemorative Rally with 60 Minis following a similar route to that used in 1964?

Robert Clayson, Vice Chairman of the Mini Cooper Register, together with John Wilkins and his team of enthusiastic helpers, organised this event with

Le circuit de Reims, temple de la vitesse !

Le Circuit de Reims. The stand opposite the pits could accommodate up to 4500 spectators. (Courtesy Robert Clayson)

The press box which is currently being restored to its former glory by motor racing enthusiasts. (Courtesy Robert Clayson)

The original mosaic BP Petroleum sign found inside the BP press room.
(Courtesy Neil Burgess)

the aim of driving the same route as that used in the 1964 event, and many other Monte Carlo Rallies. The event was not run in the depth of winter, when the alpine roads would have been covered in snow and ice, and neither was there freezing fog and ice forming on the inside of the windscreen, or any night driving.

The role of D555 GRX on this event was to be Course Opening Car, driven by Donald Farr, one of its two current owners (Dave Tippett being the other), with John Wilkins alongside. John was the person responsible for transferring all of the original recce information into tulips (a method of

The main straight at the now disused Reims Grand Prix Circuit, with many of the entrants lined up in front of the pits. (Courtesy Robert Clayson)

Minis parked by the lakeside at Aix les Bains, five of the ex 'works' cars in the centre of the picture. (Courtesy Robert Clayson)

rally navigation introduced by the Dutch), and finally printing the route book.

The route started from Dover, with cars headed for the first halt at the historic Reims Gueux Circuit, last used in 1969 for car racing, with motorcycle racing continuing until 1972. The lap record stood at 142.33mph when the circuit was deemed unsafe for racing due to the speeds that were being achieved.

The drive on day two was from Reims to Mulhouse, with day three making progress through to Aix les Bains. Just before reaching Aix les Baines, Donald Farr hit a pothole rather hard, shearing the offside front tie rod.

Day four saw the route heading south with a steady climb out of Aix les Baines

Chris Tennant standing, with Donald Farr assessing the damage to the off-side of the car (Courtesy Robert Clayson) Inset: Bag jacks are 'worth their weight in gold', and so quick. (Courtesy Robert Clayson)

The clouds hanging in the valley after the steep climb out of Aix les Bains. (Courtesy Elizabeth Purves)

Unfortunately, Basil Wales misjudged a corner, putting his car in a ditch. Valerie and Basil had to climb out of the passenger door window. (Courtesy Dave Richards)

toward the Cols, passing through the Parc Naturel Regionnaire, the Col de Barrioz at 1083 metres, and Col des Ayes at 944 metres. The end of the day saw the event arriving at Gap.

Day five was the final Leg from Gap to Monte Carlo following the 1964 seventh Stage from Gap to Seynes les Alpes, where the ideal time was 1 hour 21 minutes for the 80km distance, which included a Competitive Section of 17.5km between Chorges and the end of the bridge at

No.	Km.	Inter.	Miles	Inter.	Tulip Direction	Signpost / Information
73			156.61	0.55		Turn right at X roads S/P D537 - Superdevoluy
74			160.94	4.33		Follow D537 Superdevoluy
75			160.97	0.03		**Route Check 2** What is the name of the river?
76			161.20	0.23		Road number changes from D537 to D937 at department boundary
77			162.63	1.43		Straight on S/P - D937 Agniers 6
78			164.15	1.52		Follow D937 S/P - Agniers-en-Devolly & Veynes
79			165.94	1.81		S/P - Veynes & Gap
80			167.36	1.42		Follow D937 S/P Veynes & Gap
81			173.09	5.73		Tunnel - lights on
82			175.58	2.49		Fork left S/P - D937a Montmaur
83			177.73	2.15		Turn right at T junction S/P - D994 Veynes
84			179.77	2.04		Turn left over railway - **CARE** S/P - D320 Furmeyer

Page 7

Page 7 of the route book. Number 77 was the start of the first timed section in the 1994 Rallye Monte Carlo, 28km to Montmaur. The handwritten notes are the navigator's calculations, done when the Halda decided not to work.
(Courtesy Elizabeth Purves, car number 9)

Basil Wales relating his experiences at the final dinner in Monte Carlo.
(Courtesy Robert Clayson)

Two of the 1960s 'works' cars parked at the top of the Col de Turini. (Courtesy Robert Clayson) Inset: The Hotel des Trois Vallees at the top of the Col.
(Courtesy Elizabeth Purves)

Savines. This was followed by the next Stage from Seyne to Arnot, the ideal time being 2 hours 21 minutes for the 139km. The final stage was into Monte Carlo and also the start of Competitive Section 5 over the Col de Turini to Moulinet.

Lord Mayor's Show 2004
Date: 13th November 2004
Venue: London, England

Participation in the 2004 Lord Mayor's Show was down to the organization of Donald Farr, who was asked by the Mini Cooper Register if he would be prepared to organise 45 different Mini derivates to participate in this event to celebrate the 45th Anniversary of the start of Mini production.

Given the many problems that Donald encountered, with several entries unavailable due to last minute changes in circumstance, he was constantly calling upon his reserve list, and as a result, only 44 cars actually took part.

Sponsorship amounted to £3000 from Deutsche Borse, arranged through Hartmut Klein. BBC Television – which covered the event – was supplied with the running order of the cars, plus a brief description of each, with attention being drawn to noteworthy examples – generally of rally fame – including Donald in D555 GRX as the lead car, still bearing the Monte Carlo livery from 1996 and the Minis to Monte rally plate.

Lombard Revival Rally 2005
Date: 24-27th November 2005
Distance: 1200 miles with 52 'Selectives'
Entrants: 129
Finishers: 94

In 2004 Philip Young came up with the idea of a new event following the format of the former Lombard RAC Rally, which he was to call Endurance Rallying, and founded The Endurance Rally Association.

The idea was to use small, cheap cars with a maximum capacity of 1400cc

The Mini procession is always a favourite with the crowd. (Courtesy Robert Young Photography)

normally aspirated, or 1700cc diesel engines. Firm guidelines outlined what modifications were allowed, and there were mandatory safety requirements relating to fire extinguisher, seat belts, laminated front windscreen, mud flaps on all four wheels, and rollover protection. All cars had to be fitted with one make of tyre which was specified as the Colway remould Road Plus. A maximum average speed of 40mph was prescribed, whether on or off the public highway. The intention was to offer a challenging and inexpensive form of motorsport with the amateur in mind, and the RAC Rally's original sponsor, Lombard, agreed to sponsor the event, together with CSMA, Colway and *Motorsport News*.

Only two Minis took part in the event in 2005, whereas in 2004 there had been five Minis. As participants, Tim and I found

Multiple spot lights featured on Minis in the 1960s. Current regulations now permit only two spots. (Courtesy Gerard Brown)

An external fuel filler fed the ATL fuel cell in the boot. (Bryan Purves Collection)

D555 GRX being prepared for the rally at Southams Mini and Metro Centre. (Courtesy Peter Barker)

A fully loaded boot. (Courtesy Peter Barker)

On the right-hand rear a large Mini Cooper Register logo featured. (Bryan Purves Collection)

it a little hard on the cars, especially as we were running on 10 inch wheels. Stalwarts Peter Barker and Willy Cave were competing in Peter's recent aquisition, D555 GRX (number 40), and James Tyson and Neil Harrison in their 1970 Cooper 'S' (number 63).

D555 GRX, the car driven by Tony Dron in the 1996 Monte Carlo Rally, was originally built to Group 'A' specification with a Bill Richards engine which, unfortunately, did not conform to Technical Regulations Appendix A for this rally. Southams Mini

to be the third weekend in November, the traditional slot for the original RAC Lombard Rally – the teams departed at 7.10pm from the Kassam Stadium, Oxford, with D555 GRX and start number 40. By the time of the night halt the front number plate was already hanging off, and volumes of mud were baked onto the exhaust.

Day two saw the team starting in 45th place en route to the Silverstone Rally School where the crews encountered muddy gravel and icy puddles on a testing and demanding circuit. The teams then headed toward Bruntingthorpe and Fermyn Woods near Corby. By now it was becoming obvious that the timing for the event was too adventurous and cars were beginning to run behind schedule. The Clerk of the Course was, in many

and Metro Centre was contracted to strip out the engine and rebuild the unit to conform with the regulations, which meant that the pistons and cylinder head had to be replaced with standard parts. This, in turn, meant that the Weber Alpha engine management computer had to be re-mapped to what amounted to an 83bhp engine. Some of the original graphics on the bodywork had to be removed, as well as the PIAA four-lamp pod which was replaced by a pair of Cibie Tango fog lamps.

On 24th November – which happened

Weston Park with a loose-fitting fuel filler cap! (Courtesy Monty Watkins)

Slip-sliding away was the order of the day. (Peter Barker Collection)

headed up to the Peak District leading on to night stages at the Prestbury Sewage Treatment Works, Arley Hall and Knowsley Hall, and to the final control at Chester, the Barker/Cave Mini making the control with just seconds to spare though, unbeknown to them and many of the other crews, the road section penalties had been scrubbed.

cases, forced to give a time allowance to several crews who were finding the going difficult.

Next came Woolaton Park, a Stage that all crews enjoy, and then the rally

The Barker/Cave team had a 8.10am start on the Saturday morning from Parc Ferme heading into the first Selective in the somewhat slippery Llandegla Forest, with many cars going off the track. A

Willy Cave ensuring that Peter Barker is heading in the right direction. (Peter Barker Collection)

further Stage at Combermere Abbey was cancelled due to game shooting. The event then went on to Twemlows Hall airfield which encompassed circuits of the rally training stages. Weston Park, near Telford, now saw the car losing petrol on every corner due to a loose filler cap.

Heading into the afternoon, snow began to fall and both Ceri Forest and Radnor Forest proved difficult for the Mini which, by now, was sliding about on its sump guard with the wheels constantly spinning. Being a showroom car category rally, fitting a limited slip differential or snow tyres was totally prohibited, and, in any case, all cars had to be fitted with Colway remould tyres taken from its 'Road Plus' range. (Peter Barker commented that his 12 inch Colway tyres did not have the same pattern as those of the other cars; we also noted this fact whilst on the 2004 Revival Rally.)

Further into the night the Selectives at The Vallets, Athelstans Wood, Trellech and Chepstow Park were a combination of snow, gravel and mud, with many cars leaving the road. The final 'sting in the tail' were two Selectives in the former military training area of Caerwent, which saw numerous cars off the track, with one Rover 25 on its side and six cars having to be dragged out with broken suspension and driveshaft problems.

Come Sunday morning, and lying in 40th place overall, the Barker/Cave team set out for another session in Caerwent. If you have never rallied in Caerwent we must add that it is an experience! With changed front tyres and a burned-out light switch replaced, Caerwent presented yet another challenge to the Mini, with vast patches of sheet ice making driving extremely difficult, causing several cars to come off the road. Fortunately, Peter spun the car only once, managing to retain control and without damage.

Leaving Caerwent the rally headed for Chepstow Park, Trellech Woods, and then via Brecon to the Eppynt Ranges. By now the snow was coming down in earnest, the combination of this and ice making the Stages extremely slippery. Esgair Dafydd Forest was totally covered with snow. The rally continued on to the Mid Wales Activity Centre where a Selective on the snow- and ice-covered go-kart circuit was absolutely lethal. It was here that several cars hit the Armco, some so hard that they went straight through it! This Selective was eventually closed when yet another car hit the barriers and the co-driver cut his head.

Sweetlamb was the next venue, and, as darkness fell, the cars headed for Dolgellau, and then on to what many crews considered to be a very nice Selective in the Coed y Brenin Forest. Tarmac Selectives made pleasant driving into the control in the Bala town car park. A long drive to Llandudno via a couple of Selectives came next, then on to the final fast and dry tarmac Selective 'The Great Orme' before the finishing ramp.

The Barker/Cave Mini finished 27th overall and 8th in the 1300cc Class. Tyson/Harrison, unfortunately, did not complete the rally due to electrical problems at MC2 1.

MODELS

Fujimi.
(Courtesy
Fujimi)

Presented in year of manufacture and
release onto the market.

Fujimi
Model: Neko Mini Cooper 1.3i
Model number: LWS7
Issued: 1994
Scale: 1/24

Tomica. (Courtesy Miguel Plano)

Vitesse. (Courtesy Miguel Plano)

Tamiya. (Courtesy Tamiya)

Vitesse. (Tim Brenchley Collection)

Tomica
Model range: Tomica Tomy
Issued: 1994
Scale: 1/64

Vitesse
Issued: 1995
Scale: 1/43
Model number: V012L

Tamiya
Model: Mini Cooper Monte Carlo RTR
Model number: 57736 RC PRO
Issued: 1995
Scale: 1/10

Corgi
Model number: 04406
Issued: 1996
Scale: 1/36
Limited edition of 5700

04406 MINI - 1996 MONTE CARLO RALLY - TONY DRON

Corgi
Model number: 04407
Issued: 1997
Scale: 1/36
Limited edition of 5500

04407 MINI - 1994 MONTE CARLO RALLY - PADDY HOPKIRK

Corgi
Model number 04408
Issued: 1997
Scale: 1/36
Limited edition of 5500

04408 MINI - 1996 MONTE CARLO RALLY - KEITH BIRD

Corgi. (Courtesy Corgi)

04414 ## MINI - 1996 24 HOUR NURBURGRING

Corgi
Model number 04414
Issued: 1997
Scale: 1/36
Limited edition of 6300

Hongwell
Issued: 1997
Scale: 1/43

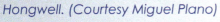

Hongwell. (Courtesy Miguel Plano)

Corgi
Model number: 04418
Issued: 1998
Scale: 1/36
Produced for Great Universal Stores
Limited edition of 5000

Corgi
Model number: 04422
Issued: 1998
Scale: 1/36
Not limited

Vitesse
Model number: SKC99008
Issued: 1998
Scale: 1/36
Limited edition of 2500

Piranha
Model number: P 02
Issued: 1999
Scale: 1/43
Self-assembly kit
Limited edition of 250

Corgi. (Courtesy Corgi)

Corgi. (Courtesy Corgi)

*Skid Vitesse.
(Tim Brenchley collection)*

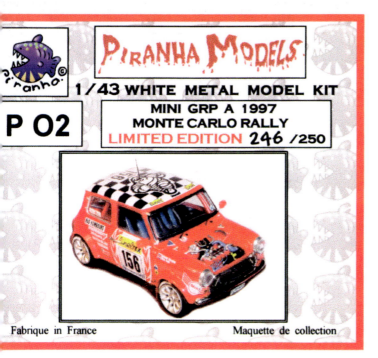

Piranha. *(Courtesy Piranha Models)*

Scale Model Technical Services.
(Bryan Purves Collection)

Scale Model Technical Services Ltd
Model number: V3C/DLE
Issued: 2000
Scale; 1/36
Numbered limited edition of 500
Signed by Paddy Hopkirk and John Cooper

British Motor Classics
Model number: MCC 423/P37A MC94 No 37
Scale: 1/43

British Motor Classics
Model number: MC 423/37B MC94 No 37
Scale: 1/43
L33 EJB no bonnet spotlight pod

British Motor Classics
Model number: MCC 423/101 MC94 No 101
Scale: 1/43
Rover Japan: Timo Makinen/ Paul Easter

British Motor Classics
Model number: MCC 441/24   RAC 94 No.25
Scale: 1/43
Brookes/Wilson 1994 Network Q RAC Rally

Hongwell
Scale: 1/43

Hongwell. (Tim Brenchley Collection)

Hongwell
Scale: 1/43

Hongwell. (Courtesy Miguel Plano)

Kyosho
Scale: 1/10
Radio-controlled

Kyosho. (Courtesy Miguel Plano)

Bburago
Model number: 34109
Scale: 1/18

John Ayrey
Model number: JLC991-R
Scale: not to scale

Bburago. (Bryan Purves Collection)

Ayrey. (Bryan Purves Collection)

Bburago. (Courtesy Bburago)

Bburago
Model number: 55159
Scale: 1/24

Hongwell
Model number: 171C
Scale: 1/72

Schuco
Model number: 331 6218
Scale: 1/72

Hongwell
Scale: 1/36

Hongwell. (Tim Brenchley Collection)

Schuco. (Bryan Purves Collection)

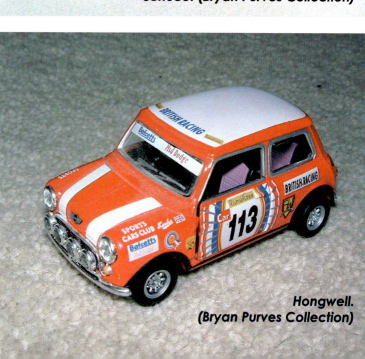

*Hongwell.
(Bryan Purves Collection)*

THE END
OF AN ERA

Having spent many long hours researching and also rebuilding the last two of these wonderful cars, we hope that you have enjoyed reading about our work. We hope, too, that we have been able to give you an insight into the last 'works' Minis of the 1990s, and the opportunity to appreciate the work that went into preparing and modifying the last two cars, at enormous expense in both time and parts in order to finally produce what can only be called the ultimate in 'works' prepared Minis.

The Mini – though at the end of its production life – will continue as part of our lives for many years to come. It will always be an icon in the world of motoring; still be raced and rallied throughout the world, and modified in many ways, but most importantly will still be there for future generations to admire and enjoy.

What went wrong with the 1990s British Motor Heritage Special Tuning Department; did BMW/Rover pull the plug? We might also ask: did BMW not want Rover to compete on the track or on the rally circuit? Were the cars over-developed, and was too much money changing hands? Was it due to internal politics?

Ten years on, hindsight makes it easy to see the mistakes made by Rover in its ill-fated return to racing and rallying. Essentially there were four major players: Brigden Coulter Motortsport; D R Engineering Consultants; Coventry Automotive, and Enterprise Racing, all given the chance during a very short period of time to develop a car and to promote the Rover Group. Each company in its own way developed the car as far as possible, be it dash displays, suspension, transmission, wiring, etc. Each year something else was tried and, to a degree, each car succeeded.

Consider this scenario, though: what if one of the companies, with good cost control and management, had received a budget of one million pounds over a four-year period? Answer: the world would have seen a classic, fully computer-controlled Mini that could develop 140bhp, with a six-speed sequential gearbox, have a lighter and strengthened bodyshell with welded-in roll cage, lightweight wiring,

Pat 'Tish' Ozanne driving with Nicky Gilmore in the navigator's seat seen here taking part in the 1960 Rallye Monte Carlo in the Standard Touring Class. (Courtesy Bryan Purves Collection)

a suspension that worked, and ... the list continues. Oh, what if!

With the support of many specialist manufacturers and suppliers – and especially as British Motor Heritage Limited is making new replacement bodyshells, panels and sub-frames – there is no, absolutely no reason for the Mini to fade away. No wonder it was hailed as The Car of the Twentieth Century. Now it can be revealed that the last two 'works' cars were the most expensive factory Minis ever built.

Visit us on the web – www.velocebooks.com
New book news • Gift vouchers • Details all books in print • Special offers

THE LAST WORD
BY DAVID PAVELEY

An honour and a privilege

It was a privilege to be asked by Bryan and Tim to pen a few words and summarise their research in bringing together the history of the last 'works' Minis. In the past, volumes have been written about the 1960/70s 'works' rallying and racing cars, but the final years of Mini production and activity have been overlooked until now. Credit must go to both Bryan and Tim for compiling this record, as well as restoring the last two – what can only be described as ultimate 'works' cars – built and with which I have had the pleasure of being associated.

When I was approached to be part of

David with the 1997 Rallye Monte Carlo Trophy for the Best International Finisher in Class Group 'N'. (Bryan Purves Collection)

the Mini programme I was obviously aware of the Mini's statistics as a competition vehicle of the 60s and early 70s, but, as we all know, statistics do not tell the whole story. I was soon to become acquainted with the Mini's character, not only as a competition vehicle but also an iconic road car with an incredible worldwide enthusiast base.

Following a brief and chance encounter, a very persuasive Brian Cameron invited me to drive the weather car on the 1996 Rallye Monte Carlo. This quickly turned into an adventure, as happens with all things Mini, full of drama and excitement as we sped through breathtaking scenery and classic Stages supporting Tony Dron, for whom I have the utmost admiration as both driver and individual. It was fitting that Tony was involved as he has almost as much heritage and as many stories to tell as the Mini!

After the adventures of the 1996 Monte it was obvious that structure and planning were necessary to take the project forward. I was given a full-time place in the organization, alongside some wonderful people, including the hard-working Southall brothers, without whom the '97 Monte project would not have come to fruition. It was little known at the time that Brian Cameron's and Mike Southall's vision resulted in many vehicles which never saw the light of day, due to the politics of German-owned Rover, slowly being laid to rest well before the Phoenix era. One of these cars was the Rover 620Ti, which had the Cameron/Southall makeover; an MG a full five years before the MG Z range was born, but that's another story ...

My first real chance of contributing to the history of the Mini occurred during mine and Andy's ill-fated outing on the Mull Rally of 1996 – the first event to shape the team and specification of the car. At scrutineering I was approached by a foreign gentleman who had flown many miles to see the first of the last 'works' Mini

rally cars in action; a true enthusiast, who left me quite speechless when he took a photograph of me next to the car, and then said that he would frame it and put it on his lounge wall with the words: "Luckiest man in the world" underneath!

By the time of the '97 Monte outing. the Mini had evolved into something quite special. The six-speed Group 'A' car was now capable of giant-killing with 144bhp, and I was looking forward to a top 20 finish. As the event drew closer, Dron was assigned the Group 'A' car and I – much to my disappointment – the Group 'N' car, as it was felt that Dron's previous experience of the rally would give him a better chance of a good result.

Tony was acquainting himself with the six-speed Group 'A' car on the Concentration Run when the car suffered a dropped valve on the road section; as I said, with a Mini everything is an adventure!

At that point between Bad Hombourg in Germany and Monaco, the rally really started for me and Andy Bull, my co-driver of considerable talent. The support vehicles were involved in trying to fix the Group 'A' car so a walletless pair of Englishmen somehow pleaded their way through tolls and petrol stations to get to Monaco with a failed clutch cylinder and a noisy gearbox, and the special Stages were still a day away!

The cars were totally legal for 1997, so the gearbox in the Group 'N' car was the new overdrive unit, meaning that 4th gear was only any good on the downhill sections. Unfortunately, this stifled the car's performance, although we were very fast on the down hill sections. Even with our excitement-dampening gear ratios, there were still plenty of thrills for car 222; I think we were the only team that had the police stop our service van, let the sniffer dogs on board, and sit back and watch the dogs eat all our provisions – then throw one of our mechanics into jail! The bail bill must have taken some explaining to the Rover board ...

By the end of the five-day event Andy and I were quite exhausted, but during this time we had absorbed the very essence of the Mini. Gifts were quite literally bestowed upon us from complete strangers because we were the 'Mini crew'. There was a special magic connection between the Mini and the Monte; old friends that had once again become reacquainted, with Andy and I part of the supporting act. The rally itself left me with mixed feelings about what might have been. Having tested both Group 'A' and 'N' Minis in the build-up to the rally, I knew the cars better than anyone, but was unable to do the recce as I had to stay behind to sign off the cars! Fortunately, the navigational skills of Andy helped us over that hurdle, except even Andy can't see around blind corners and what might be lurking there!

The Monte Carlo project was sunsequently scrutinised by the board; I quote: "... will have to stop because it is making the old car too popular and we have a new model coming out". There would be no PR following on from the Monte, and I was asked not to promote my involvement. So that was it, but not before one final fling ...

The team asked me to drive the Group 'A' car – all but a kit car, minus any real technical modification to the rear suspension – in a one-day rally. We were out to prove the Group 'A' car had real potential against an entry of capable vehicles. The Mini was

Morgan has kept a keen eye on the proceedings, and overseen the project throughout the rebuild and the writing of this book. Purr-fect! (Bryan Purves Collection)

running well for Stage 1 and we were really flying; a good result looked certain only for the clutch cylinder to go on Stage 2. The six-speed gearbox was not one for being forced without the clutch so we limped back to the service area knowing deep down that it was really all over, together with the opportunity of proving to the board that it had a winner on its hands. With this in mind Stage 3 was to be maximum attack, orders from above! I said to Andy on the start line that the rear suspension would be our downfall on a bumpy section and could be our undoing – and it certainly was. We set off into the Stage, reeling in our much faster Cosworth Sierra competitor over 1 minute in less than 7 miles. We entered the last bumpy section flat out, then oscillation took over and the car literally leapt into the air back first; we had a bird's eye view of the marshals running as we rolled through the air before crashing back to the ground. I kept my word to the team, didn't lift off the accelerator and we gave it our all. It was a sad end but at least the team went out fighting.

That was the last ever official outing of a classic 'works' Mini. I feel privileged to have been involved in such an exciting – though trying – programme which I will remember for many years to come.

David Paveley

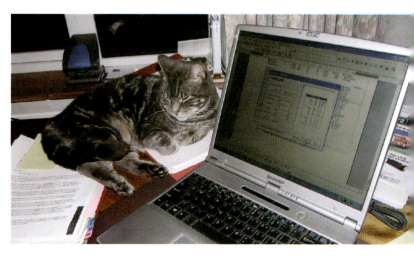

APPENDICES

APPENDIX 1

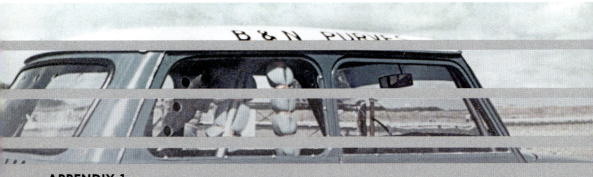

Mini 'Special Tuning' Development - Project 11 (BMH Forward Strategy 1996-2002, 15 Mar '96)																
Cashflow 000s	1996 Q1	Q2	Q3	Q4	1997 Q1	Q2	Q3	Q4	1998 Q1	Q2	Q3	Q4	1999 Q1	Q2	Q3	Q4
R&D																
Budget	0	30	30	30	30	0	20	0	0	0	0	0	0	0	0	0
Actual/LIC		59	26	34	12	0	0	10	0	0	0	0	0	0	0	0
Marketing - see separate projects																
Investment																
Budget	0	0	0	0	0	0	0	0	0	0	0	0	0	0	0	0
Actual	0	0	0	0	0	0	0	0	0	0	0	0	0	0	0	0
Revenue					447	298	149	298	402.3	268.2	134.1	268.2	362.07	241.38	120.69	241.38
Contribution	0	0	0	0	150	100	50	100	135	90	45	90	121.5	81	40.5	81
Cum cash flow		-59	-85	-119	19	119	169	259	394	484	529	619	740.5	821.5	862	943

British Motor Heritage Forward Planning 1996 – 2002 (15th March 1996).
(Courtesy British Motor Heritage/Rover)

APPENDIX 2

Mini Development - Parts Analysis									
Part	Retail	W/sale	Cost	Volume Y1	W/sale Rev	Cost of Sales (@ +5%)	Contrib'n	Source	RTM
Sports parts									R'Sport/Unipart
Bodyshell	2730	2100	1500	25	52500	39375	13125	BMH	
Subframe - front	273	210	150	40	8400	6300	2100	BMH	
Subframe assy - rear	973.7	749	535	60	44940	33705	11235	BMH	
Spring/damper unit	455	350	250	150	52500	39375	13125	WP	
Brake hose kit	1001	770	550	40	30800	23100	7700	ER	
Brake duct kit	245.7	189	135	50	9450	7087.5	2362.5	ER	
Rear disc kit	600.6	462	330	100	46200	34650	11550	ER	
Hydraulic h/brake kit	218.4	168	120	30	5040	3780	1260	ER	
Fuel Tank	1718.2	1562	1420	35	54670	52185	2485	ATL	
Fuel pump kit	436.8	336	240	35	11760	8820	2940	ATL	
Fuel lines & fittings	873.6	672	480	35	23520	17640	5880	ER	
Roll cage	1519.7	1169	835	25	29225	21918.75	7306.25	Tarcal	
Fire Extinguisher	284.35	258.5	235	25	6462.5	6168.75	293.75	SPA	
Fascia	400.4	308	220	40	12320	9240	3080	ER	
Instruments	1392.3	1071	765	25	26775	20081.25	6693.75	Stack	
Steering rack	564.2	434	310	40	17360	13020	4340	ER/Rover	
Wiring loom assy	3276	2520	1800	25	63000	47250	15750	MM	
General parts									Specialists
6-speed gearbox	2184	1680	1200	400	672000	504000	168000	Tran-X	
Sequential unit	982.8	756	540	150	113400	85050	28350	Tran-X	
F2 universal joints	109.2	84	60	800	67200	50400	16800	Tran-X	
PIAA Headlight kit	109.2	84	60	400	33600	25200	8400	PIAA	
Lamp pods	561.6	468	360	50	23400	18900	4500	PIAA	
Front valance	145.6	112	80	50	5600	4200	1400	ER/Rover	

Part	Retail	W/sale	Cost	Volume Y1	W/sale Rev	Cost of Sales (@ +5%)	Contrib'n	Source
Wheel arch kit	145.6	112	80	500	56000	42000	14000	ER/Rover
Heated front screen	171.08	131.6	94	150	19740	14805	4935	Triplex
Radiator	200.2	154	110	200	30800	23100	7700	Serck
Metro hub assy	81.9	63	45	320	20160	15120	5040	Rover
Brake disc/caliper unit	455	350	250	320	112000	84000	28000	AP
Brake pads	81.9	63	45	160	10080	7560	2520	AP
Wheels	72.8	56	40	800	44800	33600	11200	SCParts
Window handle set	91	70	50	200	14000	10500	3500	ER
Interior panel kit	191.1	147	105	50	7350	5512.5	1837.5	ER
Passenger footrest	45.5	35	25	40	1400	1050	350	ER
Front seat - sports	1183	910	650	70	63700	47775	15925	Recaro
Branded harness	109.2	84	60	70	5880	4410	1470	Willans
Steering wheel	109.2	91	70	100	9100	7350	1750	Momo
Engine								
Gp N	TBA							
Gp A	TBA							
Gp A Kit	TBA							
Parts	TBA							
Total					1310210	436903.75		

The Mini development parts and sales analysis for 1997.
(Courtesy British Motor Heritage/Rover)

APPENDIX 3

Mini special editions 1989 to 2000
(Some production figures not stated due to lack of data)

1989 Mini Thirty
June 1989
3000 built
£5599 purchase price

(Courtesy Austin Rover Cars Ltd)

Built to celebrate the 30th Anniversary of the Mini. Available in luxurious Pearlescent Cherry Red (2000 units), or Black (1000 units)

1990 Flame
February 1990
£5455

1990 Racing Green
February 1990
£5455

1990 Checkmate
February 1990
£5455

A total of 2500 Flame, Racing green, and Checkmate models were built for the UK market. All examples of the three models had white roofs

1990 Studio Two
12th June 1990
2000 built
£5375
A design project using young designers' ideas. Three colours were available: Nordic Blue, Storm Grey and Black

1990 Mini Cooper (re-introduction)
10th July 1990
1650 built with 650 exported to Japan

£6995
Sunroof and John Cooper signed bonnet stripes

1991 Neon
February 1991
1500 built
£5570
A special edition with bright badging in Nordic Metallic Blue

266

1992 British Open Classic
June 1992
1000 built
£7195
British Racing Green with a full-length, electrically-operated sunroof

1992 Italian Job
October 1992
1750 built
£5995
Red, White and Blue plus Green to make the Italian colours. White-painted alloy wheels. 1000 units for UK distribution and 750 for Italy

1993 Rio
June 1993
750 built
£5495
Polynesian Turquoise Metallic, Caribbean Pearlescent Blue and Black with interesting decal

1993 Cabriolet 1.3i
Combined total built 1080
30th June 1993
£12,250
20th December 1993
£11,995
Available in Nightfire Red and Caribbean Blue with Grey hood and 12 inch wheels. In 1994 British Racing Green became available. All cars were fitted with 12 inch wheels

1993 Tahiti
6th October 1993
500 built
£5795
Tahiti Blue paint

(Courtesy Rover Cars)

(Courtesy Rover Cars)

1994 Cooper 1.3i
April 1994
£7195

1994 Mini 35
June 1994
1000 built
£5695
The Mini produced to celebrate its 35th anniversary. Available in Nevada Red, White and Arizona Blue

1994 Monte Carlo
20th July 1994
200 built
£7195 (January)
£7995 (July)
Celebrating the 30th anniversary of the Mini's first Rallye Monte Carlo win. Colour: Flame Red or Black with red and cream interior

(Courtesy Rover Cars – sales brochure)

1994 Sprite
1994
Number built 17,830
£5395

1994 Mayfair
1994
£6795

1994 John Cooper Grand Prix Mini
1994
35 built of which 34 were in British Racing Green and one in Tahiti Blue.
£13,495
Produced to celebrate the 35th anniversaries of Mini and Mini Cooper Racing cars winning the Formula One World Championship

(Courtesy Rover Cars)

MINI

Cooper's Grand Prix Return

(Courtesy Mini World)

(Courtesy Rover Cars)

1995 Sidewalk
June 1995
1000 built
£5895
Available in Kingfisher Blue, Charcoal Grey and Diamond White. Blue tartan interior checks on the trim

1995 Cooper 'S'
October 1995
£9975
£10,350 (April 1996)
The first Cooper 'S' available for 25 years. Unique chassis plate.

1996 Equinox
April 1996
750 built
£6195
The sun, moon and stars available in Amaranth Purple, Charcoal and Platinum Silver

(Courtesy Rover Cars)

John Rhodes takes the famous chicane at Goodwood. (Courtesy Rover Group Ltd)

1996 Cooper 35
May 1996
200 built
£8195
Commemorating 35 years of the Mini Cooper. This model used the latest paint technology to recreate one of the original colours, Almond Green. Porcelain Green interior trim with leather upholstery

1997 Rover Cooper with optional Sport-Pack
1st October 1997
Standard £8995
Number built: 1650
Additional supplement for Sport-Pack: £800

(Courtesy Rover Cars)

1997 Mini Cooper S LE
November 1997
£10.995
Fitted with Jack Knight 5-speed gearbox. Only available from John Cooper Garages

1997 Mini
1st October 1996
Standard £8995
A model with optional electric fabric sunroof (£800), and plastic wheelarches

1998 Paul Smith LE
March 1998
300 built
£10,200
A blue interior matched the external paint colour

1998 Natashia Caine Designer Mini
Lovely legs, gold bullion, legs, gold bullion ...
1 built

1998 Mini Cooper Sport LE
100 built (70 Green, 30 Black)
£10,525
Brooklands Green or Black. Green leather interior. Vita racing style 'V' on the front wings

1999 Cooper 'S' 'works'
May 1999
25 built
Price subject to package, starting at £12,495, rising to £14,595
Offered with a very wide options package

(Courtesy John Cooper Garages Ltd)

1999 Cooper 'S' Sport 5
May 1999
Only 5 built
£14,450
Fitted with a five-speed Jack Knight gearbox as standard

1999 Cooper 'S' Touring
May 1999
Price subject to package, starting at £11,595, rising to £13,650
Offered with a very wide options package

1999 John Cooper LE
Autumn 1999
Number built: 300
£10,995
Produced to celebrate the 40th year of the Mini and the 40th anniversary of the first Cooper Formula 1 World Championship win. Only available in Brooklands Green, OEW roof. Grenadine red leather interior

(Courtesy John Cooper Garages Ltd – sales brochure)

(Courtesy Rover Group Ltd)

1999 Mini 40 LE
July 1999
Numbers built: 150 in Mulberry Red Metallic (£10,795)
50 in Old English White (£10,495)
50 in Island Blue (£10,495)
Full leather interior, 13 inch wheels, twin-point injection, gold-plated bonnet badge

(Courtesy Rover Group Ltd)

2000 Mini Classic 'Se7en'
15th March 2000
£9495
1.3-litre, fuel-injected, 12 inch Premium style alloy wheels, Tartan red carpets and cream cloth interior. Solar Red, Old English White or Black paintwork

2000 Mini Classic Cooper Sport
15th March 2000
£10,895
Black leather interior, alloy dash, alloy fittings, 13 inch wheels. Solar Red, Anthracite, Tahiti Blue and British Racing Green, all with a Platinum Silver roof, bonnet stripes and mirrors

(Courtesy Rover Group Ltd)

811 ACO

(Courtesy Rover Group Ltd – sales brochure)

489 UAP

2000 Mini Classic Cooper
15th March 2000
£9895
Part leather and cloth seats, 12 inch alloy wheels. Colours: Solar Red, Anthracite, Tahiti Blue, British Racing Green, all with a White roof

2000 Cooper Sport 500 LE
May 2000
500 built
£10,995
The last 500 Minis to come off the production line, each complete with a certificate of authenticity, Mini merchandise pack and Cooper Sport 500 plaque mounted on the glovebox face

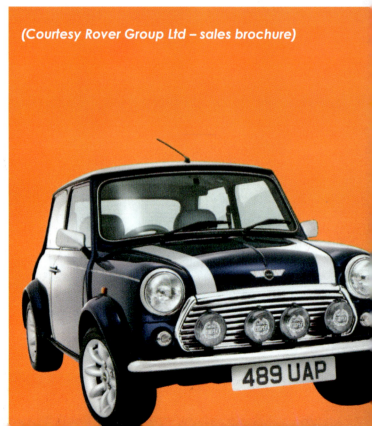

Production of the Longbridge built Mini finally came to an end in October 2000.

Farewell to the Classic Mini:
August 26th 1959 to October 4th 2000.

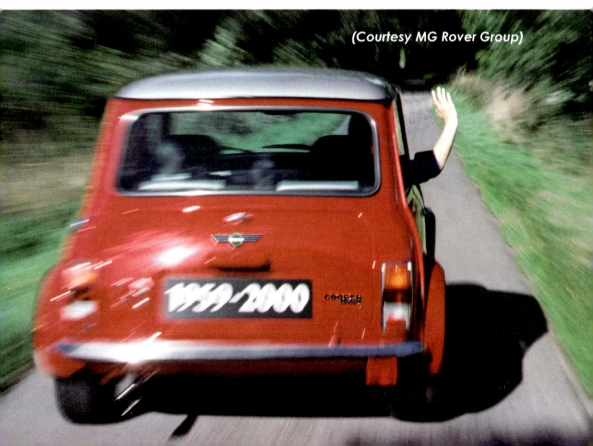

Brigden Coulter Motorsport Ltd

BRIGDEN COULTER MOTORSPORT LTD

BRINGING THE MINI BACK TO THE MONTE

Project Mini Monte Carlo

Our company built and prepared Paddy Hopkirk's Mini Cooper, L33EJB, for the 1994 Monte Carlo Rally. It ran in the top 50 during some of the stages and was placed as high as 3rd in class and 52nd overall, proving that the Mini is still competitive in World motorsport.

We can now offer the following parts that we developed for this car to Group A specification.

GpA Rally Car

Complete car to full GpA specification as run on the Monte Carlo Rally. Bodyshell is fully seam welded, subframes are seam welded and 20-point roll cage fitted, painted to match car colour.

Engine is full GpA giving guaranteed 100bhp +, Jack Knight five speed dog engagement gearbox as standard, with choice of drop gears, final drives and LSD. Drive is through Hardy Spicer joints and special Monte Carlo drive shafts. The car is fitted with the Weber Alpha injection system.

Front suspension is adjustable and rose-jointed, the rear suspension is adjustable for negative camber.

The interior is fully equipped with black dashboard, instruments as required, fuses, rally seats, fire extinguisher and extra interior lighting.

The price includes the Monte Carlo lamp pod which is essential for night rallying.

The car is fully rally prepared with many other items too numerous to list.

Complete car @ £25,000

Engine

Complete unit with our own in-house designed camshaft, Weber Alpha fuel injection system and a guaranteed output of 100bhp. This is the state of the art unit, offering a reliable yet powerful unit for competition use. £6,750

Brigden Coulter Motorsport Ltd 41 Robyns Way Sevenoaks Kent TN13 3EB Tel: 0732 740216 Fax: 0732 462359
Registered Office: 41 Robyns Way Sevenoaks Kent TN13 3EB. Registered in England: No 2339288

(Courtesy Stephen Smith)

-2-

Gearbox

4- speed. Straight cut/Straight cut dog box for the ultimate gearchange. Choice of ratios. £875
5-Speed Jack Knight, rally proven gearbox. Straight cut/Straight cut Dog engagement box with choice of ratios. £1,650

Engine & Gearbox Accessories

Custom-built Monte Carlo exhaust systems including down pipe and centre exit system skidded, painted. £267.25
Our own adjustable steady bars, with Monte Carlo bushes £38.65
Group A driveshafts including larger CV joints - virtually indestructible £350/pair
Final drives - wide range to choose from, depending on your application.
Road, Rally or Race From £187.00
Hardy Spicer joints for extra strength in competition £125.56

Body

Bodyshell. GpA Monte Carlo specification with full 20-point rollcage and 30 hours seam welding for maximum strength. In primer. £4,250
Sprayed to your own colour. Add from £650

Lamp Pod complete kit. Monte Carlo type with four PIAA lamps, rings, bulbs and wiring loom. Painted to order or in black or white. £426.78
Lamp pod only without lamps etc, painted to order or black or white. £115.48
Subframes, genuine, strengthened   Front £229.54
                                    Rear £214.54
Sumpguard. Monte type. Dural short. £48.65
Dural Extension piece for Minis £38.46
Sumpguard. Monte type with extension. £65.87
Roll bars GpA. As Paddy Hopkirk Monte car £685.60
                        Painting to your colour £158.76
Road/National/FIA cage   Front £107.65
                         Rear £116.78
                         With detachable diagonal £148.43
                         Painting £85.65
Wheels. 13in 5.5J. Alloy Monte wheels with sleeve nuts as used by Paddy Hopkirk £73each

-3-

Interior

Monte Carlo black trim kit: Includes door panels, wheel arch covers, rear quarter panels and rear parcel shelf. £75.10
Black head-lining kit including C-post panels £43.61
Black sun visors £22.78/pair
Black carpet set £64.90
Driver's foot rest £27.84
Throttle pedal extension £18.68
Monte Carlo dashboard in Kevlar £198.45
                 in fibreglass - Kevlar lookalike £95.98
Heated front screen £195.85
Heated windscreen with loom and switches kit £288.98

Suspension

Hi-Los: Ground clearance height adjusters Front £56.98/pair
                                         Rear £61.68/pair
Monte Carlo bump stop kit, front £12.95
Monte Carlo adjustable front suspension kit per side including bottom arms, tie rods, rose joints and special stainless bottom pins £245.43
Rear negative camber kit £58.98

-##-

Prices exclusive of VAT and delivery.

To order please phone: + 44 (0)732 740216. Fax: + 44 (0732) 4622359

APPENDIX 5
The competition
The Mini's main rival on both the race track and in rallying was the Fiat Cinquecento, an urban 'yuppie' vehicle. The car was technically superior to the Mini with a higher top speed enhanced by its five-speed gearbox. The Fiat's handling characteristics were also superior as a result of non-stop testing and development at Fiat's test track.

Overall much lighter than the Mini, the Fiat sported larger brakes and modern suspension geometry designed to suit its wheel size. With choice of tyres critical on the Monte, the Cinquecentos were able to use a narrower tyre in tune with its handling characteristics when encountering snow and ice.

APPENDIX 6
Semi-permanent fixings
The majority of the nuts, bolts, screws and washers used in the assembly of the 1996/97 cars were made of stainless steel or, to use the technical term, chromium-nickel/austenitic steel. This type of steel is categorised by three grades and it was the A2 grade, or 18/8, that was used for all temporary fasteners; where possible they were Allen head socket or socket button head. This grade of stainless steel has outstanding corrosion resistance under normal atmospheric conditions, including wet surroundings, impervious to the effects of oxidising and organic acids and many alkali and salt solutions.

APPENDIX 7
The specification of the AP Racing-manufactured discs and callipers used on the 1996/97 Group 'A' Rover Coopers were as follows (all dimensions in mm):
Part number: CP4136-48
Outside diameter: 267
Thickness: 21.00
'M' PCD: 139.7
Eight bolt mounting: 6.4 diameter
'C' eye: 155
'D' inside flange: 125.8
'H' mounting flange: 5.6
Maximum pad depth: D54
Number of vanes: 36
Air gap: 9.3
Weight: 4.4kg
Face type: G4
Disc face type: type G4, 8, 12, 24. Straightforward facing grooves. The number specifies the grooves per face.

Under hard driving conditions the disc bulk temperature should normally be maintained in the 400 to 600 degree Centigrade range for best performance.

Discs and callipers used on the 1996/97 Group 'A' Rover Coopers. (Courtesy A P Racing)

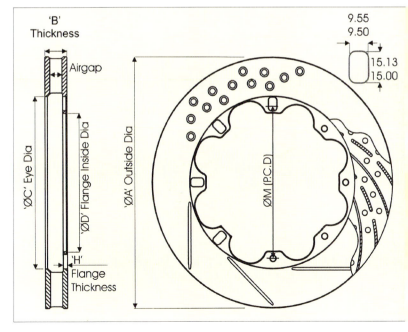

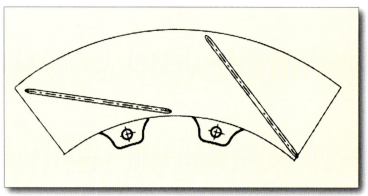

Disc face type. (Courtesy A P Racing)

The brake pads have a part number – CP2340D43 – which can be broken down as follows: CP2340 defines the pad shape and thickness, and D43 the radial depth. Pads are available from four manufacturers who offer different friction materials: Ferodo 4003F and DS2500; Mintex M1166 and F4R; Pagid RS42 and RS421; and finally Raybestos ST41, ST42 and ST43.

CP3228
4 PISTON CALIPER

TYPICAL APPLICATIONS
- Group A Race & Rally for ventilated discs.

FEATURES
- Lug mount (Blank)
- To suit Ø280.0.0mm x 23.0mm disc.
- Two piece aluminium alloy body, machined from high quality die casting.
- Aluminium pistons standard.
- High temperature seals.
- Hard anodised surface treatment.
- Stainless steel bridge pipe, pad abutments & wear plates fitted.
- 4Lb anti-knockback springs fitted.

PART NUMBERS
- CP3228-26S4 RHT.
- CP3228-27S4 LHT.

CALIPER HANDING
It is important to select the correct 'hand' of caliper. See note on page 6 for guidance.

TECHNICAL SPECIFICATION
- Piston Sizes	Ø38.1mm x 4
- Disc Diameter	Ø280.0mm
- Disc Thickness	23.0mm
- Weight (Less Pads)	1.7Kg
- Hydraulic Threads	3/8" x 24UNF
- Mounting	Blank Lug
- 'PL' Dimension	81.0mm Max
- Seal Repair Kit	CP4518-JJ
- Bleed Screw Tightening Torque	17Nm (12.5lbs/ft)

PAD FAMILY
CP2340D51
Pad Area = 43.4cm²
Pad Depth = 50.8mm
Pad Thickness = 15.9mm

SPARE PARTS
- Pistons   CP3228-103
- Pad Retainer   Clip
- Retainer P/No   CP3228-104
- Bleed Screw   CP3720-182
- Fluid Pipe   CP3228-4

APPENDIX 8

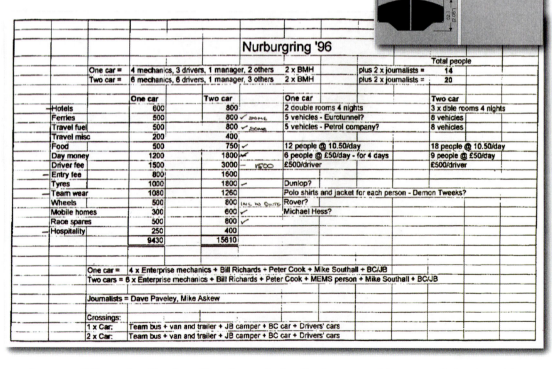

		Nurburgring '96						
	One car =	4 mechanics, 3 drivers, 1 manager, 2 others		2 x BMH		plus 2 x journalists =	**Total people** 14	
	Two car =	6 mechanics, 6 drivers, 1 manager, 3 others		2 x BMH		plus 2 x journalists =	20	
		One car	Two car	One car			Two car	
Hotels		600	800	2 double rooms 4 nights			3 x dble rooms 4 nights	
Ferries		500	800 ✓ some	5 vehicles - Eurotunnel?			8 vehicles	
Travel fuel		500	800 ✓ some	5 vehicles - Petrol company?			8 vehicles	
Travel misc		200	400					
Food		500	750 ✓	12 people @ 10.50/day			18 people @ 10.50/day	
Day money		1200	1800	6 people @ £50/day - for 4 days			9 people @ £50/day	
Driver fee		1500	3000 1500	£500/driver			£500/driver	
Entry fee		800	1600					
Tyres		1000	1800 ✓	Dunlop?				
Team wear		1080	1260	Polo shirts and jacket for each person - Demon Tweeks?				
Wheels		500	800 inc no quote	Rover?				
Mobile homes		300	600 ✓	Michael Hess?				
Race spares		500	800 ✓					
Hospitality		250	400					
		9430	15610					
	One car =	4 x Enterprise mechanics + Bill Richards + Peter Cook + Mike Southall + BC/JB						
	Two cars =	6 x Enterprise mechanics + Bill Richards + Peter Cook + MEMS person + Mike Southall + BC/JB						
	Journalists =	Dave Paveley, Mike Askew						
	Crossings:							
	1 x Car:	Team bus + van and trailer + JB camper + BC car + Drivers' cars						
	2 x Car:	Team bus + van and trailer + JB camper + BC car + Drivers' cars						

A copy of the submitted costing for entering just one and two cars into the 1996 Nürburgring 24 Hour Race. (Courtesy Enterprise Racing)

```
Date          : 14/8/1996
Registration No.: YELLOW   Run No.:  001
Owner         : ENTERPRISE RACING
Make          : ROVER        Model      : MINI COOPER
Engine size   :              Mileage    :

Carburettor      :
Pilot jet size   :
Main jet size    :
Emulsion tube    :
Cam shaft        :
Wheel size       :
Tyres            :
Spark plugs      :
Distributor      :
Exhaust          :
Air filter       :
Ignition timing        :
Ignition at full advance :
```

| | Wheel | Flywheel | |
Rpm	Bhp	Bhp	Torque
3500	50	62	93
3750	54	67	94
4000	56	70	92
4250	60	75	93
4500	62	78	91
4750	63	79	87
5000	62	77	81
5250	70	87	87
5500	70	87	83
5750	71	89	81
6000	71	89	78
6250	71	89	75
6500	70	88	71
6750	70	87	68
7000	68	85	64
7250	70	88	63
7500	70	87	61

```
            Maximum            Rpm
         FlyWheel Values

   Bhp      91              6085
   Torque   291             3178
```

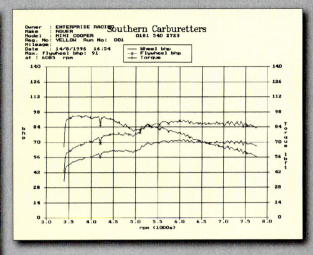

(All courtesy Enterprise Racing)

APPENDIX 9

The rolling road report on the Nürburgring car with the Yellow sun-strip.
The rolling road report on the car with the Red sun-strip.

```
Date          : 14/8/1996
Registration No.: RED    Run No.:  002
Owner         : ENTERPRISE RACING
Make          : ROVER        Model      : MINI COOPER
Engine size   :              Mileage    :

Carburettor      :
Pilot jet size   :
Main jet size    :
Emulsion tube    :
Cam shaft        :
Wheel size       :
Tyres            :
Spark plugs      :
Distributor      :
Exhaust          :
Air filter       :
Ignition timing        :
Ignition at full advance :
```

| | Wheel | Flywheel | |
Rpm	Bhp	Bhp	Torque
2750	10	13	24
3000	18	23	40
3250	47	59	95
3500	51	64	96
3750	54	67	94
4000	57	71	93
4250	63	79	97
4500	67	84	98
4750	69	86	94
5000	68	85	90
5250	72	90	89
5500	74	92	88
5750	76	95	87
6000	77	96	84
6250	79	99	82
6500	79	99	80
6750	74	92	72
7000	77	96	72
7250	75	93	67
7500	77	96	67
7750	74	93	63

```
            Maximum            Rpm
         FlyWheel Values

   Bhp      99              6671
   Torque   291             3178
```

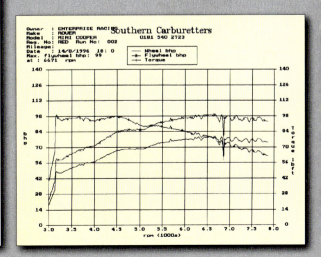

The enquiry is complete
The vehicle details for N679 TOK are:

Date of Liability	01 10 1997
Date of First Registration	10 10 1995
Year of Manufacture	1995
Cylinder Capacity (cc)	1275CC
CO_2 Emissions	Not Available
Fuel Type	Petrol
Export Marker	Not Applicable
Vehicle Status	Unlicensed
Vehicle Colour	RED
Vehicle Type Approval	

The information contained on this page is correct at the time of enquiry.
Vehicle Excise Duty Rate for vehicle

6 Months Rate	£60.50
12 Months Rate	£110.00

Please be aware that if the vehicle has recently been relicensed or a SORN declared, these details may not yet be updated on the vehicle record.

If you think that the details on the vehicle record are incorrect please write to:
VCS
DVLA
Swansea
SA99 1BA

Home   Enquiry

Including the incorrect V5C Registration Certificate for amendment.

APPENDIX 10

Car N679 TOK was the UK car from which the cloned registration number was to be used for homologation. It was also the chase car on the 1996 Rallye Monte Carlo.

Registration number: N679 TOK
Date of first registration: 10th October 1995
Make: Rover
Model: Mini Cooper
VIN: SAXXNNAYCBD068866
Colour: Red
Year of manufacture: 1995
Engine number: 12A2EF77268236
Fuel type: petrol
Engine capacity: 1275cc

282

1996 Rallye Monte Carlo chase car. (Courtesy Richard Franklin)

Homologation specifications: a brief resume

Group 'N'

A Group 'N' vehicle is a car prepared to exacting standards, the engine having the capacity of a production car of the marque. A minimum number of 2500 production cars must be manufactured within a time frame of 12 consecutive months.

The fuel tank may be homologated without a production minimum, providing the location of the tank is the same as that of

the series production model, or is in the boot.

Suspension can be strengthened, and appropriate safety equipment must be fitted, including a roll bar. For rallying the minimum permissible weight of any car is 760kg.

Group 'A'

A minimum of 2500 units must have been produced within a consecutive 12 month period. Seat specifications are specifically set out, along with foot space dimensions for all occupants. Spoilers must be rigidly fixed to the sprung part of the car's bodywork. The fixation points of the suspension may be changed provided that the suspension remains unmodified.

Jim Bamber's design for a possible Mini 'Kit Car' to contest the International rally scene. (Courtesy Car and Car Conversions)

If the cylinder capacity of the car is greater than 1300cc the engine must be positioned forward of the middle of the vehicle's wheelbase.

Engine and gearbox modifications are permitted. Braking systems can be modified. For rallying the minimum permissible weight of any car is 790kg.

Group 'VK' (Variant Kit) or Kit Car

These variants are authorised only for models in Group 'A' with two-wheel drive and normally-aspirated engines to a maximum capacity of 2-litres. These models must be taken from a 'family' of 25,000 units produced within 12 consecutive months. The cars must be registered for road use.

At least 20 examples of the 'Kit' must be produced within 12 consecutive months and made available for sale. Only one kit may be homologated for each car and each 12 month period.

The following parts may be homologated in the kits:
Inlet and exhaust manifolds
Injection/carburettors
Crankshaft and flywheel
Engine sleeving/boring
Diameter of valves for engines with 2 valves per cylinder
Con-rods
Brakes
Fuel tanks
Transmission
Suspension
Front and rear aerodynamic devices
Grille opening
Increase in wing widths by a maximum of 140mm
All 'Kit' parts must be marked legibly with the name of the manufacturer and dated

Group 'WRC'

The cars can be built to VK standard and may then be further modified to incorporate turbocharging and four-wheel drive.

APPENDIX 12

Marque/Make: Mini Modèle/Model: Cooper 1.3i N° Homol. **A-5560** N° Ext. **01/01 VO**

Page ou ext. / Page or ext.	Art. / Art.	Description / Description

603 Gearbox - manual

1. Part no:- 4 speed ~ HMP 141076   No change to casing.

e. Ratios.

	No. teeth	Ratio	Synchro.
1	31 × 15	2·362	O
2	26 × 18	1·651	O
3	23 × 21	1·252	O
4	Direct	1·000	O
Rev.	17×15 & 33×18	2·375	None
Constant	24 × 21	1·143	—

f. Gate:~

```
 1   3
 |   |
 2   4   R
```

2 Part no:~ 6 speed ~ HMP 141074   Photo. 16

e Ratios

	No. teeth	Ratio	Synchro
1	28 × 14	2·000	No
2	25 × 17	1·471	No
3	23 × 19	1·211	No
4	21 × 21	1·000	No
5	19 × 22	0·864	No
6	18 × 24	0·750	No
Rev.	15×14 & 33×18	1·864	No
Constant	—	—	—

f. Gate:~

```
 1   3   5
 |   |   |
 2   4   6   R
```
or sequential ~ mounted central, floor or adjacent to steering wheel.

Page / 22/20

Marque/Make: Mini Modèle/Model: Cooper 1.3i N° Homol. **A-5560** N° Ext. **01/01 VO**

Page ou ext. / Page or ext.	Art. / Art.	Description / Description

Reduction gears, part of 6 speed unit:~

No. teeth	24 × 18	24 × 19	25 × 17	26 × 17	26 × 16
Ratio	1·333	1·263	1·471	1·529	1·625

605 Final drive ~ alternative ratios:~

b Ratio	3·105	3·200	3·429	3·444	3·467
c No. teeth	59×19	48×15	48×14	62×18	52×15
b Ratio	3·667	3·692	3·765	3·769	3·846
c No. teeth	55×15	48×13	64×17	49×13	50×13
b Ratio	3·929	3·938	4·000	4·000	4·133
c No. teeth	55×14	63×16	64×16	56×14	62×15
b Ratio	4·154	4·167	4·231	4·250	4·267
c No. teeth	54×13	50×12	55×13	51×12	64×15
b Ratio	4·308	4·333	4·385	4·500	4·500
c No. teeth	56×13	65×15	57×13	63×14	54×12
b Ratio	4·636	4·666	4·727	4·750	4·818
c No. teeth	51×11	56×12	52×11	57×12	53×11
b Ratio	4·917				
c No. teeth	59×12				

803 Brakes

		Front	Rear
Caliper ~ RBLH ~ Part no.		HMP 141082/3	HMP 141084/5
	Photo.	17	18
e No. cyls. per wheel		4	2
e1. Bore		38·1	36·0
Disc	Part no.	HMP 141086	HMP 141089
	Photo.	19	20
Caliper mat.l		Al. alloy	Al. alloy

Page / 23/?

Homologated 4 and 6 speed gearbox ratios. (Courtesy FIA Homologation A-5560. 1997)

Homologated reduction gears and alternative ratios. Brake details. (Courtesy FIA Homologation A-5560. 1997)

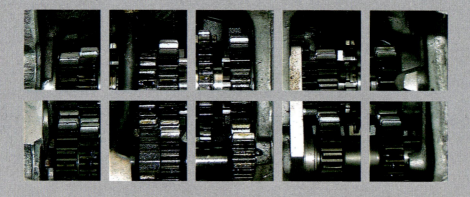

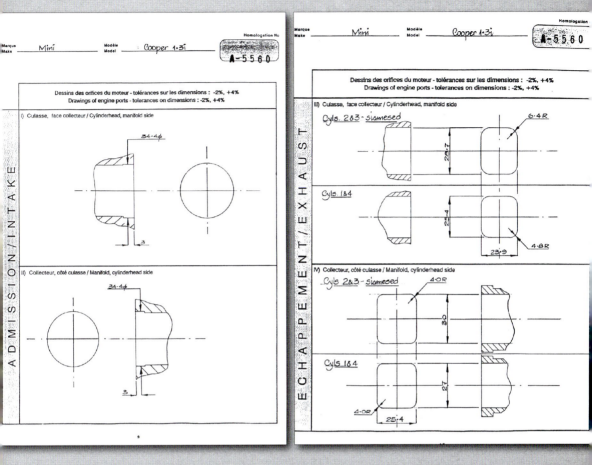

Homologation details of the cylinder head inlet ports. (Courtesy FIA Homologation A-5560. 1997)

Exhaust port homologation details. (Courtesy FIA Homologation A-5560. 1997)

CERTIFICATE OF COMPLIANCE

ATL SAFETY FUEL CELLS

Aero Tec Laboratories Inc, certify to the original purchaser of this new ATL FUEL CELL that it conforms with FIA FT3 specifications.

This certificate shall become Null & Void if the Fuel Cell has been subjected to accident, negligence, disassembly, alteration, abuse, misuse, improper installation, or unsuited uses.

AERO TEC LABORATORIES INC.

DATE of Manufacturing ...4/Q/96...

TYPE of Cell ...CUSTOM...

SERIAL No ...829553...

ORIGINAL Capacity ...

AUTHORIZED SIGNATURE...

DATE...24/12/96...

REDUCED to ...

With No... ATL volume displacement blocks...

AUTHORIZED SIGNATURE...

DATE...

APPENDIX 14

All ATL fuel cells are issued with a certificate of compliance. This relates to the cell fitted to one of the Monte Carlo cars. The fuel cell comprises an impact resistant rubberised 'bladder' filled with explosive suppressant foam baffling and then fitted with a leak-tight cap and fittings. Roll-over valves are fitted and a further aluminium container on the outside helps deflect any impacts and also as a flame shield. (Courtesy ATL Ltd)

The description of the volume displacement balls as used in the ATL fuel cells. (Courtesy ATL Ltd)

AERO TEC LABORATORIES INC.

VOLUME DISPLACEMENT BALLS

ATL are proud to announce their new lightweight Volume Displacement Balls. Where complete fuel system capacities have to be accurately calculated to comply with homologation regulations, these ATL Volume Displacement Balls are perfect for fine tuning.

Manufactured from Polypropylene in three different diameters (see table below), ATL Volume Displacement Balls are completely spherical with no protruding rims. The additional benefit is that the smooth surface of the rimless ATL Volume Displacement Balls will not cause scratching or marking to neither balls nor the ATL FIA/FT5 and FIA/FT4 Fuel Cell fabrics.

Part No	Diameter of ball	Average weight of ball	Volume Displaced (litres/Imp gallons)
VDB01	70mm	16.0 gr	0.18 litres (0.04 gal)
VDB02	100mm	40.0 gr	0.52 litres (0.11 gal)
VDB03	150mm	100.0 gr	1.77 litres (0.39 gal)

For volume displacements where a number of ATL Volume Displacement Balls are to be used, we can also provide our new ATL Mesh - Net which can comfortably retain the balls.

Supplied in tubular form, the balls are simply retained within the ATL Mesh - Net using cable ties at each end.

Depending on the number and the configuration of ATL Volume Displacement Balls, the ATL Mesh - Net is available in two sizes (see table below)

Part No	Diameter Range	Colour
MN001	50mm - 100mm	Red
MN003	100mm - 200mm	Green

For more information on the above and our existing Racing Fuel Cell product range please contact our Sales Department at the address below.

Michelin studded tyres in preparation for the ice and snow. (Courtesy Enchapment)

The Bibendum Man was originated in 1898 and has remained the legend of the Michelin Tyre Company ever since. (Courtesy Michelin Tyres Ltd)

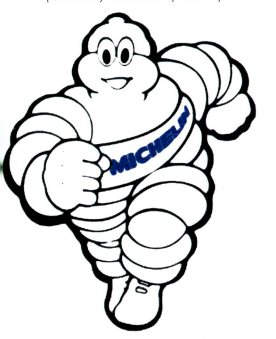

APPENDIX 15

Michelin rally tyres

The tyres used and fitted to the BCM Rallye Monte Carlo cars were supplied by Michelin and, in the majority, were from its Asphalt Rally Tyre Range. Michelin also manufactured a Gravel Rally Tyre Range which covered all surfaces that were not either asphalt or snow, but these were not suitable for this particular event. Besides the former tyre, Michelin also manufactured a G and D specification tyre which could be fitted with studs for use in heavy snow and when driving on ice. It is so very important when rallying to ensure that the service crew is correctly stocked with tyres for the various weather conditions that the rally is likely to encounter, especially when competing in winter events.

Tyre choice has always in the past been something of a sporting affair which has now become a lottery. Prior to the days when the stages were recced, drivers had to make a valued judgement of tyre choice subject to what they thought

(Courtesy Michelin Tyres Ltd)

Asphalt Rally Tyre Range

would be the ensuing driving conditions. Today entrants must run the special stages in pairs, and service points between the Stages are not permitted. With the numerous, consecutive alpine Stages on this event, altitude can vary by several hundred metres. The drivers have their ice note crews running ahead through the Stages, advising on upcoming conditions, but this still means that the drivers have to make value judgements on which tyres to fit for each group of stages.

A typical scenario is where conditions have been described on the first Stage as dry asphalt with maybe just a dusting of snow and occasional ice patches; the second Stage possibly higher in altitude with snow-covered roads. By the time the ice crews have been through the second Stage, the temperature could drop and the surfaces change to a full covering of ice. The question is: does the driver select studded ice tyres, making the first stage difficult to drive, and with the guarantee that some of the studs will be shed prior to reaching the iced section? Using 'thermal' ice tyres without studs could possibly work on the second Stage, but because of their soft tyre compound they will almost certainly have 'gone off' well before halfway. Well, what about tarmac slicks, which could gain time on the first Stage, but then there's the ice on Stage 2 ...

The numerous forces that a tyre is subjected to when being driven hard on asphalt will, in most cases, push its structure to the limit. The contact area between rubber and tarmac through which power is transmitted is no greater than the palm of a hand. Also a consideration are the lateral forces generated when cornering hard. Tyre design must be such that it will optimise all factors for the extremely short period of time that the tyre is in contact with the road. When driving on a wet road, a tyre must be capable of clearing up to at least 20 litres of water per second.

In order to explain the tyre markings we will work off a typical rally tyre fitted to the cars:

Example: 1453-13 X TL N20
14 = tread band width (cm)
53 = external diameter of the tyre (cm)
13 = rim diameter
X = radial tyre
TL = tubeless tyre
N = tread type
20 = compound

Key to coding

N = dry asphalt with excellent performance on damp roads in warm and dry conditions
N01 = as above with a temperature range of between 2 and 20 degrees C
N20 = as above with a temperature range of between 15 and 35 degrees C
TA – T1A = damp asphalt but the facility to be re-cut for improved grip in deeper water. TA 00 range of between 2 and 20 degrees C
P and B = wet asphalt. Full rain tyre for use between 2 and 20 degrees C

A compound code is also moulded into the tyre casing.

TA00 = soft compound. Extra cuts for wet conditions. Good for smooth tarmac

(Courtesy Michelin Tyres Ltd)

Gravel Rally Tyre Range

(Courtesy Michelin Tyres Ltd)

TA20 = medium compound. For dry conditions only and rough tarmac

TA40 = hard compound. Less grip with increased lifespan

M, L and FB range for good traction and transversal grip. This tyre is recommended for autocross and rallycross

Z range is asymmetric left and right, with a fairly closed pattern for increased ground contact

ZA tyres are asymmetric left and right, with a fairly open pattern giving better traction on slippery surfaces

ZE again is asymmetric left and right, with a more open pattern to clear loose stones

This range of tyres is available in various compounds with a 7 rating for mud and sand, whereas soft gravel is either 4 or 8.

Compounds 5 and 9 are best suited to hard surfaces and on buried stones

The GA tyres are best suited to full snow and ice of between 70 and 100 per cent coverage

The GE rated tyres are asymmetric left and right

The D tyre is built with sipes and is studable.

G50 is a studded snow tyre 1057-13 with a maximum rim size of 5 inches

XM+S 200 is a non-studded combination tyre which is good on patchy snow, forest stages, broken tarmac and gravel

APPENDIX 16

The House of Grimaldi

Many centuries ago Monaco was just a small, inhospitable, rocky peninsula which offered natural harbours to the local villages along its coastline. From the early part of the 12th century, however, the history of Monaco and the Grimaldi family became intertwined.

A TA20 tyre fitted to the rear of the 1997 Group 'A' rally Mini. (Courtesy British Motor Heritage – Rover)

The Grimaldi fortress stands high upon a rock, sheltering many generations of the family, and was built in 1191 in order to defend the western Riviera from attack by Saracen naval vessels.

The House of Grimaldi originates from Genoa in Italy at around the time of the first Crusade. During the 12th and 13th centuries, rivalry between political factions led to unrest in Genoa, forcing the Grimaldis – at the time leading the Guelphic political party – to abandon the state and re-settle in the country, and both the fortress of Monaco and the Provence region of France were ideal places in which to do so. Unfortunately, another faction also sought refuge in Monaco – the Ghibelines – and there developed military clashes between opposing political factions, which ended when Charles Grimaldi gave financial compensation to the Ghibelines and threw then out of the region. The fortress – and now established port – had become a bastion of trade and political activity in the region, and its position in the Mediterranean provided a good, sound base for raiding passing trading ships from Italy and Greece.

By the middle of the 15th century and with the increasing family affluence, the Grimaldi family had formed an albergo, or corporation, liberating the finances to explore the world's trading opportunities and form powerful inter-family alliances. Land was acquired and the sovereignity of the family established through relationships between Monaco and adjoining neighbours.

In 1454 John Grimaldi established the Rules of Succession for Monaco, which state that the first in line to succession is always a male, whether or not legitimate, by primogeniture. In the absence of a male heir, a female – whether or not legitimate – by primogeniture, succeeds, provided that she marries a man legitimately born of the Grimaldi lineage. If this is not the case, succession passes to the most closely related member of the Grimaldi albergo. In the case of there being two or more Grimaldi eligible relatives, the eldest is chosen.

Claudia, granddaughter of John, did not have a brother, so according to the rules of succession, in 1465 she married her cousin, Lambert Grimaldi of Antibes, retaining her position on the throne with Lambert becoming Lord of Monaco. It was Lambert who established the independence of Monaco, for which he received widespread admiration. His favourite expression: "With God's help", became the Grimaldi motto.

Politically, this was a difficult time in Monaco's history. Lambert had to defend it and the nearby Menton region with his sword from many takeover attempts. This was achieved with the assistance of his brothers of Antibes, who were always on hand to give military help when required. All attempts to de-establish or conquer Monaco were always foiled, and Monaco always kept its door open to the Grimaldis of Antibes.

Over the centuries the generic title of Lord slowly gave way to numerous other distinctive titlesm and it was now that a hierarchy of titles began to emerge. In Antibes the Grimaldis successively bore the titles Lord, Baron and Marquis, and in 1612 Honore II Grimaldi, Lord of Monaco, began to use the title 'Prince'. This was accepted in both France and Spain, and has continued as the recognised title from that day forth.

Honore's son, Prince Louis, and his wife became good friends with Louis XIV of France, and spent a considerable amount of time at the Court of Versailles. Louis fought numerous campaigns against both England and Spain for the French. His favourite place of residence was either Monaco or Genoa, although he and his family enjoyed the highest distinction at the King Louis' Court as a foreign prince and peer of France. With all his connections and the manner in which he lived, Louis was always keen to impress his host, and it is said that he enjoyed a very lavish lifestyle. With his extended family in Genoa he was made Ambassador of France to the Holy See, and had the task of pleading the King's case in connection with the succession of Spain.

Prince Louis' son, Anthony, lived in Monaco; a broken marriage and a son meant he endured a penniless lifestyle. Given the Grimaldi tradition of succession, Anthony encouraged his daughter, Louise-Hippolyte, to marry her cousin of Antibes, whom he regarded as a son. After much intrigue, however, the marriage plans were cancelled and Louise-Hippolyte eventually wed a Normandy nobleman, Jacques de Goyon Matignon, who aspired to his father-in-law's peerage, which was one of the most coveted in France. Anthony died quite soon after the wedding.

Anthony was survived by his nephew, Archbishop Honore-Francois, who died in 1748. Upon his death, the line of Grimaldi came to an end in Moncao.

Disregarding the rule of succession, and with approval from the King of France, Jacques de Goyon Matignon succeeded his father-in-law to become Jacques I Grimaldi, taking the name and coat of arms of the ancient Mediterranean family. Members of the Grimaldi family made forceful protest, in spite of the inherent legal and political difficulties, but to no avail. Jacques Matignon then elected to live in Paris as opposed to Monaco, leaving his ambitions largely unfulfilled.

During World War I the succession rule of the Grimaldi family was once again disregarded, when the French government wanted someone on the throne of Monaco that would not be a threat to France's security. With an unmarried Prince who had no direct descendents, the French government sought to elect an heir from among the Prince's relations. The illegitimate daughter of Prince Louis Matignon-Grimaldi, who was born in Algeria, was the solution and in 1919 was adopted by the Prince. Ms Charlotte Louvet then took the Grimaldi name and in 1920 married a French nobleman, Pierre de Polignac, who changed his name to Grimaldi. To them a daughter, Antoinette de Massy, was born in 1920, followed by a male heir – Rainier Polignac-Grimaldi – in 1923. In 1956 he married the film actress Grace Kelly and in 1957, Caroline was born; in 1958, Albert II Polignac-Grimaldi; and in 1965, Stephanie. Upon the death of his father in 2005, Albert II inherited the throne of Monaco.

APPENDIX 17

Footnote
The 1997 ST Special Tuning catalogue, which shows P246 WFH on the front cover and on the pages inside, is, in fact, incorrect but necessarily so! Artistic licence has been used in the production of this brochure. Rallye Monte Carlo number 222 was the number issued to the Group 'N' car; the Group 'A' car was number 156. What you see in the catalogue is the Group 'A' car with the names of Dave Paveley and Andy Bull on the wings, 222 on the doors and roof, and the Serck Marston sticker in the rear quarter windows. The workshop photograph shows the Group 'A' car being prepared in the background, and the Group 'N' car with the registration number N679 TOK in the foreground. The latter was then re-registered P246 WFH, along with P245 WFH, on 14th January 1997 just prior to the Monte Carlo Rally. The action photographs are correct and are of the Group 'N' car.

The Monte Carlo car number 222 was rolled and damaged at the Curborough Sprint Circuit immediately after the rally. BMH was now well into promoting its services and products. A free issue of the new ST catalogue accompanied the May 1997 edition of *MiniWorld* magazine.

With a little artistic licence the ST catalogue promoted Heritage products. (Courtesy British Motor Heritage/Rover)

Timing was a consideration so it made sense to transfer the requisite details to the other car; the general public was unlikely to notice the difference at a glance! (Obvious visual differences are the presence of rear mud flaps, Group 'A' logo on the A-post quarter panel, racing-style door mirror,s and spacing of the 222 door numbers.)

The 80-litre fuel cell was used in both cars for the 1996 Nürburgring races, replaced with 45-litre cells for the Rallye Monte Carlo, after which the larger cells were reinstated.

In the background of Enterprise racing workshop the Monte Carlo Group 'A' British Motor Heritage car is being prepared. The car in the immediate foreground is N679 TOK, which was to have the registration changed to P246WFH. (Courtesy Richard Franklin)

Current Reg. Number	Original Reg. Number	Date first Registered	Original Body Colour	Colour Change	Date of Colour Change	Number of Keepers
	H410FWK	16/08/1990	BLACK/WHITE	RED/WHITE		
						3
C3EJB	L54CVP	01/08/1993	RED/WHITE			
D555GRX						
						4
	L283APL	20/08/1993	RED/WHITE			
L333EJB						
						3
	L408AUE	27/08/1993	RED/WHITE			2
	L33EJB	19/11/1993	RED/WHITE			2
	8204 TK 26		RED/WHITE			2
	L66LBL	14/01/1994	RED/WHITE			3
	M963PJW	01/06/1995	RED/WHITE			1
	389 BHV 95		RED/WHITE			2
	N855HAF	01/08/1995	GREY/WHITE	RED/WHITE		
K33EJB						
K764VKM						
						3
	N679TOK	10/10/1995	RED/WHITE			1
	AL 555 CW		RED/WHITE			
	572 BTX 95		RED/WHITE			2
	757 BVV 95		BLUE/WHITE			3
			GREEN/WHITE	RED/WHITE	00/11/1996	3
P245WFH		14/01/1997				
			GREEN/WHITE			
N679TOK LATER CHANGED TO P246WFH		14/01/1997		RED/WHITE	00/11/96	

APPENDIX 18
Overview of all the 'works' Minis & registrations used between 1994 & 2005

APPENDIX 19
Useful contacts

Aero Tec Laboratories Ltd
1 Patriot Drive
Rooksley
Milton Keynes
Bedfordshire MK13 8PU
England
Tel: 01908 351700
Email: atl@atlltd.com
Website: www.atl.com

Aymami Foto Racing
Avda
Rafael Casanova 70

Notes	Part works Sponsored	Works Sponsored	Responsible for build	Group	Country of Entry	Competitive events entered	Entry number	Drivers	Navigator	Final Result
AMAGED TOTAL LOSS. OT STOLEN	YES									
NGE OF KEEPER			BCM							
NGE OF KEEPER				PRODUCTION		COMPETITION PRIZE				
R PLATE CHANGE										
NGE OF KEEPER	YES		BCM/BARRETTS	A	UK	1994 NETWORK Q RAC	24	RUSSELL BROOKES	NEIL WILSON	6TH IN CLASS. 72ND OVERALL
R PLATE CHANGE										
NGE OF KEEPER			BCM		UK	1995 NURBURGRING 24 HOUR	89	TONY DRON, JOHN BRIGDEN AND JEREMY COULTER		9TH IN CLASS. 92ND OVERALL
				A	UK	1996 RALLYE MONTE CARLO	113	TONY DRON	ALISTAIR DOUGLAS	2ND IN CLASS. 67TH OVERALL
NGE OF KEEPER			SOUTHAM ENGINEERING		UK	2005 LOMBARD REVIVAL	40	PETER BARKER	WILLY CAVE	8TH IN CLASS. 27TH OVERALL
NGE OF KEEPER										
R PLATE CHANGE	NO		BCM/BILL RICHARDS							
R PLATE CHANGE										
NGE OF KEEPER	YES		D.R. ENGINEERING	A	UK	1994 RALLYE MONTE CARLO	101	TIMO MAKINEN	PAUL EASTER	RETIRED
			MINI SPARES	A	UK	1995 NETWORK Q RAC	148	KEITH BIRD	TONY GRAHAM	RETIRED
			MINI SPARES	A	UK	1996 RALLYE MONTE CARLO	111	KEITH BIRD	ROBERT DYSON	16TH IN CLASS. 65TH OVERALL
	YES		BCM	A	UK	1993 RALLYE BRITANNIA COURSE CAR		PADDY HOPKIRK	RON CRELLIN	
				A	UK	1994 RALLYE MONTE CARLO	37	PADDY HOPKIRK	RON CRELLIN	4TH IN CLASS. 52ND OVERALL
		YES	BCM	A	FRANCE	1994 RALLYE MONTE CARLO	44	PHILIPPE CHEVALIER	MOINS BERNARD	RETIRED
EN/RECOVERED	YES		D.R. ENGINEERING			1994 RALLYE MONTE CARLO				
SCRAPPED	YES		ROVER GROUP	PRODUCTION	UK	1997 MONTE CARLO CHASE CAR				
		YES	ROVER FRANCE		FRANCE	1995 RALLYE MONTE CARLO	32	JEAN-CLAUDE ANDRUET	MICHEL 'BICHE' PETIT	RETIRED
PLATE CHANGE. TION USED ILLEGALLY NDONA 1994 MONTE			BCM	A	SWITZERLAND	1994 RALLYE MONTE CARLO	40	PHILIPPE CAMANDONA	FRANCINE CAMANDONA	3RD IN CLASS. 47TH OVERALL
RATION USED ON NA 1994 MONTE CAR. NOT BEEN ISSUED BY DVLA										
NGE OF KEEPER										
		YES	ROVER GROUP	PRODUCTION		1996 MONTE CARLO CHASE CAR		DAVE PAVELEY	NIGEL BOWLER	
ST V5 ISSUE										
		YES	ROVER ITALY	A	ITALY	1997 RALLYE MONTE CARLO	153	CLAUDIA PERONI	LILIANA ARMAND	RETIRED
		YES	COVENTRY AUTOMOTIVE	N	FRANCE	1997 RALLYE MONTE CARLO	223	FREDERIC VIE	LIONEL CURAT	52ND
		YES	COVENTRY AUTOMOTIVE	N	JAPAN	1997 RALLYE MONTE CARLO	219	YASOU KUSAKABE	OSAM MORIKAWA	RETIRED
		YES	ENTERPRISE RACING	A	UK	1996 NURBURGRING 24 HOUR	88	MICHAEL HESS, THOMAS BAYER, MARK HALES AND JOACHIM WEBER		2ND IN CLASS1400 CC
			ENTERPRISE RACING	A	UK	1996 NURBURGRING 6 HOUR	409	JOACHIM WEBER, MICHAEL HESS, THOMAS BEYER		1ST IN CLASS 1400 CC
			ENTERPRISE RACING	A	UK	1997 RALLYE MONTE CARLO	156	TONY DRON	ALISTAIR DOUGLAS	RETIRED
			ENTERPRISE RACING	A	UK	1997 NURBURGRING 24 HOUR				
REG NO. P246WFH			ENTERPRISE RACING	A	UK	1997 WESTON PARK	12	DAVE PAVELEY	ANDY BULL	RETIRED
			KERNAHANS	A	UK	1998 RALLYE CATALUNYA	74	MARTIN KERNAHAN	SIMON AYRIS	RETIRED
NGE OF KEEPER			WEST PENNINE	A	UK	1999 SEAT JIM CLARK RALLY	76	GRACE OWEN	ALI BOHM	RETIRED
			WEST PENNINE	A	UK	1999 STENA LINE ULSTER RALLY	94	GRACE OWEN	ALI BOHM	RETIRED
NGE OF KEEPER			WEST PENNINE	A	UK	1999 SONY MANX RALLY	78	GRACE OWEN	ALI BOHM	RETIRED
ATION USED ON NEW BODY		YES	ENTERPRISE RACING	A	UK	1996 NURBURGRING 24 HOUR	87	TONY DRON, PAUL TAFT, STEVEN WARBURTON AND JOHN BRIGDEN		1ST IN CLASS 1400 CC
			ENTERPRISE RACING	A	UK	1996 NURBURGRING 6 HOUR	408	TONY DRON, PAUL TAFT		2ND IN CLASS1400 CC
			ENTERPRISE RACING	A	UK	1996 PHILLIPS TOUR OF MULL	50	DAVE PAVELEY	ANDY BULL	RETIRED
				N	UK	1997 RALLYE MONTE CARLO	222	DAVE PAVELEY	ANDY BULL	BEST OVERSEAS FINISHER GROUP N 1300 CC CLASS. 4TH CLASS 59TH OVERALL
NGE OF KEEPER			ENTERPRISE RACING	A	UK	1997 NURBURGRING 24 HOUR				
NGE OF KEEPER										

08206 Sabadell
Barcelona
Spain
Tel: 0093 727 26 58

Bill Richards Racing
Unit 24
Ellingham Ind Est
Ashford
Kent TN23 6JZ
England
Tel: 01233 624336
Email: billrichardsracing@virgin.net
Website: www.billrichardsracing.com

BG Developments Ltd
Unit 9 West Court

Buntsford Park Road
Bromsgrove
Worcestershire B60 3DX
England
Tel: 01525 873716
Email: info@bgdevelopments.co.uk
Website: www.bgdevelopments.co.uk

Bremax Electronics Ltd
Castle View
Eccleshall Road
Great Bridgeford
Stafford ST18 9SQ
England
Tel: 01785 281025
Email: m.mosam@bremax.co.uk
Website: www.bremax.co.uk

Brijak Videos (1996 Monte)
Staddlestones
Stanville Road
Cumnor
Oxford OX2 9JF
England
Tel: 01865 863297
Email: xwast@yahoo.com

British Motor Heritage Ltd
Cotswold Business Park
Witney
Oxfordshire OX29 0YB
England
Tel: 01993 707208
Email: davidjane@bmh-ltd.com
Website: www.bmh-ltd.com

Bryan Purves Ltd
Applegarth
Holtye Road
East Grinstead
West Sussex RH19 3PP
England
Tel: 01342 315065
Email: bry@purves.ndo.co.uk
Website: www.bryanpurves.co.uk

Corgi Classics Ltd
PO Box 2001
Southampton
Hampshire SO14 0HS
England
Tel: 023 8024 8844
Website: www.corgi.co.uk

Coventry Automotive
Shilton Lodge Farm
Leicester Road
CoventryCV7 9LZ
England
Tel: 01455 221313

DR Engineering Consultants
10 New Ash Drive
Allesley Green
Coventry
England

Tel: 02476 404614
E.mail: dreng@dsl.pipex.com
Website: www racecar.co.uk/gripper

John Edge Signs
16 St Agnes Road
East Grinstead
West Sussex RH19 3RP
England
Tel: 01342 324587
Mobile: 07801 965469

Endurance Rally Association
5 Ashbrook Mews
Westbrook Street
Blewbury
Oxon OX11 9QA
England
Tel: 01235 851291
Email: mail@endurorallycom
Website: www.endurorally.com

Lifeline Fire and Safety Systems
Burnsall Road
Coventry CV5 6BU
England
Tel: 024 7671 2999
Email: sales@lifeline-fire.co.uk
Website: www.lifeline-fire.co.uk

Lynxsigns Ltd
Unit 5
Addington Business Centre
Vulcan Way
New Addington
Croydon
Surrey CR0 9UG
England
Tel: 020 8239 9099
Email: info@lynxsigns.co.uk
Website: www.lynxsigns.co.uk

Mini Cooper Register
Kim Bromage (Secretary)
31 Coralin Close
Chelmsley Wood
Birmingham B37 7NE
England

Tel: 0121 680 1814
Email: secretary@minicooper.org
Website: www.minicooper.org

Mini Magazine
Future Publishing
Beaufort Court
30 Monmouth Street
Bath BA1 2BW
England
Tel: 0870 8374 773

Mini Spares
Cranbourne Ind Est
Cranbourne Road
Potters Bar
Hertfordshire EN6 3JN
England
Tel: 01707 607700
Email: sales@minispares.com
Website: www.minispares.com

Mini Sport Ltd
Thompson Street
Padiham
Lancashire BB12 7AP
England
Tel: 01282 778731
Website: www.minisport.com

MiniWorld Magazine
IPC Leon House
233 High Street
Croydon CR9 1HZ
Eng;and
Tel: 020 8726 8364
Email: miniworld@ipcmedia.com
Website: www.miniworld.co.uk

Paint Box
4 Mealcheapen Street
Worcester
WR1 2DH
Tel: 01905 619944
Email: paintbox@lineone.net
Website: www.paintboxgallery.com
PIAA
PIAA (UK Ltd)

Bridgewater Road
Lympsham
Weston Super Mare BS24 0BN
England
Tel: 01934 818430
Email: sales@piaa.co.uk
Website: www.piaa.co.uk

Piranha Models
6 Bisrue des Brandons
77630 Saint Martin En Biere
France
Email: piranha@club-internet.fr

Recaro UK Ltd
Holly Farm Business Park
Honiley
Warwickshire CV8 1NP
England
Tel: 01926 484111
Email: info.gb@recaro.com
Website: www.recaro-seats.co.uk

Southern Carburettors
Unit 6
Nelson Trading Estate
Morden Road
Wimbledon
Surrey SW19 3BC
England
Tel: 0181 540 2723
Email: sales@southerncarbs.co.uk
Website: wwwsoutherncarbs.co.uk

Speedsport Photography
Frank Williams
Haulsan
Llanbedr.O.C.
Ruthin
Denbighshire
LL15 1UT
Tel: 01824 703743

Stack Ltd
Wedgewood Road
Bicester
Oxon OX26 4UL
England

Tel: 01869 245500
Email: sales@stackltd.com
Website: www.stackltd.com

Kernahan of Witney Ltd
Staple Hall Garage
Newland
Witney
Oxon OX28 3JD
England
Tel: 01993 703935
Email: s.ayris@tesco.net

Swiftune Engineering
Long Corner Farm
Bethersden
Ashford
Kent TN26 3HD
England
Tel: 01233 850843

Email: sales@swiftune.co.uk
Website: www.swiftune.co.uk

Terratrip
Ship Farm
Horsley
Derby DE21 5BR
England
Tel: 01332 880468
Website: www.terratrip.com

West Pennine Motorsport
The Green Building
Bentgate Street
Milnrow
Rochdale OL16 4NU
England
Tel: 01706 290768
Email: sales@wpm.co.uk
Website: www.wpm.co.uk

(Courtesy Bertrand Glineur)

INDEX

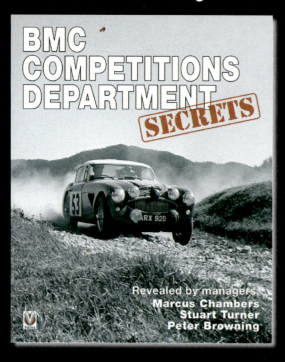
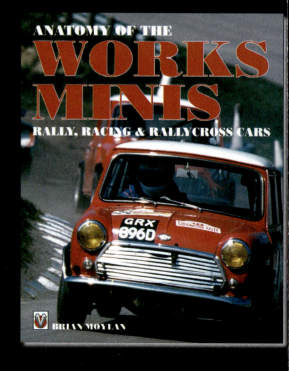